CAREFREE DIGNITY

Discourses on Training in the Nature of Mind
by Drubwang Tsoknyi Rinpoche

RANGJUNG YESHE BOOKS · WWW.RANGJUNG.COM

PADMASAMBHAVA · *Dakini Teachings* · *Advice from the Lotus-Born*
Treasures From Juniper Ridge

PADMASAMBHAVA AND JAMGÖN KONGTRÜL · *The Light of Wisdom, Vol. 1*
The Light of Wisdom, Vol. 2

YESHE TSOGYAL · *The Lotus-Born*

GAMPOPA · *The Precious Garland of the Sublime Path*

DAKPO TASHI NAMGYAL · *Clarifying the Natural State*

TSELE NATSOK RANGDRÖL · *The Heart of the Matter* · *Mirror of Mindfulness*
Empowerment · *Lamp of Mahamudra*

CHOKGYUR LINGPA · *Ocean of Amrita* · *The Great Gate*

JAMGÖN MIPHAM RINPOCHE · *Gateway to Knowledge, Vol. 1*
Gateway to Knowledge, Vol. 2 · *Gateway to Knowledge, Vol. 3*

TULKU URGYEN RINPOCHE · *Blazing Splendor* · *Rainbow Painting*
As It Is, Vol. 1 · *As It Is, Vol. 2* · *Vajra Speech*
Repeating the Words of the Buddha

TRULSHIK ADEU RINPOCHE & TULKU URGYEN RINPOCHE · *Skillful Grace*

KHENCHEN THRANGU RINPOCHE · *Crystal Clear* · *Songs of Naropa*
King of Samadhi · *Buddha Nature*

CHÖKYI NYIMA RINPOCHE · *Present Fresh Wakefulness* · *Indisputable Truth*
Union of Mahamudra & Dzogchen · *Bardo Guidebook* · *Song of Karmapa*

TSIKEY CHOKLING RINPOCHE · *Lotus Ocean*

TULKU THONDUP · *Enlightened Living*

ORGYEN TOBGYAL RINPOCHE · *Life & Teachings of Chokgyur Lingpa*

TSOKNYI RINPOCHE · *Fearless Simplicity* · *Carefree Dignity*

DZOGCHEN TRILOGY COMPILED BY MARCIA BINDER SCHMIDT · *Dzogchen
Primer Dzogchen Essentials* · *Quintessential Dzogchen*

ERIK PEMA KUNSANG · *Wellsprings of the Great Perfection*
A Tibetan Buddhist Companion · *The Rangjung Yeshe Tibetan-English
Dictionary of Buddhist Culture*

CAREFREE DIGNITY

Discourses on Training in the Nature of Mind
by Drubwang Tsoknyi Rinpoche

Compiled and translated by
Erik Pema Kunsang *and* Marcia Binder Schmidt
Edited by Kerry Moran

RANGJUNG YESHE PUBLICATIONS
BOUDHANATH, HONG KONG & ESBY

Rangjung Yeshe Publications
Flat 5a, Greenview Garden,
125 Robinson Road, Hong Kong

Address letters to:
Rangjung Yeshe Publications
P.O. box 1200,
Kathmandu, Nepal

www.rangjung.com
editor@rangjung.com

First edition 1998
Printed in the United States of America
on recycled acid-free paper
5 7 9 8 6 4

Publication Data:

Drubwang Tsoknyi Rinpoche. Translated from the Tibetan
by Erik Pema Kunsang and Marcia Binder Schmidt.
Edited by Kerry Moran.

isbn 962-7341-32-0 (pbk.)
1. Carefree Dignity. Eastern philosophy —
Buddhism. 3. Vajrayana — Dzogchen. I. Title.

Cover art: Rolf A. Kluenter

"A lot of energy in the form of teaching, translating, editing and sponsoring has gone into the making of this book. I would like to dedicate this energy so that the precious bodhichitta which is naturally present in us all will be expressed through carefree dignity in our thoughts, words and deeds, for the benefit of all beings, and to bring forth the basis for peace and happiness."

— Tsoknyi Rinpoche

CONTENTS

FOREWORD

This book is a compilation of talks given by Tsoknyi Rinpoche in 1996 at the retreat center Rangjung Yeshe Gomdé, Denmark, and at Nagi Gompa, Nepal. We have tried to present as closely as possible, while being encumbered by the written word, the vividness and humor of Rinpoche's teaching style. Wherever possible we left in the play between Rinpoche and his audience. To highlight his directness we included gestures and examples. Sometimes Rinpoche's way of speaking had a poetical quality, sentences filled with beautiful profundity. To retain some of that flavor, we have phrased it in the style of poetry. This book also includes a guided meditation, which is meant to be used as an enhancement to the reader's practice session.

Tsoknyi Rinpoche was recognized by His Holiness the 16th Gyalwang Karmapa as a reincarnation of Drubwang Tsoknyi, a renowned master of the Drukpa Kagyü and Nyingma traditions. He was brought up by the great master Khamtrül Rinpoche. Among his other teachers are Kyabje Dilgo Khyentse Rinpoche, his late father Kyabje Tulku Urgyen Rinpoche, Adhi Rinpoche of Nangchen, and Nyoshul Khen Rinpoche. Rinpoche is the head of the Drukpa Heritage Project which works to preserve the literature of the Drukpa Kagyü lineage. He is also the abbot of Ngedön Ösel Ling in the Kathmandu Valley of Nepal, and of Gechak Gompa, one of the largest nunneries in Tibet. He has been teaching students from around the world since 1991.

Carefree Dignity came into being as a unified effort with Rinpoche, the translators and the editor Kerry Moran. In addition to thanking her, we would like to thank the transcribers, Dell O'Conner and Jennifer Appave, the proofreader Shirley Blair, the cover artist, Rolf A. Kluenter, and the printing sponsor, Richard Gere.

For those readers who have received the pointing-out instruction, please use these teachings as a reminder for what you have already recognized. For those readers who have not received the pointing-out instruction, please use these teachings as an inspiration to encourage you to find a qualified master and request the pointing-out instruction in person.

May the freshness offered here be the cause for beings to awaken to the great perfection in actuality.

Erik and Marcia Schmidt

CAREFREE DIGNITY

Discourses on Training in the Nature of Mind
by Drubwang Tsoknyi Rinpoche

OPEN AND FREE

WHEN WE RECEIVE TEACHINGS, we need to have a pure attitude. There is a lot to say about this pure frame of mind. Basically it means to embrace the act of listening and teaching with *bodhichitta*, with the wish that it may bring benefit to all beings. It's possible you could have some kind of preconceived idea, some kind of personalized version of the view that you want to solidify and prove by means of the teachings. You must realize, though, that anything built on such a close-minded foundation automatically becomes impure. When listening to or reading teachings, it's best to set aside any version or concepts that you may already possess. Whether they might be correct or incorrect doesn't really matter. Just set them aside for now and carefully listen to or read what is being presented.

Some people say, after listening to a spiritual discourse, that the teacher was really good — that how he taught and what he said was excellent. Often what inspires them to say this is that what they heard fit in exactly with their preconceived ideas. The teachings simply reaffirmed the way they thought things fit together. But all this proves is that they had some preconceived ideas — some notion of how things are that they considered very special. Someone may also comment after receiving teachings that the way the teacher taught and what he said didn't make sense, or that it wasn't very important. All this means is that the teachings didn't fit with the preconceived ideas that he already had. Which says more about his attitude than about the teachings!

There is another possibility here, based on the sense of total certainty that comes from having recognized the view and faced one's own nature in actuality. Such a person has resolved that this is really so in his or her own experience. Possessing this kind of real confidence in liberation, or even being on the verge of such confidence, creates a kind of unshakable certainty within oneself. This type of confidence based on actual experience remains unshaken, no matter what kind of Dharma talk one may hear.

Any other kind of conviction we may have is a patchwork stitched together from what we have read in books and heard people say, along with all sorts of various thoughts and insights we have had at different points. These are all pieced together to create a web of intellectual ideas. This kind of patchwork is of no use to us when listening to spiritual teachings, because it will never serve as the basis for true confidence. Therefore, it's very important to listen with a totally open mind. That is the attitude with which to listen to the Dharma.

So, first we need to listen with this open mind and really hear what is being said, rather than immediately judging and jumping to conclusions. We can and should, of course, *think* about what is being said, and how it makes sense. But even that is not enough in itself. We need to try out what is taught, try to get some taste of it by using it, by training in it. Once we have a certain amount of personal experience, we can then accurately judge whether or not there is real value in that teaching. The true judgment of a teaching comes when we taste it through experience. If we only evaluate a teaching by trying to see how it fits with the ideas we already have, we're being too hasty. We cannot immediately decide to discard or accept a teaching only by hearing it. If a teaching never moves further than the intellectual realm — if it never really seeps in — we will never have the real experience of the teaching.

If we are studying some scientific theory, it's probably okay to immediately judge, discriminate and discard or accept it and leave it at that. But with the subject I am presenting here, known as the 'resting mediation of a *kusulu*,' a simple meditator, we need to actually allow it to become part of ourselves so that we can taste it within our own experience. At that point we can accurately judge the value of this approach.

Let's look at the subject of approach in more detail. I try to teach according to the simple meditative style of teaching; what is known as the *kusulu* approach. How good I am at it is not so sure. You're trying to listen and assimilate in the way of a simple meditator. Whether you're successful or not is also not sure.

There is another style that is especially well-developed in the Gelukpa and Sakya traditions, known as the 'analytical approach of a *pandita*,' a great scholar. Kagyü and Nyingma followers also use this approach to some extent, but it's not their primary way of training. In the analytical approach, you try to make everything your business. You try to figure it all out — you want to clearly understand, explain, prove and disprove by intellectual argument. You pull your rosary up on your left arm like this and say, "All right! Now let's discuss the topic of the omniscient state of enlightenment. How is that realization? Explain this subject." And then you slap your hands together, stamp your feet on the ground, lift your head and swing it around. It can be very interesting to refine one's understanding in this way. But you must remember it's not experience. It's theory. A person who practices in this fashion is not necessarily a meditator.

If you really want to train in that way, it's best to go to a philosophical college. I trained a little bit like that in the past. I slapped my hands together so much they became red and swollen! We would pair off two by two. One person would stand up and ask the questions, while the other sat down and tried to answer. The standing one tried to catch the seated one contradicting himself. Sometimes two monks stood up to debate, and all the other monks sat in line and listened.

In the morning, the *khenpo*, the Buddhist professor, explained a certain topic, probably four lines of teaching. That little bit was enough; in fact, it was very impressive, because he could elucidate it in such great detail. For example, this verse:

May the precious mind of enlightenment
Arise where it has not arisen.
Where it has arisen, may it not wane,
But further and further increase.

What is meant by the precious mind of enlightenment, the enlightened attitude of bodhichitta? What does it really mean? How is it defined? How does it improve, and how does it worsen? How does it grow, wane and so on? The few lines discussed are thus connected with a lot of other different topics, and the khenpo can shed light on the subject from all sorts of different angles. In the afternoon the students debate on the topic they heard that morning. It's actually quite a good method, because it really clarifies what the intent of the Dharma is. Anything one is unclear about can be clarified. For each matter in which a doubt arises, there's another thought that can reply to that. And it goes on and on like that — there's always a possible response for every doubt.

My style is not like that. It is possible that the method I am giving might seem very simple, or maybe a little too simplistic. But on the other hand, the outcome of using it can be very deep, in the sense of bringing about profound insight. If we immediately reject that simple method the moment we hear about it, thinking "This is too superficial," we will never achieve the results that come through using it. As I said before, it's too early to make a judgment based merely on listening. One should listen to the teachings on Dzogchen, the Great Perfection, with a very open mind, without any prejudice or preconceived ideas. Why? Because the Dzogchen view is very open-minded; thus, when listening to and receiving those teachings one should be open-minded as well. If you listen in a very narrow-minded analytical way, like trying to fit everything into a pinhole; you will never be able to accommodate the vast openness of *dharmadhatu*, your basic state.

The real understanding that arises from experiencing our innate nature in actuality is something that comes about through specific causes and circumstances. These include the blessings of the lineage masters, one's own open-mindedness, one's intelligence, and the instruction of one's teacher. All these factors come together to create an atmosphere in which it is possible for the innate nature that is already in ourselves to be totally revealed, completely laid open.

This is how true realization occurs. It is a combination of factors, the meeting together of which allows for true understanding. It is not that we have to assemble different pieces of information into some kind of architectural structure, or a jigsaw puzzle, and that when that is complete, we have the view. It's not like that at all. It's more a sense of allowing everything to fall into place by itself: the blessings, one's own discriminating intelligence and ability to see clearly, one's open-mind-edness, and the power of one's past karma, as well as past and present aspirations.

In order for us to know about the view, to learn about the view, some explanations need to be given. We need a complete presentation of the perspective, how to train in it, how it use it in various situations and how it relates to our behavior, and what the result of that training is — traditionally known as the view, meditation, conduct and fruition. In this context we also need to know about ground, path, and fruition.

When learning about the view, the first thing one needs to learn is how to recognize the nature of mind. The second is how to actually see or experience the nature of mind. Finally, you need to know how to free any kind of thought or emotion that manifests in your mind. All these details need to be presented correctly. The main point of all this is liberation. We need to know how to be free, but in order to know how to be free, we need to know first what the free state is.

People seem to believe that Dzogchen is this, Dzogchen is that — that Dzogchen is something to do, Dzogchen is something to imagine, something to hold in mind. Some focus on Dzogchen as being an object to keep your mind focused on, somewhere outside, maybe over there. *(Rinpoche points).* Others try to concentrate inwardly on Dzogchen as inside themselves. Some try to keep a state in between these two, and call that the Great Perfection. These days it seems like Dzogchen is being pulled around in all different directions. It's like tying something onto the tail of a dog, writing "Dzogchen" on it and seeing what happens. It may end up on the golden spire atop a temple, or it may be dragged through the gutter. Nobody really knows where it will end up.

My point here is that it is not good enough to invent some personal idea of Dzogchen and then train in that. If you do that, Dzogchen becomes something fabricated, something you've made up. You try to achieve something and you call that Dzogchen; or you cultivate something and what comes out of that, something you imagine in your mind, that is Dzogchen. None of these different kinds of pretense are the genuine, authentic Great Perfection.

If you want to penetrate to the real meaning of the Great Perfection, you need to place it high on your list of priorities. We need to pay special attention to something that we feel is important, which means setting aside time. If something is really important to us, we will spend time first finding out about it, then applying ourselves to it. We need to find a teacher, a master with whom we can really penetrate to the very core of what the Great Perfection is. That takes effort and dedication. It may involve some sense of sacrifice, but that is the only way to go about it. Dzogchen is not something we grab at and get in a matter of a few moments.

I see a lot of people — Tibetans, Chinese, Europeans and Americans. They all come and say, "I am practicing Dzogchen, I am training in Dzogchen. This is what I experienced. This is what I understand." Then they tell me something of what their experience is. What they are training in isn't necessarily Dzogchen. They have formed different ideas of their own. Some kind of flavor of Dzogchen does permeate their experience to an extent, but it's not the real thing.

Some people think that Dzogchen is when they lean back and take a break in the midst of their busy activities. Or that it's when they have eaten a delicious meal and their senses are really awake and wide open. They think, "Now I've got it!" Or maybe when they feel compassionate towards other beings or feel devotion towards their guru, they shed a few tears and feel really good about themselves and think "Wow! Now I understand Dzogchen!" But all these experiences are just a fragment of the big picture. It's really important to get the whole picture.

We should be extra-careful that we don't fool ourselves, because that's really not okay. It might be alright for somebody else to fool us, but if we fool ourselves it's definitely not okay. We should be smart about how we use our time. Maybe we worked really hard to save up a lot of money, and finally managed to buy an airplane ticket to come all the way to India or Nepal. We stayed here for a while, but when we look back afterwards we might realize that all we really did was hang around. Perhaps we didn't really apply ourselves to learning genuine meditation practice, because we got carried away by this and that. The sun was too hot ... it was too dusty and tiring ... so we went home and took a nap. Looking back afterwards, we realize that we only spent a small fraction of our time learning how to genuinely practice. That's what I mean by being not so smart.

Simply repeating what we heard is also not good enough. Dzogchen is not made up of pieces of information that we can collect and take home. Dzogchen teachings are about how to be *totally free*. It's not sufficient to only receive the teachings. It is essential to apply them, to live them. Right now we are enveloped in deluded experience. We have created a cage for ourselves out of our own disturbing emotions and duality, and we sit in it, day in and day out. We can remain in this cage — or we can use the Dzogchen instructions to break it open and become totally free. That is what the whole purpose is. I am working with this as well.

Similarly, it's not enough that we merely make a name for ourselves, that we go home and become known as someone who went to Nepal and got Dzogchen teachings. Actually, if you feel like that *is* enough; it's not so hard to do. We can go home and tell stories and be known as the person who studied in Nepal. But honestly, the Dharma is meant to go much deeper than that. It is meant to be used to become totally free. Not a little bit free, but *completely* free — waking up one hundred percent from this dream, this confusion that we have been in for so long. This may sound like I'm scolding you, but honestly it's not scolding, not at all. Please don't misunderstand.

The instructions that I am giving in this seminar and that are presented in this book are meant to help you to become free. These teachings belong to Vajrayana — in particular to Dzogchen, the Great

Perfection. The term 'Great Perfection' means that all conditioned phenomena, without any exception whatsoever, are perfect and complete. Nothing is excluded from the sphere or the basic space of your unconditioned nature.

The word *Dzogpa* in Tibetan can be understood in two ways. One meaning is 'finished' in the sense of perfected, that all conditioned experience is completed or finished within the unconditioned basic space. Another interpretation is that all experience is totally included or contained within that basic space. Either way, the point being made is that all conditioned experience is mistaken and deluded. When one sees through this delusion and exposes or reveals its very substance, everything dissolves into the ultimate, into the unconditioned basic space. So, you can say that the Great Perfection is something that is totally complete and doesn't exclude anything at all. In itself it is not made of any concrete substance whatsoever, not even so much as an atom; yet it is totally complete, nothing missing. That is the general definition of the Great Perfection.

What I was just describing could be called the view, in that it is something that we try to realize or achieve or attain. Within this Great Perfection itself, however, categories such as ground, path and fruition or view, meditation and conduct do not really exist as separate entities. On the other hand, in our personal experience as individuals who have not yet realized the view, the different aspects like ground, path and fruition, or view, meditation and conduct can be quite helpful. It is said that the categories of ground, path and fruition or meditation, view and conduct are like different levels in space. In space itself, of course, there aren't really any different levels. But on the other hand, our way of experiencing things is not yet beyond conceptual mind. Because we are still on this side of conceptual mind, we have to operate with practical concepts like ground, path and fruition.

In this book I will outline ground, path and fruition in the hope of helping you gain some understanding about your basic nature, your own mind. This nature of mind is always present, and it can be called different names: the natural state, the basic nature, the real condition, the enlightened essence, or buddha-nature. This basic nature is what is meant by ground.

Path is a state of confusion which is not recognizing this ground, our basic state, to be as it is. Conceptual mind and time are both present during the path. But when your mind is pure, free of these, that is called fruition, and that is what is to be attained. To reiterate, confusion is called path. This confusion can be cleared up. There are three methods to clarify confusion: view, meditation and conduct. By means of the view, meditation and conduct we reveal what is already present. Slowly and gradually, we uncover more and more of the basic state. This process is what I will try to explain.

THE GROUND

THE MOST IMPORTANT ASPECT in Buddhism is mind, and mind means attitude. We need to form a genuine attitude about engaging in the Buddhist path. Once we've decided to enter it, we should think, "What a fortunate situation I've encountered! I'm very happy about this, and I'll make full use of it. I'll use this situation not merely to make me temporarily happy or to achieve something for myself, but in order to diminish my disturbing emotions and progress towards enlightenment for the sake of all sentient beings." This kind of attitude is something we need to train in.

Having formed this attitude, we need to work on realizing that everything is pure just the way it is. Everything is intrinsically free and perfect, and this is not just our imagination. The very nature of all things is an original purity. Whether we are talking about the nature of mind or the nature of all things, it is basically pure. This purity is not somehow separated from the impure aspect of things. Nor is it some product that we need to create or achieve. It is a natural purity, already present. Do you understand this principle? This is very important.

This original purity is not to be regarded as a product, a creation of something new, something that is not already present. It's not like that at all. Original purity is not something created or accomplished. We may imagine that because we so obviously experience impurity that there must be purity somewhere else that we can get to, as if we are in a foul-smelling room and we imagine a beautiful fragrance in another place. That's not it. This purity does not fall into any category; it belongs to neither samsara nor nirvana. In this context, it is not as if samsara is some impure state and nirvana is some pure place somewhere else. The purity of our intrinsic innate nature is present throughout all states — not falling into the category of samsara, not falling into the category of nirvana, but pervasive throughout. I will talk more about this later.

This term, innate nature or basic substance or basic element, buddha nature, essence of all buddhas — this is what buddhas actually are. This is what the purity is, and this is what the training is in, what the Dzogchen training is all about.

Ground, path and fruition — all of these terms are basically about this innate nature, which is not confined to only to samsara or only nirvana. Our basic state is something which is present in every situation, whether samsaric or nirvanic, without belonging to either. In a way one could say it's the shared or common ground of these two states. So that is the purity, the purity of the basic state. The most important thing to understand at first is the ground, the basic state.

This nature, what is it? It is pure. Purity. Is this something that we can accomplish? No, it isn't. Does it belong to samsara? No. Does it belong to nirvana? No. Yet it's present throughout all states. That basic nature is what we should fully realize. It's difficult to find an accurate example of how this innate nature really is. One comparison that is often used is space. Space is not limited to being only between the walls and the pillars, not just between the floor and the ceiling — space is throughout everything.

I would now like to define the word 'mind.' The Tibetan word is *sem*. Basically it means *that which knows*, that which thinks that things are "nice" or "not nice." Because there is some sense of knowing, there is some identity, some property of that which knows. Exactly what is it, how is it? In essence, it is your innate nature, which is all-pervasive, ever-present.

Most important is to remember we don't have to think of mind as a concrete 'thing.' It's really more a quality of knowing — of knowing and thinking. This word 'mind' is going to be used a lot, but please remember every time you hear or read it that it simply means some act of knowing or thinking. It's really pretty simple. Knowing, just that.

There are many ways that knowing takes place. There can be dualistic knowing, or knowing which is free of duality. In either case, our mind is simply just knowing. The word *sem* means dualistic knowing. Maybe you feel like a lot of words are being thrown out at you right now, but please just catch them and keep them. We will put them together later.

Now let's look at ground, path and fruition. Earlier I briefly discussed ground, our basic nature. This basic nature is described as something which does not belong to either samsara or nirvana, and yet is present throughout all states, whether samsaric or nirvanic. It doesn't belong to either, yet is all-pervasive. Ground is something which is present as the very nature of this knowing mind. You can say this knowing is something which is empty and yet cognizant. These two aspects, emptiness and cognizant, are indivisible — you can't separate them. Sometimes three indivisible aspects are described: empty in essence, cognizant by nature and unconfined in capacity. This indivisible nature of mind is always present and it is called by different names: the natural state, the basic nature, the real condition, the enlightened essence or buddha-nature. Regardless of what name it goes by, this is what is meant by ground.

Path, in this context, is called confusion. From the Buddhist perspective we are not talking about only one lifetime of confusion, but innumerable lifetimes. The basic confusion is this: not recognizing the basic state, the ground, to be as it is, one confuses it or mistakes the basic state for being something other. An example would be if I mistook the rosary that I am holding in my hand for something else, believing it to be a snake, or a piece of rope, mistaking its concrete physical form, smell, texture, and so forth.

This process of solidifying that which obscures our basic state has gone on for many, many lifetimes, not just for a short while. Our confusion is long-term. It's through training in the view, meditation, and conduct that we rediscover what is already present. Through training, we are reintroduced to the basic state.

Ground means the nature of our mind, our basic state, which has the capacity to be enlightened, to be awakened. By 'enlightened' we mean able to be free. Everyone has this kind of potential. That is our ground.

The ground is the nature of things.
This nature, dharmata, is self-existing.
This dharmata nature is not fabricated.
It's not something that was once constructed.
It is not something that originally didn't exist and was then created.
It is not something that we can improve or modify in any way.
It simply is what is.
What naturally is.
The natural state, itself.
Not made by the Buddha.
Not made by sentient beings.
Not made by the four elements.
It is a nature which just is, by itself.

The Buddha did not come into this world and create this basic nature. Everything is naturally pervaded by emptiness. Likewise, mind is naturally and always pervaded by a nature which is empty and cognizant. By 'everything,' I am referring to material or concrete things as well. They're all permeated by an empty quality, and it is this very quality that allows things to come into being. That empty quality is still present even when things exist. In the same way, all states of consciousness are permeated by a nature which is both empty and cognizant.

The empty quality of things means the openness that allows for the thing to come into being, to unfold, to be present. You can move your hand around in mid-air because the space is open, right? Another word for this open quality is 'empty.' Here's another example: this stick I'm holding in my hand can disintegrate. It has a perishable nature, right? The fact that its existence is impermanent proves that it is empty in

25

nature. These examples provide a rough idea of what empty quality means in this context.

Our nature — and now we're back talking about mind — this mind right here — is something which is basically both empty and cognizant, indivisibly. What happens in a normal moment of perception, when we are looking at a flower, for example, is that our basic identity, this unconfined, empty cognizance, becomes confined in the moment of perceiving. Somehow the empty quality becomes limited to being the perceiver, while the cognizance of the perceived, of what is present, is confined to being the object. The original unconfined and empty cognizance becomes apparently split up into perceiver and perceived, subject and object.

Of course, this isn't really the case; it just *seems* like that. This mistaking of what seemingly is as being real is confusion. That is what confusion really is: mistaking something that seems to be for what it isn't. At the same moment, one fails to recognize what actually *is*. Delusion is this ongoing, moment-to-moment conceptualizing activity of fabricating a subject and object that don't really exist.

It's as if we see a colored rope lying on the ground, mistake it for a snake, and panic. The rope and the snake look alike, and because of not directly seeing what is what, we become confused. On the other hand, when we recognize that the rope is simply a rope — when we recognize it for being what it is — the notion that it is a snake vanishes. That is only possible because the *snakeness* doesn't exist in any way whatsoever in the rope. Therefore, that which so terrified us was merely a construct created by our own thoughts.

That is why it is said that disturbing emotions have no real existence in the ground itself. Disturbing emotions, which are the basic cause of samsara, only come about during path through mistakenness, through delusion. Path is synonymous with being confused. Path is to be mistaken. Ground is our basic state, which is pure in nature. It's because we don't know this purity — because we don't acknowledge it — that we confuse it with impurity. So, confusion occurs on the path. When this confusion is cleared up, that's called fruition.

Among these three, where are we right now? We are at the path stage — being confused. Why do we practice the Dharma? Because we have the basic state, the essential nature as ground. It is like the oil present in sesame seeds, which can be released with the proper procedure of pressing. It's not something completely nonexistent or imaginary, like oil in sand. All that is necessary is to acknowledge what we have as what we have. We need a method for recognizing this, and such a method does exist.

What do we need to recognize? We need to recognize our basic state, the ground. This basic state encompasses enlightened body, speech and mind — body present as essence, speech present as nature and mind radiantly present as capacity. Because the enlightened body, speech and mind are already present as the identity of the ground, as a mere dependent relationship with that, right now, when we are on the path, our identity is one of having a body, a voice and a mind.

To go back to the example, without the rope there wouldn't be the notion of snake. In fact, it would be impossible to have the notion of something being this snake if there wasn't a rope. In the same way, enlightened body, speech and mind, in the form of essence, nature and capacity, are already present as our basic state, the ground. Only because of this is it possible to be mistaken about what we are. In a country where there is no rope, you would never mistake a piece of rope for a snake, because there would be no basis for misunderstanding.

Let's go one step deeper into exploring our confusion. Because we've failed to acknowledge that the enlightened body is present as essence, it has turned into a physical body. The enlightened body as essence lies beyond arising and disintegration, birth and death. It has not been acknowledged, and now it appears in the form of something that takes birth and later dies. It is the same with our voice and mind.

To reiterate, the path stage is one of confusion. We are on the path right now and this confusion needs to be clarified. The method used to clarify confusion on the path is threefold: view, meditation and conduct. This is where recognizing *rigpa* comes in.

This rigpa which needs to be realized is actually an aspect of the ground, an aspect of our dharmakaya nature. But rigpa can also be considered something to be recognized during the path. In this regard, path and ground are identical in essence. It is only a difference of one's essential nature being covered by confusion, or not covered by it.

When recognizing the naked state of rigpa, we are like this *(Rinpoche shows a piece of blue cloth)*. This is the ground, but it is covered by the path *(Rinpoche covers the blue cloth with pieces of white, green, red and yellow paper)*. You can see there are many different types of coverings, including emotional obscurations and cognitive obscurations. The notions we have — first 'I,' as in 'I am,' which is followed by 'my,' 'mine' and so forth — these notions are like opaque veils that cover the basic ground.

There are various ways to remove these obscurations, including the meditation practices of shamatha and vipashyana, the development stage, training in the completion stage with attributes, utilizing the key vajra points of channels, energies and essences, and so forth. A single meditation technique removes a single layer of obscuration. When at some point we arrive at what is called the first *bhumi*, also known as the 'path of seeing,' realization dawns in our stream of being. Gradually all the covers are removed, so that eventually the ground is totally revealed. That is the realization of dharmakaya.

It's generally believed that this process takes a tremendously long time. There must be a more direct method than gathering merit and purifying obscurations through three incalculable aeons! The Dzogchen approach to removing obscurations and uncovering our basic nature is indeed direct and quick. The Dzogchen view involves cutting through to primordial purity. The Dzogchen teachings have three sections: mind section, space section and instruction section. Within the instruction section there are two aspects: *kadag trekchö,* the cutting through of primordial purity, and *lhündrub tögal,* the direct crossing of spontaneous presence.

From the Dzogchen perspective, everything that covers or obscures the pure basic ground is called thought, or conceptual mind. Regardless of whether it is karma or habitual tendencies, it is contained within conceptual attitude. Trekchö is the thorough cut of cutting through, cutting the obscurations completely to pieces, like slashing through them with a knife. So the past thought has ceased, the future thought hasn't yet arisen, and the knife is cutting through this stream of present thought. But one doesn't keep hold of this knife either; one lets the knife go, so there is a gap. When you cut through again and again in this way, the string of thought falls to pieces. If you cut a rosary in a few places, at some point it doesn't work any longer.

If you cut Tsoknyi Rinpoche's head off, and cut his arms and legs off, and continue cutting, cutting in this way, at some point there is no longer any Tsoknyi Rinpoche. If you only cut off Tsoknyi Rinpoche's head, you can say here is Tsoknyi Rinpoche's head and here is his body, those two pieces. But if you cut the head up again and say here are the cheeks and here are the eyes and so on, soon you won't be able to call those pieces a head any longer. And if you cut those pieces up really finely, if you mince them up completely, finally there are no separate things left at all. Eventually it becomes emptiness. There is only the name left of Tsoknyi Rinpoche, there is no thing to attach that to. If Tsoknyi Rinpoche is not that famous, after a few generations even the name vanishes as well. Everything vanishes, even the name.

Confusion needs to be chopped into pieces in the same way. The conceptual frame of mind is not one solid lump; it's not a single concrete thing. It's actually made up of small pieces which are connected in a vague sort of way. You can call that vague sort of connection karma, or habit, or the thinking mind. But if you know how to really recognize, a gap immediately appears. Then it's like your obscurations have been removed, allowing a little piece of your basic nature to be visible. So it gets covered again, and again you need to recognize rigpa. You'll find that as you chop more and more, the ability of the obscurations to return actually becomes less and less.

Even if only a little piece of the basic state is visible, if it is the genuine, real thing, that is the recognizing of dharmakaya. But whether we actually recognize or not is dependent solely upon ourselves. The

Dzogchen teaching on how to recognize is available and is being taught. But how it is applied by a person is something entirely up to the individual. One cannot say that everyone recognizes or everybody doesn't recognize — exactly who recognizes and who doesn't is not fixed. We can know that for ourselves.

We need to recognize in a way that is not mixed up with concepts, with attachment, with clinging, with resting or dwelling on something. And in a way that is not mixed up with analysis either. Everything is perceived, yet we are not stuck in the perceiving. This is a very important sentence: "Everything is perceived, yet we are not stuck in the perceiving." The natural expression of the basic essence of mind can move or manifest in two different ways. One is as a conceptual frame of mind, a thought. The result of that is confusion. The other is the expression showing itself as intelligence or knowledge. That becomes original wakefulness, which results in liberation.

I'm using the word conceptual a lot here. A concept is a thought formed about a subject and object. A conceptual attitude is based on this holding onto of subject and object. The subject and object can be many different things. Most obviously, they can be material objects that we see or hear. For instance, when looking at this mandala plate in front of me, the mind fixes its attention on the plate as an object. Through the medium of the eyes occurs the visual cognition of the mandala plate as by a perceiver, the subject, and inevitably some thought is formed about it. The process is the same for all the senses. That is an example of conceptual mind at work.

There is another, more subtle way conceptual mind operates. Basically, conceptuality implies duality — duality of this and that, of subject and object. This does not only refer to external material things: it could also be that the previous thought is the object and the present thought is the subject. Conceptual also implies the notion of time, whether it be in the gross materialistic sense of an external interaction, or the more subtle internal sense of one thought looking at the previous thought, or looking back into a past memory. While it's not overtly dualistic, there is still some lapse there, some sense of time. The sense of time is always conceptual. Something which is temporal is always conceptual; thus, the notion of time is conceptual. The notion of time is a conceptual state. Is that clear?

Now I will introduce what is meant by the path. Path here refers to not knowing the basic nature — thinking of our basic state as being something other than what it actually is. That is called path. Path is delusion. This delusion or confusion essentially means we fail to know our basic nature as it is, and instead mistake it for something else. That is the confusion. Not recognizing what is to be what it is, but regarding it as something other. Mind, and the nature of mind, is fundamentally pure. When we fail to recognize the identity or nature of what knows as something pure, free, egoless and insubstantial — and when we instead regard the nature of this knowing as being 'me' or 'I,' and hold onto that concept — this is a small view, and it is confused, mistaken. Introducing the idea of me/I is mistaking our essential nature for something that it isn't.

At some point, by means of some method, we are introduced to our basic nature and recognize what is to be as it is. When confusion has thoroughly been cleared up, that is fruition. When this mistakenness is dissolved; where does it go? Nowhere, because the confusion never existed in the first place. If the confusion was a real entity, then when it went away we could follow it and see where it went. But it wasn't real at all.

Among these three, ground, path and fruition, ground is purity, pure. Path is confusion, and fruition is being free from confusion. If anybody asks us what is spiritual practice about, we should reply that it is to clear up confusion. If someone asks what is confusion, what are you going to say?

STUDENT: Conceptual thought.

RINPOCHE: What is conceptual thought?

STUDENT: Delusion.

RINPOCHE: What is delusion?

STUDENT: Thinking something to be that it isn't.

RINPOCHE: How do you know what is to be what it is? What is the use of being free from confusion? What is wrong with confusion?

STUDENT: It is suffering, and knowing that is the path.

RINPOCHE: The Buddha said that, didn't he? Okay, let's hear from somebody else: what is the use of being free from confusion? How many of you agree that we are confused? Why are we confused? Why do you accept this?

STUDENT: Although we intellectually understand what you said about things to be as they are, we don't have the personal experience.

RINPOCHE: One more answer?

STUDENT: Not getting what we want causes pain.

RINPOCHE: Just because what you want doesn't happen, does it mean there is something wrong with what you want? Who decides how things should be? Who knows whether that's right or not?

TRANSLATOR: Can I just interject that when Rinpoche uses the word *trül*, I translate it in three different ways: delusion, confusion or being mistaken.

RINPOCHE: There is being confused and there is being free. What do you understand by being free?

STUDENT: No thought.

RINPOCHE: That's one point of being free.

STUDENT: Not falling under the power of habitual tendencies.

RINPOCHE: Good.

STUDENT: Being awake and having an open heart.

RINPOCHE: How do you explain being awake and having an open heart?

STUDENT: Doing virtuous activities for the benefit of beings and avoiding the negative.

RINPOCHE: These are all aspects of freedom. Free of confusion means being free from the bonds of karma, whether it be good karma or bad karma. To be free and independent. Freedom *means* independence, a state in which one is totally unassailable, not impeded or obstructed by anything. Not even the tiniest little thing can obstruct your freedom in the least. That you can call true freedom.

Feeling at peace is of course a freedom, or at least has the flavor of freedom, but real freedom, total freedom, means to be completely independent, not subject to or conditioned by anything whatsoever. In the complete realization of the three kayas — dharmakaya, sambhoga-kaya, nirmanakaya — one is free to send out 100, billion nirmanakayas simultaneously or not, as one pleases. One is also able to dissolve all of them at will. To be totally in charge, to have full mastery over all that appears and exists in this way — that you can say is complete freedom, total freedom.

In order to attain this freedom, we need to abandon conceptual mind. Honestly, conceptual mind belongs to the path; it is mistaken, it is confused. Conceptual mind is temporal, it belongs to time, it is bound, it is bondage. This is something to think about.

You are probably all tired by now after all this discussion. Relax, make yourselves comfortable! Be unoccupied, but not in a dry, rigid way, being very stiff and unmoving, not like that. Try to be unoccupied and kind of moist with some inner joy, so that a little smile can come out, like that.

Questions?

STUDENT: Are the ground and rigpa the same?

RINPOCHE: In one particular context, ground is identical with rigpa, nondual knowing. In this context, however, ground refers to our basic state, while rigpa is something recognized while on the path. Once rigpa is fully recognized, one realizes that rigpa and ground are identical, not two different things. It's like when we look towards the moon on the first day of the lunar month. We see only a thin sliver, right? Our view changes as the moon waxes fuller and fuller, but it remains the same moon.

Likewise, right now, regardless of whether we call what we recognize rigpa or dharmakaya, it's still only a sliver; a brief glimpse. But once the strength of our realization has been fully perfected, we can truly say that rigpa and ground are indivisible. At that point there is no more talk about view, meditation and conduct; no mention of ground, path and fruition. All that belonged to the path.

VIEW

WHEN WE DISCUSS THE WAYS to be free, we begin with three aspects: view, meditation and conduct.

There are basically two types of view, conceptual and nonconceptual. Conceptual view is when we start with shamatha training, cultivating a mind that is still and quiet. Our mind becomes more and more quiet, more and more subtle until there remains only a single moment, called the 'indivisible instant of consciousness.' According to the *shravaka* perspective, there are two absolutes, the indivisible atom of matter and the indivisible instant of consciousness. Meditation practice gradually eliminates the dwelling on coarse things, until only those two absolutes are left. As a shamatha meditator, one reaches a state where all sensation and thought ceases — at least to a certain degree. It is possible to get stuck in that state of cessation, but more importantly, we should recognize that this whole process belongs to conceptual view. Seen from the Dzogchen perspective, the entire process, beginning with the materialistic frame of mind and continuing until it's quieted down to this single instant in time, is still based on a conceptual view.

According to Dzogchen teachings, then, this is not the true view, because the end result is not unconfined, unimpeded mind, but merely a state of cessation. This is a very important point. If we begin with letting our attention rest on something, of course we will go beyond disturbing emotions and gross thoughts. However, some sense of dwelling on the present moment, the present awareness, remains, even though it may become more and more subtle.

While keeping to the shamatha meditation, this sense of resting or dwelling on something is never really relinquished. Thus, the 'being in the present' is never true freedom, real liberation, because there is no freedom from the present moment. Sure, this state is pleasant, it is tranquil, it is quiet. But it is still *bound*, bound by the sense of nowness which is subtle and conceptual way of directing the mind. There is no strong movement of the attention, there is no sense of being occupied with thoughts of the past or hopes or fears about the future. Everything has been quieted down. There is no strong fixation on anything, no sense of hope or expectation or fear — and yet a very subtle dwelling on the nowness remains. So the question arises, is this state that of a meditation gone wrong? We can't say that it has completely gone wrong, because after all, it does remain a meditative state in the sense of being undistracted. It's just not the perfect state. Keep that in mind.

Now we will discuss the real thing — nonconceptual view. Right now we will be concerned not so much with what has happened in the past, or what is going to happen in the future, but just about this present moment. This present moment you do have the capacity to know. That sense of knowing is what we call mind.

Where is this mind and what does it look like? We can look for it, but it's very hard to pin it down to a specific location. On the other hand, this ability to know does undeniably exist. If the mind was a concrete thing it should be possible to locate it and say "This is where it is," but mind is not concrete. It is inconcrete, but at the same time you cannot say that there is no mind. It is inconcrete and yet present.

There *is* mind, because we do know, right? We have thoughts like this: "Oh, my back is hurting. My meditation last night wasn't that great. The sleep wasn't that nice either." The sense of knowing that the insulation pad in your tent wasn't that insulating after all — this knowing is called mind. It is not the brain that knows. Mind is not brain, although there is some close link between the mind and the brain. But mind is not matter, it is inconcrete, and yet it still most definitely exists. We can understand the mind to be this capacity of knowing.

This knowing sometimes occupies itself with visible physical form, sometimes with audible sounds, sometimes with smells, sometimes with tastes, sometimes with textures. It alternates between paying attention to and perceiving these different things, now one, now another. Mind works in conjunction with something seen, heard, smelled, tasted, or felt. The knowing of these things is what we call mind. This knowing involves subject and object: object being sights, sounds, smells, tastes and textures, subject being that which knows these things. Objects include tangible material objects, as well as more subtle objects involving memory. "Before I did such-and-such." "I thought such-and-such" — this kind of thinking involves a subsequent thought recalling a previous thought. In Tibetan, we call this kind of dualistic conceptual mind *sem*. Sem always involves a conceptual knowing by means of subject and object.

Now I will make an important distinction between the thinking mind and mind-essence. Mind and mind-essence are the same, yet they are not identical. It's like the front and back of a hand — it's the same hand, but different aspects. Mind and mind-essence are one, but not the same, rather like ice and water.

Mind-essence has three qualities. It is empty in essence; there is no identity there, it is utterly empty. At the same time, its nature is to be cognizant, able to know. Finally, the way this essence works or operates is unimpeded, totally unconfined. Certainly this is an intellectual way of talking about mind-essence, but sometimes intellectual comprehension is necessary. Let's examine this further. 'Empty essence' means that when one looks for it, there is no finding, no center, no edge. There is no place out of which mind-essence came, there is no place it goes to or disappears into, and there is no place it is right now. Nevertheless, it is present throughout, in an all-pervasive way. Empty essence is just like that.

'Cognizant nature' means that an awake quality exists simultaneously with this emptiness. This quality is the ability to know. In the context of mind-essence, cognizant nature means knowing that the essence is empty, that it has no center, no edge. In contrast, right now our sense of knowing involves *sem*, in that there is a center and an edge. We know that "I'm here and you're there," that there is a top and bottom and so forth. All these concepts can be termed 'cognizant nature,' but this type of cognizance involves the knowing of dualistic and conceptual mind, of *sem*.

The knowing involved in mind essence, on the other hand, is simply acknowledging that the essence is empty — that there is no center and no edge. This involves knowing how this essence is in actuality, right now. In other words, it is the knowing of the basic space of things, traditionally called *dharmadhatu*. It is out of this knowing that the omniscient quality of buddhahood is slowly revealed. Please don't misunderstand this as the empty essence being the object which is known by a subject called cognizant nature. It's not like one observes the other. Now, the third aspect of being unconfined is also by definition indivisible from the first two. While being empty, the knowing of that is not separate from it.

Let me repeat some points, since the view is so very important. The view depends on our state of mind, so we need to know what this mind is. There are two aspects of mind — the thinking mind and mind essence. These two, to repeat the example, are like water and ice: same nature, different form. It is possible for water to be ice. It is also possible for ice to be water. The same substance can appear as both ice and water, right? In the same way, our ordinary thinking and mind essence are not two totally separate things. They are interrelated in a fundamental way. So we begin with finding out what is thinking mind; then we discover the nature of this thinking mind — mind essence.

First of all, mind is not a concrete or material thing. It is something which is immaterial and also very powerful. So you can say it is immaterial, and yet it exists. It is no thing, yet it is. Okay? How does this thinking mind work? What does it do? We have five sense organs: eyes, ears, nose, tongue, body. Apart from these senses, there exist sights, sounds, smells, tastes, and textures. Consciousness perceives through these five senses by seeing, hearing, smelling and so forth. There is also a sixth way of noticing, which is through memory or thought. So there are a total of six ways of knowing or perceiving. All of these involve the workings of mind through subject and object. These two words, subject and object, are very important in the Dzogchen context, along with thinking mind and mind essence.

Now, this thinking mind is something very sticky. It's always latching onto something. The attention reaches out through one of the five senses to catch hold of a particular object, or it conjures up a memory from the past, or anticipates something in the future. It's always catching hold of something either in the present, through the senses, or in the past or future, through conceptual thought. Thinking mind doesn't remain and relax freely; it's always busy taking hold of something. Constant activity is how the thinking mind works.

We can also say thinking mind is unstable in itself. It doesn't simply remain. Whenever a beautiful form manifests *(Rinpoche whistles a tune as an example)*, it immediately catches hold of that and falls into attachment. When it perceives something unpleasant, it feels aversion towards that, falling in another direction. When there is something that is pleasant, our attention is immediately attracted, while with something unpleasant, we feel dislike. When there's something in between, then we don't care. We shut off. Sometimes that movement of attention is very subtle, as when for instance you feel faintly attracted towards something. At other times, very strong attachment or aversion can arise. Regardless of the magnitude, the attention is always busy moving towards something or away from something. That constant movement is how mind works.

Like, dislike, and indifference are the famous three poisons, and thinking mind is always under their spell. In other words, mind is not independent, because it's always caught up in something. It is controlled by circumstance, and is thus unfree. It's not independent and free in itself. Thinking mind is always facing away from itself, extroverted. Do you understand this? As an example, think of someone you might know who is constantly engrossed in external affairs and never pays any attention to what's going on inside him or herself.

In our modern times, with the development of more and more gadgets, our attention is even busier, occupied, caught up in things. There are simply more things to be caught up in! It's like being absorbed in what's going on TV. When you watch television or a movie, you can totally lose yourself. Your attention is totally caught up in what's taking place on the screen, which can feel so real that it can seem like an entire world. It's the power of mind, of consciousness, that makes the screen into such a big landscape. When our attention is caught up in another area — let's say two kilometers out into the distance — then there is no real sense of being just what one is, where one actually is. Losing track of oneself like this creates some kind of instability, which can give rise to anxiety and fear. Mind is split up into something other, far away, and there's no real knowledge of what mind actually is.

Instead of reacting in this fashion, what we really need to do is to acknowledge exactly what this mind is — our essence, our own buddha nature — by recognizing it. We've looked at how the thinking mind works. Now we need to know mind essence. In fact, you know very well how thinking mind works through your experience of daily life, every day and every night! So there's no need to talk a lot about it. What we do need to know is how not to be caught up in *sem* — how to be free. Even though we are enmeshed in it now, we don't have to be like this. We can change our minds.

First, we should understand that this thinking mind has an essence, which is not a separate entity that is totally apart from it. Mind essence is linked with this thinking mind, but it is something different as well.

Like everything else, mind essence is empty. What is meant by empty? Let's talk about the emptiness of a flower. The fact that a flower can come into being is proof that it is empty of inherent being. Before it didn't exist, now it does — thus, it is impermanent. That it can remain or exist for a while means that it is empty. And the fact that it finally disintegrates or falls apart is further proof that it is empty. The fact that anything can arise, exist and then disappear proves that it is empty. That is the emptiness of external things. Similarly, just as outer things are empty, the thinking mind is also empty. It shares the same properties of coming into being, existing for a time, then disintegrating.

Mind essence, on the other hand, is empty in a different way. It is something that has not come into being. It doesn't really exist anywhere in any particular way. And in the end, mind essence does not disintegrate or vanish. The emptiness of mind essence revolves around the fact it's something which is not produced, doesn't remain and doesn't cease to be, either. In this kind of empty essence there is no center, no edge. Something that has no center has no end in any direction, does it?

Mind essence is empty, primordially and originally so.
It doesn't come into being,
It doesn't exist as something,
It doesn't cease to be.
You can say it is nothing, no thing,
But at the same time there is mind essence.
You can call it empty. That is fine.
All this is just talking about it.
When we actually experience it, what is it like?
It's a feeling of being open,
Totally wide open.
A moment of being totally open,
Unconfined in any direction.
Not a concrete thing: not at all.
It's empty — it's not made out of anything whatsoever.
That is what is called empty essence.
It is totally clear and wide awake,
So there is nothing to pinpoint as "This is it!"
It has neither back nor front; like space.
Without thoughts, nothing held in mind, no perceiver —
But it's not nothing, either.
Totally clear, like crystal —
That is the experience of the empty quality.

As I said, this empty mind essence is not a nothingness, not an absence like physical space. It's not exactly like an empty cup, because the cognizant nature, the quality of knowing, exists inseparably with this empty essence. What is known possesses no center and no edge; there is no arising, no remaining, and no ceasing. At the moment it is known, it is simply like that. Mind essence is totally clear and open, not confined in any way, yet wide awake and conscious.

If we're talking about thinking mind, there is the mind thinking of something in terms of subject and object. But in the case of mind essence, there's no need for subject and object. Instead, there's a spontaneous knowing which is natural cognizance, a 'self-knowing.' This natural knowing is like a candle flame. The flame emanates light all by itself, so that you don't need to shine a torch on it in order to see it. It's naturally illuminated, all by itself. The flame is self-illuminating. It doesn't have to be illuminated by an external force. In the same way, the mind essence is something which is empty by itself and aware by itself. It is not known because one *tries* to know it; it is naturally known. You could call this self-knowing.

When we hear this we shouldn't try to picture empty essence, like trying to imagine how open space looks like. That kind of intellectual effort is not at all necessary. It's actually much easier than that. Just let your mind recognize itself, and immediately there's an open, aware feeling which knows, all by itself. There's openness, and there's immediately a knowing of that openness. That which is aware that mind is wide open is the cognizant quality. When you simply let yourself be like that, understanding automatically unfolds. A *lot* of understanding. This insight does not arise through thought. It's not conceptual.

How do we discriminate between what is thought and what is not? Thought, in Tibetan called *namtok*, is always dualistic, involving a subject and an object. A thought is by definition about something and holds onto that something. It involves the fixing of attention on something. But in the play of natural awareness, as in the case of mind essence, there is no subject and no object. The difference between thought and nonthought is the duality of subject and object.

You might be wondering what is meant by subject and object. Thinking involves a subject thinking of an object, and a fixing of the attention. This last point is very important. If we really look into what happens when a thought unfolds, we see it is attention fixing itself. We need to release this fixing, totally and completely — because then it's simply the cognizant nature and empty essence by itself.

What is it that prevents us from being as we naturally are? It's this basic subject-object fixing of attention. But there is also the possibility of an unfolding of awareness which is independent of subject and object, and is thus unobstructed. could the Dzogchen teachings say that our capacity unfolds in an unconfined way. However it's phrased, there is some energy, some play of mind essence, and this play is the unity of emptiness and cognizance. Do you understand this?

In order to experience this, we need to get used to it by training in it. We may progress slowly, but we should start out with getting the idea of it. There's thinking mind and mind essence. The thinking mind always holds on to subject and object. It always involves some clinging, whether it be to hope, to fear, or to not knowing. Mind essence, on the other hand, has three qualities. It is empty or wide open. There is a knowing of this openness, which is natural cognizance. Out of this natural cognizance wisdom unfolds, what we mean when we speak of the wisdom of the buddhas and their unimpeded knowledge of all things. That cognizant quality has no limit; it is unconfined.

The unity of these two — the unity of emptiness and cognizance — is the capacity. Capacity means ability or power. Every person has a certain degree of capacity. You can get up and run, right? That's an example of your capacity. In the same way, mind essence has the capacity to be compassionate, to understand, and to manifest in the exact appropriate form for the benefit of others. From the state of enlightenment, emanations can appear and all kinds of incredible miracles can be performed. All these aspects are different facets of the capacity of mind essence.

Thinking mind is like ice, while mind essence is like water. You cannot say ice is not water. But ice looks different than water, doesn't it? In the same way, thinking mind and mind essence are identical, but work in different ways.

When our attention is allowed to freeze in different ways, we get stuck in different experiences: heaven, hell, hungry ghosts, the animal realm, human beings, demigods or gods. All these different kinds of experiences result from the habits of being caught up in fixed mind. Fixating mind is like ice shaped in different forms. A piece of ice can be shaped in an infinite variety of ways: like a human being, a god or goddess, or even like an ice cube.

In the same way, the thinking mind fixes itself through karma and habits into all different kinds of forms and states. When it is in a really awkward way with itself, that is called hell. Different ways may be called different realms. Sometimes the mind appears and takes rebirth in the human body and looks like a human; sometimes in other ways. There's no end to the ways that mind can solidify and freeze itself as the result of different combinations of factors and circumstances and past karma and temporary conditions. When mind has no control, samsara unfolds in all possible ways.

Thinking mind is bondage. The thinking mind is like that all the time. As soon as something happens, it catches our attention in a reactive way. The "caught" attention is not free, that's the important thing to realize. It's so easily caught up in reacting. If someone says a nasty word to you, you immediately get angry. That's not being free.

If somebody abuses you or scolds you, you immediately lose your freedom to that. But you don't have to be angry. It's merely words that are being said. Usually we blame the other person for our attention getting stuck there, but actually we're to blame. The other person didn't grab our mind and let it get caught up. We did that ourselves.

Our thinking mind is always getting caught up in this way. When circumstances are pleasant we smile, we're happy, we say "Ah, how wonderful." When things hurt or feel unbearable we cry or we get depressed. Whether we are happy or sad, we are caught up, not free. We like to blame others for our condition. What about if instead we try and be free?

It's very nice to say "be free," but how can we do this? Some mechanism is involved here, a process which may at first be a little difficult.

First, you have to notice when mind is sitting like this, ready to grab at something. *(Rinpoche shows his hand in the gesture of being ready to grab something passing by).* We're all sitting like this right now; ready to grab hold of something. We are so inclined to send our attention outwardly all the time; in fact, we do this continuously. So instead of constantly going with the outward motion — being angry at this or attracted to that and so forth — instead of getting caught up, why not slow down a little? Just let go. What is it that is angry? Recognize who is angry; recognize that which gets angry. The mind that is angry should recognize itself. Then automatically, in that instant of recognition, the anger dissolves. It happens all by itself that very second. The very instant that which is getting caught up stops and recognizes itself, there's no more being caught up.

We constantly have a presentation or show going on in our minds, which may be either pleasant or unpleasant, beautiful or ugly. It happens to us all by itself. On one side are the objects being presented all the time; on the other is mind. The objects are of course impermanent. We may think, "I don't want to be apart from it," but inevitably it vanishes — and then we feel hurt. You can become so tired, so fed up with the whole process.

Instead, just let go. Letting go doesn't mean blacking out or spacing out. The moment of letting go is open, but it shouldn't be dull. It should be wide awake, and this state of wide-awake letting go lasts for a while. It has continuity, like this *(Rinpoche rings his bell).* There is some kind of continuity of that sound; some ongoing quality to the bell's tone. In the same way, the moment you let go and acknowledge this empty awareness, that acknowledgment lasts for a while. The wide-awake knowing called openness, or unimpededness, is totally free of thought, free of anything that is held in mind.

Now I will give you two more words to understand: stability, in the sense of being stable in oneself, and continuity. Try to remember these, because there is a certain depth of meaning to them.

It's not like knowing your own essence is something that you get to after a long while. Neither is it something you slowly discover. The very moment you recognize it, it is seen immediately. You have already arrived. Why is it like this? Because mind is not a concrete thing, not a material 'something.' If mind essence was a concrete thing, you could get closer and closer to it and finally touch it because there would be a certain amount of distance between it and you. But mind is immaterial. This immaterial mind can know itself. It is seen the moment you look. And, in the moment of seeing it's free. What is freed? The fixing of attention, the fixation of subject and object, subject on object.

This empty and awake essence that lasts for a little while is called seeing the view. In the Dzogchen teachings, this is called *rigpa*, natural awareness, a very important word. in rigpa there are three qualities present. It's empty in essence, it's cognizant by nature and its capacity is unconfined. Recognizing this threefold identity is called recognizing rigpa. Rigpa means awareness. But this is not awareness that is dualistic, in terms of subject looking at object. It is nondual awareness.

In the same way that the flame of a candle is self-illuminating, the essence of mind is self-knowing. It is said, 'seeing no thing is the supreme sight.' That's how it is. It is not a mistaken way of knowing. You can call that the view, or rigpa, or mind essence, any of those three names. It is the Dzogchen view, not of any kind of viewpoint. You can also call it mind essence because this is how your mind really is in itself. Not just how it looks like or how it appears, but how it is. Because it is the innermost, it's called essence. It's innermost or secret because it is always with you, and yet not known unless it is shown or pointed out.

There is a big difference between recognizing and not recognizing this. If you recognize, it is dharmakaya; if not, it is dualistic thinking. When recognizing, that itself is the very substance for awakening to enlightenment. The not-recognizing or the not-knowing of this essence is the very root cause of continuing in samsara.

For this view to be part of our experience after we have been introduced to it, we first need to deliberately remind ourselves. After that, we need to let be without effort. Therefore, there are two words: the meditation state and the post-meditation. Meditation state is letting be in evenness. Post-meditation is when you are activated. You think "I need to do this and that; how nice, how bad, I should eat, I need a drink, I must go there." That's the post-meditation.

During post-meditation you need to remind yourself to recognize mind essence. When looking, it is seen. While seeing, there is no need to look and look and look. If you keep on looking you're not in rigpa. Rigpa is naturally present.

At the moment of recognizing you don't have to try to figure out what it is. Just totally let go of any kind of concern or worry or thought. You won't go crazy. You won't lose the ability to think, either. Don't worry about that. I can guarantee this. People think "If I totally relax I won't be able to think." Some people think "If I totally let go then I get into some kind of emptiness and I'll end up who knows where — maybe in some other world." We don't have to be afraid of that. It won't happen, because there is a natural cognizance which, because it is empty in essence, is not limited to any one place. It gets opened up.

Usually when we fix our attention
We confine this natural cognizance.
Instead of doing that, why not simply let experience unfold?
There is some energy in the beauty,
In the ugliness,
In whatever situation you are in.
Just let it unfold, and you'll know more and more.
There's no need to fix it or nail it down.
Just be carefree and let things be.
Then every single state within samsara and nirvana
Will only unfold, more and more.
When we are wide awake, anything can take place, can't it?

When an old man watches children playing, he doesn't get too caught up in their chatter — he knows they are only playing. In the same way, we experience lots of different feelings and thoughts that well up suddenly and unexpectedly, all the time. Sometimes we're happy, sometimes we're unhappy; we experience like, dislike, worry, not caring, and so forth. Simply treat this constant flow of emotion with as little concern as if it were children playing. In such a state, any possible thought, any possible emotion can unfold.

If we had to act out every single thought we had, we would go crazy. There's no need to act out every single thought. Just let them pass. There is no end to the ambitions and wishes of the mind. It is always wanting something more. Instead of getting caught up in whatever you want in that moment, try to be more stable in yourself.

Any questions?

STUDENT: What is the difference between looking at the nature of mind before having decided on it and afterwards?

RINPOCHE: You're right, there are two ways of looking at the nature of mind. One is before you have recognized it; the other is after recognizing how it is. Looking into the nature of mind after having recognized it, you realize it is not something other that what it is: empty essence, cognizant by nature, and these two indivisible, not confined to one or the other. This is the identity of rigpa, not something new, not something other. It is as it is. But when we haven't yet recognized it, we just *hear* or *read* about its empty essence and cognizant nature, and that these two are indivisible. Intellectually we try to sort out how those concepts fit together. And at some point we settle this issue. We are now convinced that this is reasonable; that this is probably and maybe definitely how it is. To settle our minds on that is called resolving. Resolving is to feel intellectually sure of the nature of mind. Recognizing it is to actually experience it.

STUDENT: When we search for the mind, we discover that it has no center or edge, and so on. We cannot find it. Is it the same with the empty essence and the cognizant nature — do we search for them for a period of time?

RINPOCHE: You keep looking into these two qualities, the *unfindability* of being empty in essence, and the wide awake quality of being cognizant in nature, until you experience that they are actually one single identity. When you try to grab hold of a piece of space, how long do you have to try until you're successful? Five years? Ten years? Or is it that you can't grab hold of space? That space is not something that is approachable; you cannot reach space and catch it. It's like that. You look, you look, you look, you try to find. When you cannot find, relax in this not-finding. You try to grab the space, you grab it, grab it, grab it — but you find that you cannot grab hold of space. So you relax, because you are already in space — as a matter of fact, your hand was never outside of space!

STUDENT: At the time of not finding, how do we arrive at the natural cognizance?

RINPOCHE: First, understand that the truth of Dharma is not something to be achieved. Instead, it is realized by a sense of letting go. Let go of this impulse to grab hold of the space that we have been trying to catch for so long. Finally we become convinced that it's impossible to catch space. At that point, just let go — and you will find space is already present. Where does the cognizant nature come from? It's already present. Isn't there a knowing that it is not something findable; isn't there a knowing of its basic unfindability? Isn't there a knowing that this is how it is? That knowing doesn't have to come from somewhere else — it's already present. Letting go is exactly like that.

Let's say that the cognizant nature is like a candle flame. Do you have to cast light on the flame with a torch? No, because the radiance of the flame is already there. Just as the flame has its own radiance, mind knows how it is in itself. Knowing by itself. The flame and its light are the same, identical. In the same way, the empty essence of mind is self-known. It doesn't have to be made known by something other. It's not like shining a torch on the Vajrasattva image: that Vajrasattva is over there, the torch is here and the moment you press the switch, Vajrasattva becomes known. It is not like that at all. It's more like Vajrasattva himself is already illuminated.

In the same way, when recognizing mind essence, the essence of what knows is seen as naturally empty and naturally cognizant. These two qualities are not separate. It's important first of all to know how to recognize mind essence. Second, it's important to see mind essence. Third, it's important to know how to let mind essence be. It is not enough to merely *know* *about* mind essence. We all already have mind essence; it's not enough to simply know about it. We need to *experience* it. What is necessary is that mind essence and its knowing need to be one, indivisible. Mingled as one in our own seat, so to speak — that is self-knowing.

STUDENT: Does this self-knowing apply to being aware of thoughts?

RINPOCHE: Just noticing that a thought arises doesn't help much. The thought needs to be liberated. Thinking, "Now there is a thought, it is a thought of such-and-such" — that is simply noticing. It's like being a shepherd watching what his sheep are doing. There is still some subject-object duality: "I wonder, maybe the sheep are getting lost," or "I need to make sure the sheep stay in the pasture." It's just like thinking, "Now there's a thought. Now this thought is thinking of such-and-such. Now it went." What is really necessary is to be in a way in which the movement of thoughts disappear without a trace, like drawing on the surface of water.

There are two ways to do this. The first, which is good for beginners, involves a thought being liberated the same moment you remember to look into its essence. — In the moment of recognizing your basic nature, the movement of thought is like the drawing on the surface of water. The second way is the moment something is thought, it is dissolved at the same time, simultaneously. This is for more advanced practitioners, and allows the attention to not be hooked by anything, not get caught up in anything.

It's not entirely accurate to call this kind of thinking thought. Let's call it a reflection instead. It's a kind of knowing of what needs to be done, what needs to be carried out, but it's not like an ordinary thought. If thinking involves a conceptual duality of subject and object there is also time, and therefore there is karma. That is not so perfect.

So, there are two ways. One is as soon as one thinks of something, one immediately recognizes the thinker, and this thinking dissolves. The other can be used when there is a good degree of stability in rigpa. Then any movement doesn't really distract from the essence. There is no sense of losing the continuity of knowing the mind essence, so that any thought that may move or not move neither helps nor harms. The essence is not caught up in anything at all. It's like a thief in an empty house, with nothing to do, nothing to take, nothing to grasp on to. Or it's like a crystal ball, where everything is reflected on the surface of the crystal, and yet the crystal doesn't go anywhere; it doesn't reach out to grasp anything. No matter what is reflected, it doesn't influence the crystal. Whatever these reflections look like, they don't help the crystal, nor do they harm it. The crystal remains as it is.

This example of the crystal points to the fact that the identity of rigpa or nondual awareness is unbroken. It is not caught up in subject and object based on what is perceived. Whatever takes place — sights, sounds, smells, tastes or textures — and whatever is understood about these doesn't obstruct in any way. All experience becomes the unfolding of original wakefulness. This is the very basis for the omniscient wisdom of buddhahood, called 'the wisdom of perceiving all possibly existing things.' Everything is unblocked, totally unblocked.

Usually a shamatha meditator blocks out everything except the nowness, and focuses his mind on just that. No thought, no nothing. Some people seem to believe training in Dzogchen involves sitting with open, glaring eyes and blocking out everything so that the attention is caught up in, or stuck in, the nowness of that moment. This seems to be a Western misconception. The Asian version is to sit and withdraw within. Different cultures create different habits, but we need to be in a way that is neither of these two. We need some kind of natural cognizance that is not caught up in subject and object but is steady in itself. Really, it's more like this:

Empty essence means very, very open
And very spacious, like a totally open sky.
Space has no center or edge.
Nothing is prevented, it is completely unimpeded.
Empty essence, like space, is not made out of anything whatsoever.
At the same time there is a sense of knowing,
An awake quality, a cognizant nature,
Not separate from the openness of this space.

Like the sun shining in daytime,
The daylight and space are not separate.
It's all sunlit space.
Nothing is confined, nothing is blocked out.
All the doors and windows are wide open.
Like a total welcome of — all possibilities—
Which doesn't get caught up in whatever happens.
It is wide open,
The unity of empty essence and cognizant nature.
This is the third quality, that of unconfined capacity.

When all the windows and doors are wide open, there is nothing that you are afraid to lose. There are no things in the house that can be stolen. Totally wide open. We don't need to be afraid at this point of being too open, like we will get lost. Don't fear that this knowing will somehow vanish because you will open up totally and somehow go crazy. You don't have to be afraid of that at all. In fact, it's only if we are *not* like that we will go crazy! Just let yourself be wide open, without any hope that you achieve something and without any fear that you will lose something. Remain completely without hope and fear.

This is how the mind essence is. We need to acknowledge that; recognize it — we need to recognize what we have. There are two contexts for this: the meditation state and the post-meditation state. Meditation state means to be as the essence, while post-meditation involves departing from that. Right now we are in the post-meditation state; from here, we need to get to the meditation state. When not recognizing, we need to recognize. Most important is recognizing.

BEGINNING MEDITATION

ONE CAN GO ABOUT MEDITATION PRACTICE in two different ways: in terms of achieving something, or in terms of getting rid of something. At this point, it's better to approach meditation practice from the second perspective, with the sense of becoming free. To have the attitude, "By meditating I will get something or I will achieve something" is not right. The basic meaning of confusion is to believe something to be in a way it in fact isn't. Meditation should allow us to realize or know the natural state — what really is. In other words, meditation is to be free from the mistakenness of believing something to be that isn't. That's why we say meditation is more a matter of getting rid of something than achieving something.

Let's make this slate clean from the beginning, free from the idea that we need to achieve something from meditation. If we think, "I must achieve something, I must get something out of this," we are already troubling ourselves in an unnecessary fashion.

How do we practice meditation? We start by sitting up in a very relaxed fashion. The body should be straight and upright, but not tight or rigid in any way — just totally free and relaxed. Don't control how you breathe; just let the breathe flow naturally. It's the same with your mind — don't hold onto anything. Simply allow yourself to be free and at ease.

Shravaka meditation is often described as the application of mindfulness, sometimes called the fourfold application of mindfulness: the mindfulness of body, of sensations, of thoughts, and of phenomena. What that means is simply being aware, letting your attention be calm, undistracted and peaceful. Be aware of how you are, what it feels like, what you are thinking — be aware of what you experience and how you experience it. Also be mindful of your sensations, of your thoughts feelings, and of the phenomena.

To apply mindfulness of body means to be aware of how your body is. When you sit, you're aware of whether you're sitting straight or whether you're leaning to one side or the other. You're aware of whether you're exhaling or inhaling. When you are walking, you are aware of your putting one foot in front of the other. You are aware of every single part involved in the activity, and the breathing as well. That is called being mindful of body.

This kind of meditation does not involve imagining anything, no fantasy. We're just being aware of how our body is. You're not visualizing anything like in development stage practice, or creating anything which is not already present, like trying to cultivate love or compassion. It simply means being aware of what is, how we are. Being aware of how your body is and what it does without losing the continuity of this awareness or interrupting it with anything is called the application of mindfulness of the body.

Paying attention to exactly what happens when you do something is a very simple training. When you drink a cup of tea, pay attention to what you are doing — reaching your arm out, taking hold of the cup, lifting it up, putting it to your lips, tasting the liquid, feeling it enter your mouth, swallowing — and after that you notice that your hand is putting the cup down again. All this actually takes place, doesn't it? It's not something we imagine or make up, it's not something mystical, it's not something that we have to try hard to do. Nor is it the ordinary way of being mindless, when we're thinking of something else while drinking the tea and are not really aware of what's going on. It's simply paying attention to what happens.

When we get used to paying attention to our physical presence, we find that we naturally stop doing a lot of useless activities that formerly occupied our time. We do what is necessary, and when there is nothing that needs to be done, we relax.

Some of my own teachers were exactly like that. They knew what they were doing when they did something. They would put a thing down in a certain place, and later when they needed it they would know exactly where they put it, because they had been aware of putting it down when they did so. There would be no confusion about it. Neither were they too involved in arranging things to look nice in a certain way, first putting it here, then putting it in another place, then moving it in a third place so it would look nicer. They simply put the object down; later, they would take it up again and use it, very simply. They were neither spaced out nor uptight and fussy. They were able to function very accurately when necessary, yet at the same time they were very relaxed.

When we practice being mindful in this way, we don't have to unnecessarily repeat a lot of thoughts and actions. I feel about thirty percent of our activities are really superfluous. We think the same thing over and over again — "I should do this and I should do that" — instead of just thinking it once, and then doing it. By training in being aware and mindful, we can get rid of a lot of unnecessary thoughts and actions.

Training in mindfulness gets rid of the two steps forward, one step back, that kind of unnecessary activity. If we're caught up in this, we don't get past five steps; we never reach six or seven. We simply go back and start from the beginning all over again for no reason. Being more mindful will get rid of that, both in relation to how our body is, how our sensations are, how our mental state is, and what we focus on as well. Mindfulness destroys the habitual tendencies.

I am speaking from my own experience here. I live atop a hill behind Swayambhu, and often I have to go down to the car and drive to Boudhanath, where I have things to do. While I'm driving I often think about what I have to do. But honestly, there's nothing that I can do while driving the car. Since I haven't yet arrived, it's totally unnecessary for me to think about the same thing over and over again. Mindfulness can relieve us of that kind of over-repeating. As a result we will find we have more free time and are more at leisure. When we are more at ease, we are automatically more peaceful.

The next is mindfulness of sensation. There might be pleasant or unpleasant sensations, but basically you feel something all the time, right? Some kind of sensation is going on all the time, like this. *(Rinpoche slurps his tea, 'Ahhhh')*. We need to be aware of what things feel like. When we wear clothing, we can be aware of whether it's rough or smooth. If there's a pain in our back, we should be aware of that. When we become clearly aware of how something is felt — whether it's painful or whether it's pleasant — then we can do something about it, if necessary. Sometimes the moment is neutral in terms of sensation. That's okay too. Just train in being aware of how you feel in terms of physical sensations.

Mindfulness of thoughts refers to your mental state. Are you angry? Then be aware that you are angry. Whatever the emotion is, whether you desire something, whether you feel proud or jealous or dull or irritated — no matter what, just be aware of the thought or emotion that unfolds. Simply notice it, be mindful of that, be aware of what happens. In this context, you don't have to prevent it or try not to think or feel something. If you feel something, just let it be felt. But if you don't feel anything in particular, you don't have to try to feel something, either. Just allow whatever happens to happen openly.

Most of our problems in life come from not allowing things to happen. We try to prevent something from happening, or if something slips away from us we try to nail it down and hold onto it so it doesn't disappear. We hope that something won't happen, or are afraid that something will happen. We are always trying to accept or reject, to hold on in one sense or another, and that creates a lot of problems. If we would just allow things to manifest and arise openly, our problems would be greatly reduced.

It's said the best situation is to look like a Shravaka but to be the Great Perfection — to embody Dzogchen. In other words, sit nicely while being totally free and at ease inside yourself. Let yourself be very open and free within, because otherwise it's very hard to really practice the Dharma. As a matter of fact, it's very hard to do anything! Settle your body in a pleasant, gentle way, and within your mind be free from hope and fear. Don't try to make yourself feel anything or think of anything. Don't try to *not* think of anything, either. Allow whatever thought or emotion that arises to simply unfold. Don't do anything to it — just notice what takes place.

Be like a mirror. If something red is held up it reflects red; if something green comes along it reflects green. A mirror doesn't prevent anything from being reflected, nor does it encourage or invite anything to be reflected. In the same way, you don't have to do anything regarding how you feel physically or mentally, other than be aware of it. Like a mirror, be aware of what unfolds in your experience — not rejecting, not accepting, not preventing anything, not encouraging anything, but being aware all the while.

This being aware, or this knowing, is something of utmost importance we will return to later. Actually, it is the main point. The *knowledge that realizes egolessness*, and, later on, *self-existing awareness*, is very closely linked with this 'knowing.' In fact, it doesn't come from any other place. The knowledge that realizes egolessness and the self-existing awareness doesn't come from any other place than this knowing. This knowing perceives subject and object, whatever takes place in our experience right now. It is this knowing that also experiences non-duality. Do you understand this? I am hinting now. The type of knowing based on perceiving something — a cup, a table, a glass — is actually something very important. That is what mind is. Mind, or consciousness, is called so many things: soul, spirit, mind, heart. Buddhism defines it as *that which knows*. This knowing that we all have — that is mind.

Things do not know. A table doesn't know itself, a flower doesn't know, a cup doesn't know. Yet within us right now there is something that is wide awake and consciousness, isn't there? That is what mind is. It is something really precious. And we need to really understand it, because that is the basis for attaining enlightenment, as well as the basis for continuing in samsara. That is what life is, actually.

In Buddhism, the term 'life' refers to this mind, not to the physical body. There is a continuity, an ongoing sense of knowing, of being awake, that goes on life after life. We practice meditation in order to improve this stream of being, which is the life of the mind, not the life of the body. It is this stream of life, this stream of knowing, that needs to be liberated.

What I would like to put across is that the remedy we use at the beginning is conceptual. Eventually we have to let go of the remedy as well. When we use a remedy; we are by definition practicing meditation, as opposed to nonmeditation.

A lot of people hear that a Dzogchen practitioner leaves his or her gaze directed towards space, the sky. So immediately they put their heads back, like this *(Rinpoche tilts his head up)*. But actually it is the eyes that gaze into space — not the neck! You don't look with the neck. Keep the head in the same relaxed, natural way and raise the eyes just a little bit, not rolled all the way up. The term 'directing the gaze' doesn't really mean looking, or staring into space; it just means leave your eyes like that. It's like putting a crystal ball in a little bowl of water — it sinks to the bottom and stays there, doesn't it? That is what is meant by directing your gaze towards space. This instruction actually applies to all the senses, to hearing and smell and so forth. You don't have to correct or alter or try to maintain a certain position within any of these. Just leave them exactly as they are.

If some of you are used to training in shamatha and feel the need to continue with that, that's okay, do that for a while. Some of you have already received instructions in Dzogchen and know how to train in that in an authentic way, so continue training like that. For those of you who are beginners here, this is how to train. Let yourself be. You don't have to do anything. When you find yourself having no thought, when you are not occupied by any thought, you don't have to panic — it's perfectly all right. We don't have to make up some thoughts to occupy ourselves. Likewise, when we do get involved in thoughts, we don't have to be terrified by that and think, "Arghhh, this is terrible, what should I do about these thoughts?" Just allow the thoughts to unfold and don't pursue them. Allow the thoughts to vanish. When after that there are again no thoughts, you don't have to think, "This is it, now I've finally got it, this is special, this is rigpa." You don't have to fixate your attention on that either. Simply allow that to happen as well. In other words, let yourself be at ease with whatever happens.

We need to allow our mind to be open. When the windows on opposite sides of a room are open, the breeze moves through the room and goes out the window. We don't have to grab at the breeze as it is passing by. Thoughts arise and vanish in the same way. We don't have to do anything to the thoughts or hold them or try to change them as they pass by. There still has to be some sense of knowing — we can call that presence of mind or mindfulness, meaning that we are not totally oblivious to what is happening. But while a sense of knowing is important, we shouldn't attach any special value to what happens or does not happen.

Sometimes, of course, our back hurts or something bothers us physically. We have to accept this as part of meditation training. You might also have some kind of expectation about experiencing a mystical, beautiful state where you feel free and open and painless. Holding on to this kind of expectation and hope actually creates obstacle for it to happen, because the more we hope to not have pain, the more it irritates us when it does occur. Be free of hope and fear. Train in a carefree way. In order to know really how to train, we need to remind ourselves to be carefree and at ease — not spaced out or dull and withdrawn, but simply at ease.

One or two questions?

STUDENT: What does 'to improve' mean with regard to meditation practice?

RINPOCHE: Earlier I mentioned that we should approach meditation from the perspective of getting rid of something. To get rid of our disturbing emotions and habitual fixation, to increasingly rid ourselves of our delusion — that is an improvement. Another improvement is to see that which is real and true more and more clearly.

STUDENT: You mentioned relaxing; however, it's difficult to relax when we experience physical pain while practicing.

RINPOCHE: That's a natural part of meditation practice in the beginning. It's a sign that you're beginning to practice meditation, so rejoice in that. After a while you get used sitting and it doesn't hurt so much, but initially there's not much to do about it. Since it's physical, you can't just do away with it. If it was a thought you could think about something else, right? But since it's physical, there's not much to do. Actually, you can keep one thought in mind: "Other people sit; so I can also sit. I can do it."

STUDENT: Rinpoche, you mentioned that meditation is getting rid of something. Does that happen immediately, or do we alternate between being free and unfree?

RINPOCHE: There are two situations, two possibilities. If you're totally free from confusion, then there's no falling back. But if you're only a little bit free, then you can go back and forth. For example, imagine that you see a piece of colored rope lying near your house and you believe it's a snake. You get scared, you run inside, you lock your door, and you are still afraid that the snake will somehow get into your house. And you will be worried until someone tells you it's not a snake, it's just a piece of rope. But simply hearing that is not enough, because you're not convinced. Only when you go and check it out for yourself and look directly at the rope — maybe even touch it — do you see it's actually just a rope, it's not a snake. After such direct experience, you are no longer confused, nor can you fall back into confusion. You're free of that confusion permanently; you're beyond it. It's like that.

This is why intellectual knowledge is not enough. We need experience, personal experience, and in order to gain that personal experience it's important to practice. It's impossible to say exactly when and how our confusion will dissolve. For Garab Dorje it happened instantaneously: from that moment on there was no more confusion. For us it will probably happen gradually: little by little, we become less and less confused. However, it's also possible that we become gradually less confused for a certain period, say one year, and then the following year we suddenly find ourselves totally free from confusion. Someone could go in retreat and meditate for ten years, and come out not liberated, while another person might meditate for one year or even just one day and become totally free. When and how one achieves liberation is an individual thing. But once you see through to the very root cause of confusion and are totally free from it, falling back is not possible. It's important to know this.

As Buddhist practitioners, our main job is to be free from confusion, simply to be free. That's what all these meditations and practices are about — being free. We tie ourselves up in all sorts of different kinds of bonds of attachment and hope and fear and concepts of accepting and rejecting — it's like covering ourselves up with all sorts of different patches of material. All the practices are just about uncovering ourselves from these patches, freeing ourselves from this situation.

The main point is that we need to allow confusion to dissolve. Confusion means to mistake something for what it is not, to misunderstand something in a way that is not actually true. The main confusion, how confusion really begins, is failing to know our own nature, what we really are. Not knowing how our nature is the essence of confusion.

When someone says something like, "Don't talk to me like that," or, "I can't take it," or "I can't bear it, it's too much," or "I can't control myself," they are afraid of themselves, and are not really in charge of how their own nature manifests. They're frightened of what they might do, because they don't know what they really are. If they did, there wouldn't be a problem at all. There's actually nothing you can't deal with when it comes down to it — there is no state of mind that cannot be released, liberated. So the root cause of confusion is found right here, within ourselves. The mind is not like a computer that somebody else has programmed and that is out of your control. It's not like that at all. In actuality, you have total control already. Acting like you do not is called 'being your own enemy,' so don't be like that.

STUDENT: Sometimes, when my habitual tendencies manifest very strongly; I feel that I actually don't have control. What should I do at that time?

RINPOCHE: Honestly, you're not totally out of control. At these times you should take hold of the practice. One way to deal with this is to realize that there is just one stream of mind, just one stream of consciousness. It's not like one consciousness or part of your mind is trying to control another part, which is so uncontrollable that the first has to give up. Really, there's just one stream of mind, and if that one stream of mind decides to practice — meaning relax and release the grip — then there is no other mind that can be out of control. The problem stops right there. That's one way. If this flower is making trouble and I let go of it, I drop it, then what is there to make trouble? Rather than one mind making trouble and the other trying to chase it and catch it and make it stop, there is just one mind. If that mind tries to be aware and relax, the troublemaker is already gone. It's simple, really. Because mind is so fast and can act so quickly, it may seem like there's more than one, but really there isn't. Simply, let this present mind totally be.

STUDENT: Is there a common mind, or does each individual have one?

RINPOCHE: Each being has an individual mind. These individual minds are experienced in dependency with the karma that is shared by many beings. Your body is a human now. You have the karma for human experience, you experience in a way similar to other human beings. But if you're reborn as an animal, then in that life you'll experience situations as an animal, due to that karma.

Being free from confusion, dissolving confusion, means being free of karma as well. In this case we are referring to karma as the basis for cause and effect, for causation — that which promotes results out of causes. It is something we have no choice about; we are not in charge of it. There's bad karma and good karma. Because we are humans we are said to have good karma. If we are hungry ghosts or an animal, then we are said to have bad karma. Among human beings there are many kinds — again, good karma, bad karma, right? Fortunate or good karma means we have all our sense faculties complete, and we are born in a time and place where we have personal freedom. If you experience such good karma, rejoice in that and be happy. Remind yourself every day how fortunate it is that you can do what you want. Although this freedom is temporary and limited, because of it we have the opportunity to practice so we can achieve ultimate freedom. Which is what we are doing right here.

TRANSCENDING SHAMATHA

INITIALLY THE ACT OF MEDITATION involves trying to keep the attention still. One beings by practicing shamatha with support, focusing the attention on one object and trying to remain mindful rather than getting distracted by one thing after another. Next comes shamatha without support, in which we don't focus or rest *on* anything, but retain a sense of mindful presence. One remains gently and peacefully, still being mindful. The very act of being mindful is the meditating. I also mentioned that we should try to be mindful when we walk around and carry out various activities. This mindfulness, the attention that is mindful of whatever we do in any situation, should be carried around with us everywhere. This type of normal mindfulness is deliberate, in that it requires effort.

In terms of conceptual view, we heard explanation about shamatha, where one forms an assumption about how it is and keeps that in mind. There are different kinds of shamatha, dense, inert shamatha, and correct shamatha. The first kind is dull shamatha, a kind of vacant or stupid stillness. It means sitting in a way in which one doesn't notice anything whatsoever, and tries to be less and less aware of whether or not there is thought movement, closing one's mind into a state of dullness. Training in that kind of shamatha is the very cause for rebirth as an animal in the next life. That is a mistaken path.

The correct way of practicing shamatha, which forms the basis or support for the true path, is mentioned in all the vehicles. It is simply presence of mind, being awake to whether one is experiencing thought movement or stillness. It is this kind of one-pointed attention which at some point allows the dividing line between thought movement and stillness to fall apart. Mahamudra terms this the 'discovery of simplicity.' Simply remaining in the noticing or knowing quality is a correct basis for true practice.

A famous example says: "In the tranquil ocean of shamatha sports the great fish of vipashyana," of insight. It is the placid or tranquil ocean of the true shamatha, not the mistaken type of stillness. This means stillness in which attention doesn't waver. The knowing quality itself remains undistracted. This steadiness provides the basis for us to inquire what this knowing is based on. What is it really? The discovery of vipashyana, true insight, comes when we discover that there is neither root nor basis for this knowing; when no concept or construct whatsoever is formed about this knowing. This type of clear insight is "the great fish sporting in the ocean of stillness."

Another famous example describes it as "no thing whatsoever, but everything is perceived." It is no thing whatsoever, yet anything can be experienced. In this context, 'no thing whatsoever' means that there is no dwelling on stillness or thought occurrence, what is thought of. Awareness is so bare and open it is like no particular thing at all. It is not a total absence of awareness, however, because the possibility exists that *anything* can be known out of this state. "No thing whatsoever, yet everything is perceived." This early stage of knowing or noticing whether there is stillness or thought occurrence is also called rigpa. However, it is not the same meaning of rigpa as the Dzogchen sense of self-existing awareness.

Great masters traditionally give something called the pointing-out instruction, which literally means bringing one face to face with one's true nature. What is this nature that is being introduced? A practitioner of shamatha who has cultivated a sense of stillness to the extent that there is no longer any dividing point between thought occurrence and simply resting experiences a certain quality of knowing or presence of mind. This knowing is what the practitioner is brought face to face with — or rather, the very identity of this knowing as being rootless and groundless, insubstantial. By recognizing this, one is introduced to self-existing awareness, *rangjung rigpa*.

In terms of experience, what is this really? When simply resting in meditation, dwelling on the nowness, there is this presence of mind. One is being asked to recognize the essence of this knowing. At the very moment no basis is found. In other words, the sense of *dwelling on* something falls apart, the *resting in* something disintegrates. This doesn't mean that the quality of knowing or being awake vanishes. It still is, but there is no dwelling on anything whatsoever. It is simply awareness *in itself*. This is the point where shamatha is transcended into self-existing awareness. It is not a sequential process that takes place over time; instead, it happens very fast. It is simply a matter of letting the focus or dwelling fall apart. When that happens, you already have arrived in self-existing awareness, in rigpa. That is what is meant by the saying that samsara and nirvana are like the front and back of your own hand. It is the difference between knowing and not knowing. In the moment of knowing, you are already there.

There is only one mind; it is not that there are two minds, one recognizing the other. In the very moment of recognizing, it is like a knot that is untied. We don't have to do anything further than that, leave it untied. In the moment of looking, it is already seen. It is not that later on we come to see. Why? Because mind and mind essence are very close. The second reason is that it is not that mind essence is something that we have to get our sights on; its not like that. It is not that we need to hold the awareness on it for a while, like one or two minutes and slowly it will appear within our experience. Since there is only one mind, the moment you recognize, it is simply a matter of letting go. That thinker or knower of that moment is just like a new knot, like a new thought. The moment you abandon it, it unties. We are already arrived at where we need to arrive at, we are already in the nature of mind.

It is possible, however to have all different kinds of expectations and ideas about what is going to happen, that now I will see something, something unusual. I'll catch hold of something, finally. We try to see something. But, if we line up rigpa as some object of our attention that we somehow will be able to sit and look at, we kind of remove rigpa away into a distance that will never be obtainable, no matter how long we continue like that. That is not necessary at all. All that is necessary is simply let the attention recognize itself for a very short while. Second, totally drop everything as if you were going to let go of a corpse; leave it exactly as it is — you have already arrived. Free from any kind of notion, like "I see it, I don't see it, this is it, this is not it." That is why it is said "Short moments, many times." Rigpa is not some state that we can prolong. It prolongs naturally by itself.

What is it that there is to see when recognizing rigpa? It has three qualities, but present simultaneously. Empty essence means there is no center or edge to see. This absence of something to see is by itself aware or awake. These two qualities are unconfined. Do you understand this? These three are seen in the moment of looking, that is what we call rigpa.

I also mention two other words: the meditation state and the post-meditation. The meditation state is when recognizing the state of rigpa, and lasts maybe one second, two seconds, or a little longer. When straying from that, it is called post-meditation. Many people they say, I spent half an hour, or one hour, in the meditation state, but this is not really true. What is true is that we spend 45 minutes or an hour *training* to be in the meditation state, but the genuine meditation state only lasts for a short while, once in a while.

When seeing the three qualities simultaneously, that is called seeing the nature of mind. In Dzogchen it is called rigpa. Or you can call it the Dzogchen view. There are different kinds of views mentioned: conceptual view and nonconceptual view. The rigpa view is a nonconceptual type of view. Rigpa needs to be seen. This seeing is not in terms of subject seeing object, it is a seeing devoid of duality. Seeing no thing is the supreme sight. It is not a thing to see because it is not made out of any concrete substance. But also, there is nothing extra remaining unseen. In the moment of looking, it is seen. That is called view. Among the three view, meditation and conduct, this is the view.

Next, when saying meditation here, it means the training in that, which means to sustain its continuity, to sustain the continuity of the view. We are not cultivating something through force or developing a thought which isn't there, by catching hold of the view and then maintaining it. We are simply allowing the continuity of seeing the nature of mind to continue. At first it lasts for a second, then two seconds, then three seconds, and so on.

During the post-meditation state — for example, right now — we experience the thought, "I got distracted. I need to recognize. Now I'm doing that." Recognizing the essence is like striking the clapper against a bell *(Rinpoche rings a bell)*. When the two parts of the bell make contact, a sound manifests. That sound illustrates the natural state that we need to just let be. First we recognize *(Rinpoche rings the bell)*; then there is a natural *ongoingness* to that state, isn't there? First comes the effort, the contacting of the two pieces, or the deliberate effort of reminding oneself to recognize awareness. When the clapper strikes the bell, it's like the moment of seeing the nature of mind. That is rigpa. And there is some ongoing quality to that, some continuity, just as the bell's tone continues to reverberate for a while. If one simply looks at the bell, there is no sound, right? Likewise, if we strike it repeatedly — if we look and look over and over again — there is no sound. Just look once, and let be in naturalness. First we need to know how to look, like how to ring the bell. After that, we don't have to worry about whether we see, or don't see, whether rigpa is achieved or lost, or anything. Just *let it be*. Training involves sustaining that ongoingness, like letting the continuity of sound reverberate.

The sound that is there at the beginning and the sound that remains a few seconds later is the same continuity, isn't it? In the same way, the first moment of seeing rigpa is the same continuity as that experienced later, for as long as the experience lasts. When we get distracted into post-meditation, it's like there is no more sound. Our mind is now busy occupying itself with perceiver and perceived, the latter involving all sorts of different sense objects. Then again we remind ourselves, "Oh, I got distracted. I must recognize again." While seeing, there is no need to make anything or create anything. We don't have to improve the sound while it is ringing, like try to make it a little nicer.

If our meditation training is like someone who continuously hit the bell to make a sound, we can get a sickness Tibetan medicine calls disorder of the wind element — *lung* — a type of anxiety that sometimes manifests as pain in the upper shoulders. It's easy to get anxious, trying to see something when there is nothing to see! But it's like spending a whole day trying to catch mid-air. The only result is that our hands hurt. In the same way, if we try to sit and meditate a whole day, trying to catch hold of something which there is nothing to catch hold of, we may develop the disorder of the wind element.

To train by simply letting the nature be, as it naturally is, is called *nonmeditation*, and it is the most eminent form of meditating. In nonmeditation, we are not tying ourselves up in a conceptual frame of mind. Rather than trying to hold something, we are naturally letting be what basically is. First we need to look, to *know* how to look, like knowing how to ring the bell. After that, we need to know how to leave it is as it is. Once we get distracted, we need to know how to recognize again; once the sound vanishes, we need to know how to ring it again. This ringing the bell again is the analogy for conduct.

First, when recognizing mind essence, there is a sense of seeing that it is no-thing. Then that seeing is allowed to continue. That is the training. After a while, it slips away and we get distracted. At some point we notice that we've gotten distracted, and remind ourselves to look once more. This reminding is the utilizing, through which we again recognize.

How should the training be in this context? It is described as undistracted nonmeditation, or not meditating. We are not imagining something or keeping something in mind, but neither are we totally carried away and absent-minded or distracted. If one meditates, that becomes conceptual, but if one is distracted, it all slips away. Therefore we let be without being distracted, but also without meditating. Do you understand what is meant by undistracted nonmeditation? What is wrong with being distracted? What is wrong with meditating?

STUDENT: It is conceptual.

RINPOCHE: Why be undistracted and not meditate? What is the reason for coupling these words together?

STUDENT: Meditation implies some effort. Rigpa involves no effort.

RINPOCHE: Yes, it is something like that. Without even a hair-tip being meditated upon, and yet not being distracted for even an instant. What can you do? What is there to do?

STUDENT: Rest naturally.

RINPOCHE: It's true that both being distracted and meditating are conceptual. Being distracted involves coarse conceptual thinking, while meditating is a more subtle type of conceptual mind. We need to be free from both. Some meditators are not distracted by outer things, because mindfulness is there. At the same time they train themselves to avoid focusing on something inwardly. But there is still a sense of resting in nowness, of keeping awareness in the present moment. And this resting or dwelling on the present moment obstructs liberation and omniscient enlightenment. In genuine Dzogchen training, we need to let go of this notion of being in the present. We need to let go of the notion of meditating, but if one simply gives up meditating and becomes like any other ordinary person, that is no use at all. One needs to have no sense of meditating and yet be totally undistracted at the same time.

Don't be upset that while we are beginners this kind of view only lasts for a very short while. If we continue the training it will slowly last longer and longer. But also we don't have to either believe "I am someone who has been involved in spiritual practice for a lot of years," or "I am just a beginner in this, so there is no way I can really approach this." It is simply a matter of knowing how to recognize the nature of mind, and then letting be in that. That is what it is all about here. It's like if someone has had the wrong key to a door, and has spent the entire day and night trying to open the door with it, compared to someone who gets the right key, goes straight to the door, and immediately opens it. In the same way, to spend months and years trying to conceptually figure out this nature of mind only muddles it up. There is not a lot of use in that.

There are some people who try to cultivate empty mind for a long time, try to empty their minds out. Others try to construct and maintain a sense of awakeness. Or they sit and face a vast space and for a long time try to be like that, until this vastness of space finally seeps into their brain and becomes a permanent construction. None of this is of much use.

Up until this point, I have explained to you how your basic state or basic nature is. I have explained to you how to recognize this basic nature.

In the moment of looking we immediately see that it is empty,
That there is no thing to see.
There is no center and no circumference.
It is wide open,
A moment of being totally wide open.
It is totally clear,
Without even a single speck of dust.
There is nothing to fix the attention on.
This is called empty essence.
But we have not become vacant;
Neither absent-minded nor spaced out —
Experience or perception is not blocked.
This is the cognizant nature.
Don't get caught up in perceiving.
Yet experience is present.
While still being empty, we perceive;
While perceiving, this perceiving is empty in essence.
It is not confined to one or the other;
Totally unimpeded, totally open.
This is the unconfined capacity.
This is how it really is, already.

In the moment of recognizing there is an acknowledging of how it is. This acknowledging doesn't remain as a separate entity, like the conceptual thought "Oh, now I see!" It's more like a knife cutting through the string of thoughts — if we keep the knife and cling to it, it becomes an obstruction. In the same way, when recognizing mind essence, no recognizer should remain. It is simply allowed to dissolve, so that there is no duality.

First comes the cut, the recognition; then immediately the realization of recognizing mind essence is allowed to dissolve. This describes an indispensable principle of Dzogchen teachings called self-existing awareness. At that moment there is no new karma or new attitude being formed; instead, it is a *dissolving* of karma and conceptual attitudes. Training in self-existing awareness melts away previous habits of thinking, previous habits of karmic attitude. This method is truly the way to solve the whole problem of samsara. The more we grow used to practicing it, the more karma is eliminated. Complete enlightenment is the point when no more karma is being formed, and when no more karmic traces remain.

Among three vital points in the Dzogchen teachings, this first point is called 'recognizing your own nature.' 'Own' here means that you yourself are the nature of dharmakaya. You are not recognizing a separate, other thing. It is literally being face-to-face with your own nature, recognizing yourself as being the dharmakaya nature.

The second point after that is to persevere in this recognition. Continue training in that further and further, and keep on receiving instructions. If we have misconceptions or uncertainties to be cleared up, we return to our meditation master and receive further instructions. Then we continue to train, again and again. We can also use spiritual books to explain things, but they have to be authentic Dharma books. Perhaps we can read a few lines that explain this nature and then apply that to our own experience. Maybe then we read a little more, and again apply that to our own experience. In this way it becomes clearer and clearer, and we feel more and more certain, until at some point we have real confidence. Ultimately we will be totally convinced that this self-existing awareness is the real way to melt away disturbing emotions and dissolve the conceptual frame of mind. With practice we will eventually discover that level of conviction, called 'king-like confidence.'

Let's use the example of being addicted to smoking cigarettes. We want to kick the habit, because we are told by others that it is bad for our lungs, shortens our life, destroys our health, clogs up our channels and so forth. We understand this, we believe it, we even remind ourselves that smoking is no good, telling ourselves, "I shouldn't be smoking, it's bad for me, it's detrimental to my health." But none of that really helps, does it? Simply having the idea that smoking is bad doesn't make us stop smoking, because we have a deeply embedded habit. Holding an intellectual idea does not terminate the habit. What is necessary is to interrupt the habitual involvement in the act, again and again.

In the same way, the forming of conceptual thought is a habit that needs to be interrupted again and again. And the only thing that can really cut through our habitual thinking, that addiction to conceptual mind, is the recognition of self-existing awareness. Once we know from our own experience that this recognition is the only thing that can really cut through, we possess some real conviction.

If the situation was otherwise, we could go into the operating room and have a surgeon remove our conceptual frame of mind, our disturbing emotions and karma. If our brain could really be opened up and those pieces could be surgically removed, that would be wonderful. But I'm sorry: it's impossible. Nor is there any kind of wonder drug that we can take to become totally free from thoughts and disturbing emotions. Nor is there any kind of bomb we can blow up to make the mind stop producing ignorant thinking and negative karma.

What it comes down to is there is no kind of material trick or deliberate technique that actually works to stop conceptual mind. The only thing that works is the recognition of self-existing awareness, *rangjung rigpa*. The habit of forming disturbing emotions is relinquished by growing more and more used to that recognition, till eventually the habit becomes totally liberated. By recognizing our own essence at the moment of experiencing a thought or emotion, that thought or emotion is naturally liberated. Through experiencing this process ourselves, we can gain some real conviction.

Using some material substance doesn't work to stop conceptual mind, because the problem is being created by something immaterial. Gadgets are formed of concrete substance, and thus do not really touch the immaterial source of the problem. Mind is insubstantial; it is not material. Everything is created out of mind. Therefore, we need to find a way in which this immaterial source of all problems is somehow stopped.

The method we are discussing here naturally dissolves conceptual mind through self-liberation.

Let be in equanimity,
Immediately there is a quality of freedom;
Unbound by concepts, thoughts, or time,
Unfettered by any view, dwelling, or prejudice.
Totally free and all-pervasive,
Belonging neither to one side or another,
Not dull or vacant.
Totally clear and awake, so that anything can unfold.
Still, whatever takes place doesn't bind us.
That is being free.

This is completely unlike the normal way of thinking or perception, in which the perceived takes charge over you. Here it is more that you are in charge of the perceived. Because everything perceived is a *personal perception*. Once you recognize that personal perception is actually devoid of self-nature, then what is perceived does not bind you. This is the kind of certainty that we need to discover. I am not talking about the dualistic intellectual certainty of, "I know that," but the nondualistic certainty that comes from experience. This is what is meant by the second vital instruction 'resolving on one point.'

This realization is not something that is handed over through words. What I am talking about cannot really be conveyed through words. But words *can* point the way towards how we can discover it in ourselves, so that at some point we feel, "Wow, this is how it really is." How and when one recognizes mind essence is not definite. We may go in and sit for half an hour, and nothing happens, but it's possible that later we're walking around outside — maybe in the shopping center — and we recognize mind essence; it becomes an actuality in our experience. Why did it happen at that particular moment? It's because of having practiced before; it's based on previous training. Perhaps we persevere in the training, meditating and meditating, and we feel nothing is happening. Eventually we think, "Maybe I should just give up." In that very moment of giving up, it is also possible to recognize mind essence! Because we've just totally let go.

So by all means, give up all this anxiety and worry. If our business deal is not going well, we have been trying hard to be successful, to make a profit, but there is a problem we try to fix, but nothing seems to help ... or if we have a problem in our relationship we're trying to fix, trying to work out if it is a really good situation between us and our partner, we're trying our best, but it only gets more complicated ... at some point we have to give up and let go of the whole thing. At that very moment it's possible to recognize mind essence. Who knows, maybe we will improve the relationship! Because usually the problem in the relationship is created by ourselves. The individuals on both sides want to prove their points and refuse to let go. That is the friction, the real problem. If you just let go, then who knows, maybe that will improve the relationship.

But before letting go you must genuinely try to recognize. You shouldn't give up too early! You need to train in meditation again and again, both inside the shrine room and outside as well. After having genuinely tried for a long time to gain some real insight, it is okay to let go, stop trying, and simply be there. Realization might take place in that moment of relaxation. You might even get totally enlightened, like Garab Dorje. We should exert ourselves, not in an uptight way, but in an open and free way, until we feel sure. And this sense of certainty shouldn't be allowed to become a stumbling block, another obstacle for rigpa. Instead, allow the sense of being sure and certain to be the expression of the essence, without holding onto that either.

Any questions? Let's have a few questions now.

STUDENT: What does 'to look' mean?

RINPOCHE: I explained the way to look; how to look. Because if we don't know how to look, we won't know how to see. It's like tuning the strings on a guitar: if you tighten them up all the way, the sound will never be nice. If you leave them too slack, it won't be good either. The best tuning point is somewhere in between too tight and too loose. There's a certain trick involved in getting them just right, isn't there? In the same way, recognizing mind essence lies somewhere in between staring in a very stiff way and being totally indifferent and not caring about it at all.

Thoughts come one after the other, like beads on a string. You don't have to prevent them; you don't have to put a box around them; and you don't have to hold on to them. Be totally free, while being awake. At some point, due to habit, a thought is formed again. Whether we are aware of that or not, thoughts start to move and do their thing, and at that moment you need some presence of mind which sees, "I got distracted." The next thought needs to be, "Well, let's recognize mind essence." And again there is a moment of finding nothing at all and letting be in that.

STUDENT: It seems that there is a sort of withdrawal of visual perception when recognizing the essence. Afterwards the visual perception returns much more vividly and clearly. Is that all right or not?

RINPOCHE: Whether that is all right or not all right is really something for you to decide. But remember this: in the moment of recognizing mind essence, it's not that we are not allowed to see visible forms. Nor do forms disappear; in fact, they become clearer and more distinct than before. But we shouldn't fixate on what is being seen — that is the most important point. We need to check for ourselves whether we are fixing the attention on what is perceived, or are simply allowing it to be. In the moment of recognizing mind essence, and in the moment of being mind essence, the experiences of the five senses are not blocked off. You are not trying to *not* perceive, to not hear or not to see anything. That kind of practice would be like shutting ourselves off from everything, like putting consciousness in a box. The approach I am talking about is the opposite, in that everything is increasingly opened up so that the all-pervasiveness of basic space is allowed for. The normal way of fixing the attention on something heard or seen is one of eliminating everything else. The particular perceiving consciousness is focused and the other five fields are excluded. In this type of situation, the all-pervasiveness is somehow hampered or blocked.

The training here is more in the sense of allowing the awake quality to be totally open and free — not caught up in one way of perceiving one particular sense object. There is perception, but this perceiving is something insubstantial and empty, and because of this, experience is allowed to continue unfolding. That is the principle of the unity of appearance and emptiness. Empty doesn't mean that there is no form; it simply means no fixation, not fixing on. All the appearances, everything that is perceived, is still present. Empty doesn't mean that everything is erased. It's more in the sense of a wide-open state where nothing is held or fixated upon.

(Rinpoche raises a flower). The very first instant there is the concept flower, you don't have to do anything more than that. Merely leave it. Normally, in the next instant we start to define: what the exact color of the flower is, what particular kind of flower it is, whether we like it or not, and so on. That process, which can go on and on, is all our doing. The perceiver is personalizing his or her experience.

In the beginning, we are training to become like a very small child in a temple hall. The child perceives everything — when he moves his head around, he sees all the colors and shapes and so forth, but no value is attached to anything. No concepts are being formed, because the child doesn't know what is what. He hasn't learned any of that. It is a very free way of experiencing. This is how we try to be in the beginning. We allow everything to take place, but we are not caught up in any of it.

Later on we will come to a point when it is perfectly all right to have certain concepts about things, but they are instantly dissolved as they are formed. Tulku Urgyen Rinpoche or Dilgo Khyentse Rinpoche could function in this world beautifully and perform all sorts of different activities without being caught up in any way whatsoever. This doesn't mean that they didn't have some kind of idea of what was going on. They were perfectly aware of what was taking place. It's like snowflakes descending onto a red-hot iron plate — the moment they touch, they are immediately evaporated, dissolved. There is no karma being formed in any way. Nothing is being kept. The snowflakes are not being stored anywhere. The moment they appear, they are simultaneously burned up and vanish. In that way, any activity or involvement of attention creates no karma and causes no obstruction whatsoever.

What usually happens is that whenever something is seen or heard, we feel that it demands our attention. We fall under the command of the visible form being seen and we feel that we have to get involved in discriminating what it is. So we stay busy attaching values and defining and pigeon-holing it. If a sound occurs, we immediately think, "I have to listen to that sound. What is it?" We get caught up again, and again, trapped in discriminating whether we like the sensation or don't like it; whether we must accept it or reject it. That very process *is* the creation of karma, right there. That is what we are trying to step out of right now through this meditation training.

In the beginning we need to be like an infant: open-minded without forming concepts. Most important is *tracelessness*. No trace left. Like walking but leaving no footprints. There may be a disturbing emotion, but it can be dissolved without creating any karma. It's just like the way certain criminals wear rubber gloves in order to avoid leaving fingerprints. Just like that! This relates to the Vajrayana principle of not rejecting disturbing emotions, but simply allowing them to be self-liberated. Tracelessness shows how it is possible to allow these emotions to arise, and yet not create karma. Like when seeing a form, it's just seeing it. It's okay, it doesn't harm anything. You don't have to think, "This is a form that I see" and hold onto that.

STUDENT: How do I avoid becoming caught up in the meditation technique?

RINPOCHE: To experience this type of problem is an indication that you are too involved in the act of recognizing. Now try totally letting be. Be awake. Simply remember rigpa. That's one concern instead of many. Try to remember only one, rigpa, quickly, instantly, instantly. Like walking and all of a sudden stopping. Try it out. We don't have to make a special custom out of recognizing rigpa, like adding it to what already exists. That just creates another habit.

If you develop a ritual where you first have to supplicate the guru, visualize the guru, dissolve into yourself, and then recognize rigpa, it is difficult to do in daily situations. You don't always have the chance to carry out the whole performance. If somebody is verbally abusive to you, do you say, "Wait a minute," then quickly supplicate, dissolve back, then recognize, then say, "Okay, go on, what were you saying?." Of course it would be nice if we *could* behave like that, but often we don't have that chance. And if we really need to perform the entire ritual and can't, then everything is lost. Rigpa is lost. We are just like an ordinary person stuck in the concepts of me and that.

Our situation right now is like learning to drive. We are in an open free space here in the driving school, and we are moving around learning to drive. There aren't many obstacles for us to bang up against. But eventually we need to be able to deal with traffic jams and crowded streets. In other words, you need to train the ability to recognize rigpa instantly, otherwise, what is the use of training? Staying in an uncomfortable tent on the mountains and sitting in the same position for forty-five minutes without moving — what is the use of that unless there is some kind of training that allows us to be able to deal with disturbing emotions later on? That is the whole point. Of course we do our formal practice after having first made supplications and performed certain visualization. But this doesn't mean we have to exclude all other situations. We should also be able to train in recognizing rigpa while we go to the toilet, while we take a shower, while having a conversation with others — in an instant, again and again.

If rigpa were our meditation object, then we would be occupied while we were in rigpa, and would be unable to deal with other things at the same time. But honestly, rigpa is not an object of meditation; it is a training. Therefore, we are totally free when training in rigpa — free to deal with everything else. That is very important. We know whether we are occupied while meditating or not. We can train while making food, but we should start with something very simple. Otherwise it might become tasteless or get burned, and then we will experience even greater disturbing emotions! That is one big reason to be free and easy about this.

It is said that the advanced practitioner's way of functioning is like a tightly knotted rope that has been burnt in a fire. It still keeps the same shape, but once you touch it, there is no real substance to it. It crumbles into ash, there's no real solidity to it. In the same way, a good practitioner can function in all situations, and may even look like he or she is having disturbing emotions, but nothing is held onto really solidly. It doesn't create any karma; no trace is left.

Any other questions? If you have no questions, that is really good. It means that you have realized this.

STUDENT 1: Why do thoughts vanish when recognizing mind essence?

RINPOCHE: Why? Okay, you answer. *(Points at another student).*

STUDENT 2: They are the expression of mind essence.

RINPOCHE: Why would a thought vanish if it is an expression of mind essence?

STUDENT 2: It is like the analogy of fire in a house and the smoke goes out the window. If you pour water on the fire the smoke disappears.

RINPOCHE: When recognizing, how exactly do you pour the water? How do you connect?

STUDENT 2: By recognizing the mind essence.

STUDENT 1: How do you recognize mind essence?

STUDENT 2: Same question again, but why is it that thoughts vanish when recognizing mind essence?

STUDENT 1: Once you recognize mind essence, thought vanishes.

STUDENT 2: That doesn't seem right to me. It seems to me that when a thought vanishes you recognize mind essence, not that when you recognize mind essence the thought vanishes. You could recognize mind essence and thought comes back and you'd again be in conceptual mind.

RINPOCHE: There is also something to understand from what you say.

STUDENT: Rigpa is without duality. Thought is duality. When recognizing rigpa, there is nothing for the thought to argue or fight with.

RINPOCHE: That's true. That's what is really meant in this statement: "All demons, obstructing forces and evil spirits of dualistic perception, enjoy this torma and disperse to your own places, in the nondual wisdom state." When nondual wakefulness really shows up in full force, the dualistic demons become very scared, very shy.

STUDENT: If you recognize nature of mind you have left behind the area of thought, so therefore thought has to stop.

RINPOCHE: Why does it have to stop?

STUDENT: Because in recognizing mind nature there's no activity, no thing, there can't be anything.

RINPOCHE: Do you mind saying it again? It's okay to repeat the same words.

STUDENT: When you recognize mind nature, your thinking and thoughts are left behind.

RINPOCHE: Why?

STUDENT: Because in the essence of mind there's no thing, there's no activity. There's nothing going on. There can't be thought.

STUDENT 3: In order to recognize rigpa dualistic thinking has to cease. Well, in order to do that you have to interrupt for a moment your concept of 'I,' the concept that you exist. If you can interrupt that concept for a moment, thinking by definition will cease and you will be in rigpa. The question I would like to ask here is what does 'I' mean?

RINPOCHE: Why do you have to interrupt that concept?

STUDENT: In order to avoid a thought. Thinking is dualistic. It requires an 'I.' It requires a self, an ego to have a thought. Thoughts don't exist without the thinker.

RINPOCHE: There's something to understand in what you're saying.

STUDENT: If the thought has nothing to stand on then there can't be another thought.

RINPOCHE: That's also right.

STUDENT: I can't stop the thoughts, but I can see emptiness.

STUDENT: How about using this example: rigpa is the ocean, and thoughts are the waves. When you dive into the water, you have no waves.

RINPOCHE: What's the meaning?

STUDENT: If you drown you can't think any more!

STUDENT: If the thoughts have no ground or root, you can't think anymore.

RINPOCHE: Why do thoughts have no ground or root? What about the all-ground, the *alaya*?

STUDENT: Originally they don't have ground or root. Rigpa has no root.

RINPOCHE: Okay, okay. This discussion demonstrated some good understanding on the part of all of you. I would like to add a few words and explain a little more what is meant by thought, conceptualizing, which in Tibetan we call *namtok*. There are two different situations. The first is from within rigpa a perception arises. The other situation involves no rigpa just thought. First of all, knowing what is, is not necessarily thought. Perceiving is not necessarily thought. Dzogchen doesn't ask you to not perceive. Do you understand this? This is very, very important, extremely important.

If we do think perceiving means thought, then when we hear 'be free of thought' we think it means no knowing or experience of anything. That is totally wrong, completely mistaken. It is never said that because there's no thought there's no knowing. The knowing and the thinking are different. It is possible to know while thinking. A knowing can also be an act of thinking. It is possible. But there's also a knowing which is free of thought. Do you understand this? One kind of knowing is a knowing which is an act of thinking; another is a knowing which is not an act of thinking.

The difference between these two depends on — and now we get another Tibetan word — *dzinpa*, which means holding or fixating. That is what the view stands and falls with in Dzogchen. The view depends on whether or not there's fixating. In the state of rigpa you are allowed to know whatever is, but without fixating. If you get involved in fixating, it becomes thinking. It becomes thought. If there's a knowing free of thinking, free of fixation, you can call that the *play of wakefulness*. Anything can unfold as the play of wakefulness, be it good or bad or anything in between. But thought is always fixating. Fixing on something. Just bare knowing is not necessarily called thought, however. Is that clear?

Thought means that there is fixation. There is, nevertheless, also a way of knowing free of thought, free of fixating. There's also a way of knowing while fixating. In the Dzogchen state of meditation, which is rigpa, there's a way of knowing free of thought, free of fixating. In the post-meditation state there's a way of knowing while fixating. The main difference is whether there is fixating or no fixating, *dzinpa* or no *dzinpa*. Dzinpa can be very subtle, very fine, but it always ends. It always finishes.

The original question was: why do thoughts dissolve in the moment of recognizing rigpa? Here's an example. You cannot have two things, like this lid and that stick, occupying exactly the same thought at the same moment. Like two pieces of solid matter cannot occupy the same space at the same time. In the same way, there's only one mind. Since there's only one mind, when this one mind stops fixating there's no thought that occupies that space.

That's one point. Another is that this mind essence is empty, is not a substantial thing. In the absence of a thought, in the absence of fixating, this empty essence is open. It's not occupied by something of substance. A thought has substance. Please understand that the word substance doesn't necessarily imply material substance. In Buddhist metaphysics, substance can be temporal, in the sense of time. Thought is a temporal substance. This temporal substance of thought occupies the space of mind essence during the act of fixating, during the act of thinking, so that the play of wakefulness is prevented, blocked; it cannot really manifest. In the absence of thought, in the absence of fixating, the innate qualities of wakefulness can have free play. Actually it's quite wonderful that our essence is empty. There's a lot more to understand with regard to this point.

According to Buddhist metaphysics, physical space does not have substantial existence. Rather, it is an openness that accommodates. Space means openness. It's not a thing that functions or operates. Because space is empty and not substantially existent, we can use it. For example, we seem to be using this space here in this room quite a lot, for all sorts of different things. In the same way, emptiness of mind is also something which is not substantially existent. Therefore, a lot of stuff can take place.

As a matter of fact, in the space of this room literally thousands of beings can move about and do things. One particular point of space may be used by many, many sentient beings right at this very moment. They don't see us, and we don't see them. It is quite amazing. This may sound a little strange, but actually it isn't strange — it's real. It is said that in a single instant, a buddha can know and perceive innumerable worlds, innumerable realms. There's a lot of deep significance in that statement. There are billions and trillions of buddhafields — they're not just limited to this solar system.

You've heard it said that "appearances are mind." We could rephrase this as "the perceived is mind." The perception is mind. If we really understand this, we will also understand that the perceived is emptiness. Everything that is perceived is emptiness. For example, another being in the six realms would not perceive this as a room. It's only something that is perceived by us humans. Therefore, we feel that we are in a room. The relativity of a particular version of reality is something worth thinking about. It has something to do with Einstein's General Theory of Relativity. There's something to understand there.

STUDENT: Einstein said that it had to do with distance travel — the same space being occupied in different parts of the universe simultaneously.

RINPOCHE: That was the previous incarnation of Einstein who said this. His next incarnation will say something a little different. *(laughter)*

Let's say that a person sleeps in a small room that is only a little bigger than his own body. While sleeping, he dreams of an elephant in a large place. If the perceived room really existed, it should exist for the dreamer as a space in which an elephant couldn't possibly enter into. But the daytime room is not real while the dreamer is dreaming. Therefore, it is possible for an elephant to enter his dream-room.

That's one point. We can get into stuff like that later, but slowly, slowly. If we start to talk too much about this, we become really smart, really clever at figuring out things. Then it all becomes conceptual — and rigpa is lost. Honestly. The smart person's obstacle is intellectual: to simply be too smart. They know everything else, but this clever frame of mind is very hard to drop. Sometimes I wonder, "Some scientists are so clever; so clear-thinking that they must be able to be enlightened." And then I wonder again, "Well, if in their clarity they won't give up this thinking, maybe they won't be able to become enlightened."

STUDENT: How long should we train each day?

RINPOCHE: Honestly, there is no fixed time for this practice. But there are two modes of training: one while your buttocks are on the cushion and one while they are not. The main training is to allow rigpa to be in equanimity. Train in the state of naked awareness, free of concepts. 'Concept' here means perceiver and perceived, subject and object. That's how it really is. If we want to set a time, then according to Tibetan tradition we should do a three-year retreat. But there's no guarantee that we will be stable in rigpa after those three years. Likewise, no one can say that you cannot attain stability if you don't do a three-year retreat.

I feel that the most important thing about the Dharma, the most vital thing, is to know what the key point is, the exact key point. How much time one spends on a certain thing is less important. Of course, spending time on spiritual practice does create a lot of merit, but the most important thing is to know the key point.

In a three-year retreat, for example, you may spend the first year focusing outwardly, the next year concentrating inwardly, the third year resting in between, and then your three years are up. At the end of the three years you're just about to know what rigpa is when you get kicked out.

So you can't say there's a fixed duration of time for practice. What we really need to do is recognize the naked, vivid quality of rigpa. The moment you recognize rigpa, there's a sense of being wide open. Awake. Free of subject and object, free of thoughts, free of the future, with no dwelling on the present either. It's like pouring water in a crystal bowl — totally clear. With the cognizance comes some clarity, some brightness. Not the brightness from the electric bulb or daylight, but an internal sense of being lucid. Totally naked the moment you recognize. Totally naked.

So, what is most important is not to practice a certain length of time, but really to know this key point well. But if you want a simple opinion, it's a good idea to spend two hours a day. Sit an hour in the morning and one in the afternoon. Some countries have two-day weekends, in which case it's good to spend one of the two days doing retreat. Spend one of the two days on samsaric, enjoyable activities, and the other uninvolved in television, newspapers or books, as well as uninvolved in washing your clothes or dishes or cleaning the house. Set the time up from morning to evening to do practice and train in this. When you feel tired and you don't feel like meditating, you can read spiritual books or take a nap. But don't look at the television or read the newspaper. Practice meditation, read Dharma books or take a nap — these three things. If you're not really sleepy but still tired, then you can daydream a little. *(laughter)*

One of the points of this kind of practice is to avoid occupying yourself with something all the time. If you are always entertaining yourself, you create the habit of always wanting to do something. You become dependent upon those things you occupy ourselves with, and you always need those things around. At some point, it feels impossible to just be. It's good to train at least occasionally in breaking this habit, this addiction to being entertained.

If you really train seriously in the best way, then in this very body and lifetime you can reach enlightenment and be liberated. Don't be lazy. Be enthusiastic about this. Practice with gladness. Actually, diligence really means to be happy about doing it. If you don't feel that glad about being diligent all the time, then push yourself, say, twenty percent. That much is okay. If it's a hundred percent pushing, you're forcing yourself, and it's like mental torture.

Dualistic mind has the tendency to stray into laziness. It likes being lazy. First we have a thought of something that we find interesting. We'd like to get into that. That itself forms the habit that makes it easier to do it again and actually occupy oneself with that something which is interesting. If you repeat it daily, then the habit becomes your personality — and then one day it is you! Change that.

Not Meditating, not Being Distracted

If the ground is like the string of this rosary, and the path is confusion, then habitual thoughts are like the beads. When we practice, we recognize the present thinker and simply let be, not following past thoughts and not inviting future thoughts. That process is like leaving a gap between two beads. In that gap we contact the ground, the string that runs through each bead.

Again our conceptual mind reasserts itself, and due to habit a new bead is formed. Training may dissolve individual thoughts, individual beads, but if we don't know how to practice authentic meditation, we end up replacing each thought with a 'meditation thought.' Many meditators do that. Instead of a bead, which is recognized as being a thought, we substitute something else which we call rigpa — something nice. To regard the experience of rigpa as something that we see or something that we achieve is simply another thought. A lot of people do that. That is called 'bound by the Dharma.' It's like walking around on the other shore of the ocean still carrying the boat on one's back. Remember, though: the view is a *method*, it is not something to achieve. Be carefree, at ease, and relaxed in your practice. Train in this for a while, and then step outside, loosen up, and shake your shoulders a little. You could do certain yogic exercises known in Tibetan Buddhism, or, if you don't know these, just move around a little bit to loosen up. Let whatever happens happen. spiritual practice is not an exercise in holding on more and more to something important. Rather,

88

it's a sense of increasingly loosening up and letting go. Keep an upright, straight body; breathe freely — then release into natural mind.

If we have made our meditation training to sit and stare outwardly, or to withdraw inwardly, or to hold a certain state in between — all these ways can make obstacles for us. Our training needs to be different. It's not simply a matter of staring outwardly, which is very easy to get into here at Nagi Gompa because of the spaciousness of the location. We shouldn't train in being as alert as a hawk which sits and tries to pinpoint somebody else to eat! It's also possible to kind of lean back into ourselves, as we might do when we are inside the temple, which is a more covered environment. It might feel very comfortable to practice like this, so that we sink further and further into that peaceful state. Eventually we will probably fall asleep. We shouldn't practice like that, either. Neither should we get caught up in the feeling of shamatha, which is a very pleasant sensation of being quiet and tranquil and holding that feeling. "Ahhhh," we might think, "This meditation is so nice. I am so happy to feel like this. I'm really enjoying it." There is some attachment to that, right? Whether you are attached to the pleasure of the calm meditation state or to anything else in the world, it is still attachment. We need to be free from all of that.

It is not that we need to shut off these things from our experience, like closing the door. We don't need to shut out the outside, and neither should we shut off the inside. Nor should we balance somewhere in between these two extremes. Simply allow yourself to be empty, an empty continuity which is also awake or cognizant. Within that state, everything can then unfold or takes place freely. Open mind is the basis. Remember, empty does not mean vacant; it means wide-open.

After recognizing the view, sustain the continuity through meditation, and resolve it through conduct. Earlier I discussed recognizing the view and meditation, as well as the difference between mind and mind essence. Mind seeing its own essence is called the view. This seeing is not in terms of subject and object. It is not a seeing in which there is a 'me' that sees. Neither is it a seeing in which there is nothing at all, no identity whatsoever. It's not a seeing of a total absence, of nothingness.

Rather, it's a seeing that there is *no thing*, no concrete thing. That is called seeing the mind essence.

In the Dzogchen context, this seeing of mind essence is called rigpa. Rigpa means some sense of knowing, an awake quality. In Tibetan we talk about rigpa and *ma-rigpa*, knowing and unknowing. This unknowing is usually called ignorance. Rigpa is the simultaneous knowing of three qualities: the quality of being empty, the quality of being cognizant, and the quality of being unconfined.

Seeing by merely looking and free by merely seeing. Remain free. 'Sustaining the continuity through meditation' is simply to remain in a free way.

At the present moment our mind faces away from itself. Mind immediately bends towards whatever we experience — sight, sound, taste, smell, texture. As soon as there is a sight, sound, smell, taste, or texture, mind leans towards it. The attention is also caught up by thoughts about the past, about the future, and about the present. In fact, it is the present mind that thinks about something in the past or future. There is no past or future anywhere, but one imagines something that will come and calls that the future. In reality, everything takes place in the present. What we call past is thinking of or remembering a past, but it takes place in the present. It's the same with the future. We plan or anticipate something in the present, and we call that the future. Actually past has ceased; it is no more. Future hasn't come yet, it doesn't exist. Everything is present mind, either remembering or imagining.

Please distinguish again between two points I have already mentioned: the meditation state and the post-meditation. You should clearly understand these two words. There's a general way of defining these terms, and a slightly different way in the particular context of mind essence. Usually, when someone sits down and doesn't move for an hour, that's called the meditation state. When the person stands up and starts walking around doing different things, that is called post-meditation. In other words, sitting down is called meditation; walking around doing daily activities is called post-meditation.

The situation is slightly different in the Dzogchen point of view, in the context of mind essence. Recognizing the view involves experiencing a sense of awakeness and allowing that to continue. That duration is called the meditation state. Whenever we get distracted and start to think of something, that is called post-meditation — regardless of whether or not we are sitting on our cushion or walking around. It's like two sides of a hand: here is rigpa, and there, facing away, is the thinking mind. Within one minute we beginners can flicker back and forth many times. For somebody who is really experienced, on the other hand, the true meditation state can last for one minute, two minutes, twenty minutes, half an hour, one hour — it's possible. So please understand that in the Dzogchen context meditation and post-meditation have nothing to do with formal practice versus worldly activity. Meditation here means the mind is unclouded by concept and thought, there is no effort, while post-meditation means mixed with concept and thought; mixed with effort.

Now it's very interesting to look at where is the dividing point between these two? Let's look at our practice. We get distracted and start to think of something, then, at some point we notice that we are distracted. We say, "Oh, I lost it. I wandered off." Then we think, "I should recognize the essence again." That's a reminding, which is still part of post-meditation. Based on this reminder, we can arrive back in the meditation state. To remind ourselves during the meditation state, on the other hand, is incorrect and superfluous. I mentioned yesterday that we don't need to carry the method with us past the point it's served its purpose, like lugging around a boat once we reach the shore. To try to be mindful while already recognizing is just like carrying along a boat. When arriving in rigpa, we should definitely be free of disturbing emotions — but we also need to be free of the method, the technique. It's like if you want to break something, you take a club and you beat it. Once it breaks, if you're still hanging on to the club, that's too much. The job has been done.

This is an extremely important point to understand. We need to overcome disturbing emotions, but in the next moment it doesn't help to carry around and hang on to the technique which helps us to do that. If you hang on, it isn't the realization of emptiness — it's constricted emptiness. Holding tightly onto the idea of recognizing is a common mistake in meditation.

Avoiding this pitfall depends first on the view, and next on the meditation. Meditation means to sustain the continuity of the view. To have the idea "I must get the view," "I need to keep the view for a long period of time," turns the whole thing conceptual. This is a mistake. That's why it's said, "Don't meditate, and yet, don't be distracted." Here, to meditate means to *do* something mentally.

So, what does meditating generally mean? It means some mental doing. What is the view? What is meant by view in this context?

STUDENT: Nonmeditation.

RINPOCHE: What is nonmeditation?

STUDENT 1: Being free from disturbing emotions.

STUDENT 2: Rigpa.

RINPOCHE: These are all words, right? You can label it all sorts of different names, like that which overcomes disturbing emotions, the nature of mind, mind essence, rigpa and so forth. But what is mind essence, really? Don't use the Dharma words now, use what you understand.

STUDENT: The nature of mind itself.

RINPOCHE: What is it like?

STUDENT: Beyond concept.

RINPOCHE: What is the definition of conceptual? What does it mean?

STUDENT: Concepts.

RINPOCHE: And what is that?

STUDENT: Distraction.

RINPOCHE: Is mind essence something you need to recognize or not? If it is all by itself then you don't have to do anything, right? And if this is so, you must have been in the state of rigpa from the time you were very young.

STUDENT: I think it's more that we're beginning to learn to see what is naturally arising.

RINPOCHE: The view means to know. Usually to know implies one knows something that one didn't know before. It's not enough that mind essence is something already naturally present within us. We need to know what is naturally present, and we need to do this by some method. How do we know whether a state is conceptual or nonconceptual? You said that rigpa or nature of mind is free from concepts, right? That implies that the thinking mind is conceptual, doesn't it? What is the real difference between the two?

STUDENT: Knowing and not knowing.

RINPOCHE: Can you describe the thing called rigpa and the conceptual mind a little more, please? How do they look? Why is one free of thought and free of concept, and why is the other mixed up in concept?

STUDENT: The difference between rigpa and conceptual mind is that rigpa is free of the conceptual frame of mind.

RINPOCHE: That's true. What is the conceptual frame of mind itself?

STUDENT: Following after subject and object.

RINPOCHE: Another?

STUDENT 2: It's grasping onto the present.

STUDENT 3: Moving, changing.

STUDENT 4: It's fixated without knowing itself.

RINPOCHE: What you are all saying is quite good. What I am trying to put across here is that the remedy we are using against conceptual mind is also conceptual, and therefore, we have to let go of it as well. When we are applying the remedy it means that we are meditating, as opposed to nonmeditation.

The act of meditating normally begins with trying to keep the attention still. First one concentrates on one object, using the method of 'shamatha with support.' You focus your attention on something, and instead of getting distracted by one thing after another, you keep trying to be mindful. Later there's 'shamatha without support,' where we don't focus on anything, but still retain a sense of trying to be mindful. Not resting on anything, remaining gently, peacefully — but still being mindful. The act of *being* mindful is an act of meditating. I also mentioned that we should try to be mindful when we walk around and carry out our daily activities. This mindfulness, the attention that is mindful of whatever we do in any situation, is carried all around with us like not being distracted by this and that, but just being mindful. This trying to be mindful is the act of meditating. The normal mindfulness is therefore a deliberate mindfulness.

In the Dzogchen context, however, we need to be free from deliberate mindfulness. But to be distracted when free from deliberate mindfulness is also not the right way. Usually our normal state is to not meditate but to be distracted. What's the use of that? The view is not to meditate on as much as a hair tip, but at the same time to be unmoved from nondistraction. This kind of mindfulness is effortless. There's a difference between being deliberate and effortless, isn't there? Deliberate means we try to do something, whereas effortless is what happens all by itself. First we remind ourselves, "I need to recognize." That's deliberate and effortful. We're still in the post-meditation; we haven't arrived at the meditative state yet.

When we recognize; it's like sounding the bell. *(Rinpoche rings the bell.)* Then let be. To recognize and then hold on to that recognition would be the same as holding the stick on the bell. There's no sound then, is there? Just recognize and let be. If you have trained in this, you'll know what is meant here. Training means to sit yourself down and try to experience what is meant. Then you gain some familiarity. Otherwise, you just think about it, and there's no real experience connected to these words. To just wonder, "What did he mean? What is this mind essence or view that he's talking about? I wonder is it like this, or like that?" — that is not called training.

The true training is phrased as "neither meditating nor being distracted," because if we meditate it's conceptual, and if we get distracted we're just ordinary. To be undistracted and not meditating, that is the real state. To see the nature of mind without a seer and something seen, and not to separate from that state — this is something we can understand only in our own experience, if we train. Otherwise we can listen to thousands of hours of talk about this, and it'll never get clear.

So sit yourself down and try to get acquainted with what's being explained here. You may be successful, or you may not, but the result doesn't matter. At least you'll get some experience. It seems we need to train more because if we just keep talking about it, the words will make it totally lost. Then it becomes like all the rest of the information we've gathered, all the teachings that we've heard, understood, and then forgotten. "Oh, a new teaching. Oh, that's very interesting. ... Now I understand!" — and then you forget. "I already understood that point the last seminar; isn't there something new? Well of course! I already understood that during this seminar, isn't there something new?"

To react like this indicates one doesn't have real personal experience. Everything is lost in theory. And to abandon true understanding in favor of theory is simply not good enough. We may even become numb at some point, jaded from too much talk. It's like the skins used to hold butter in Tibet. Leather usually has to be softened with grease or oil in order to be pliable. But butter-skins are in constant contact with butter, and yet they become totally stiff. To just pretend that we understood something because we heard it and intellectually comprehended it, that's not real experience. And if we fool ourselves like this, we'll never practice. We'll just believe we understood, until we're disturbed by some emotion and we haven't a clue as to what to do.

You may remember that earlier I said, "If you recognize mind essence, disturbing emotions are liberated." You may have heard and comprehended how to dissolve disturbing emotions, but that alone doesn't dissolve your disturbing emotions. Why not? Because you are not really used to deal with your emotions that way. You haven't really trained. You haven't really become fully experienced.

The word *continuity* is very important. I mentioned that mind essence is something wide open, not made of anything whatsoever, yet vividly clear. It's perfectly okay to perceive things in this state; in fact, nothing is blocked off. The natural cognizance ensures that sights are seen, sounds are heard, and so forth. And, as a matter of fact, whatever is perceived doesn't harm or help anything whatsoever. We don't get dragged into hell just by experiencing something. Neither are we elevated to a heavenly state simply by experiencing something. It's like what Tilopa said to Naropa: "Son, you're not bound by perceiving, but by clinging. So cut your clinging, Naropa."

When remaining as mind essence, it's allowed to see, to hear, to sense whatever takes place. You don't have to prevent that. If you prevent or inhibit it's not the self-existing state. Being empty in essence, cognizant by nature and unconfined in capacity are qualities that are naturally so. They're intrinsic; they're self-existing. All we have to do is recognize what *is* as being just as it is. Not making it into an object, not getting carried away by another object, but simply sustaining the continuity of what is, through undistracted meditation.

Any questions?

STUDENT: I'm wondering ... in the beginning, recognition lasts for such a short period of time, and distraction comes so easily. If the recognition doesn't stay very long, I don't want to repeatedly searching for it after the distraction comes. How do I avoid this problem of trying to recognize and still be able to practice? It seems like there's a little bit of tension there.

RINPOCHE: For a beginner there is some kind of clash between these two. It's like being caught in a fight between two sides. The way to overcome this is first, recognize. Then, let be. Don't worry too much about whether you got it or didn't get it, saw it or didn't see; just wait a bit. Train like this for a few months, without worrying about whether you see mind essence or not. If you immediately start thinking, "Do I see it?," or "I don't see it," you are just forming a new concept. To sit like this — "I see it!" — means that the training immediately becomes conceptual. I am happy to hear your question because it shows you have some taste, some experience. Good practice!

Take the example of water which is a bit murky. It doesn't become clear by splashing it or stirring it up, but by allowing it to settle. You need to emphasize the relaxed and letting-go quality more. When one is more relaxed and at ease, the clarity and brightness will increasingly come forth by itself, though not necessarily from the very beginning. Right now it's true what you say, that the moment of recognizing is so short. But one shouldn't get stuck in worrying about it and saying, "Now I've gotten it. Oh no, I haven't gotten it; this is bad, I must get it back. Oh no, now I didn't get it again." Really, the mind can go on and on like that. Instead, just look and let be for a few months. Recognize and drop concerns. Don't hope, don't fear, don't be anxious about seeing or not seeing. Just totally drop any preoccupation with all that.

During the post-meditation state you can look back and say, "How was it?" It's all right to examine the meditation state in retrospect, to inquire into how it actually was. But if we continuously question and analyze whether this is the real state or not during the meditation state, it's already the post-meditation.

This is how it is for beginners. With training, at some point it is said that everything unfolds as the play of wakefulness. You can reflect on events and engage in activities without losing the expansiveness of this empty awakened state. It doesn't get lost.

It's like learning how to drive. It's not spontaneous, is it? You need to hold onto the wheel, you need to think of where to put the feet, how to operate the clutch, the gear, the brake, the accelerator and so forth. You have to look where you're driving all the time. There's a lot to worry about.

When you're a trained driver, on the other hand, you don't have to worry about a thing. You just drive. I saw someone in America who was driving a car. He had his girlfriend beside him. He had a hamburger in one hand, the music was on full blast, and he was driving at top speed. They were both very happy, no problems whatsoever. He was trained.

In the beginning, when you're learning to drive, you can't have the girlfriend right there beside you. She'll complain that you're not giving her your full attention. You'll get in trouble. When you're much more stable and trained, then you can carry out all activities without any problem without ever leaving the state of emptiness. The natural cognizance can take care of the girlfriend, who by the way is the empty essence. The two can be an indivisible unity. They are the unity of means and knowledge, in which the means is the natural cognizance, which is the male aspect, while the female, the consort, is the great mother of emptiness. The traditional symbolism that involve deities in union, male and female buddhas in union, like Samantabhadra and consort, show us is that experience and emptiness are indivisible.

When you recognize mind essence, at that moment nothing is switched off. You can still see and hear and feel and so forth — very precisely, in fact, because there's no latching onto or clinging to anything at that moment. Everything is vividly clear, totally distinct. You experience exactly what is. Nothing is distorted in any way. You're not fixating on anything either. And when you grow more accustomed to that state, then you can carry out any activity from within it. Everything becomes the play of original wakefulness.

We don't have to always work at applying the method. In a flash, in a moment, arrive in rigpa. At the moment of arriving, you are already in rigpa. To use again the example of driving a car, the moment someone turns in front of you, you hit the brake. It's not like you first have to think, "Where is the brake? Now I should put my foot on it. Now I should push it down." It doesn't happen like that. You just hit it! In fact, if you drive like that you will kill a lot of people. Rather, the best way is when getting involved in a disturbing emotion, immediately recognize rigpa. The emotion is liberated, like a snake that is untied by itself. Or like drawing upon the surface of water, where the drawing and the dissolving take place at the same time. Finally it gets to the point that whether a thought stirs or doesn't stir, it makes absolutely no difference, because it is like a thief entering an empty house — nothing to gain, nothing to lose. We should make sure that we get to that point.

Just like whenever somebody runs out in front of you, you hit the brake — in the same way, whenever a thought or emotion like anger starts to move, immediately use that as a support, as a helper, for recognizing rigpa. That is the best way. You don't hit the brake unless somebody jumps out in front of you, right? It's thanks to the person appearing in front of your car that you hit the brake. In the same way, it is thanks to thoughts and emotions that we get a chance to recognize rigpa. It's due to their kindness. Once we train in that way, when any thought or emotion is used to trigger the recognition of rigpa; we can truly say that "the essence of thought is dharmakaya." There won't be a time, an opportunity, for thoughts to be activated in the normal way. Thoughts do still arise, but at that point a thought is like a burnt rope. If you try to pull the end of a burnt rope in order to use it, you get hold of nothing. In the same way, because of recognizing rigpa in the moment of thought, the thought cannot create karma. It doesn't work like before. Otherwise, a thought creates karma by holding on to subject and object and doing something out of that duality. When no duality is held, no karma is created. If you hit the brakes before the person is run down, no karma is created.

In the same way, there are thoughts and emotions, but when your practice is in such a way that they trigger the recognition of rigpa, there is no creation of karma. Even if thoughts are activated or you start to be involved in them for a few seconds, the confusion can dissolve with recognition. We need to be that quick. Otherwise, if we are too slow for each thought and emotion, we are too slow to avoid the creation of karma. Then we have a lot of karmic accidents, so to speak! Karma is accumulated, and that makes the twelve links of interdependent origination go on and on. Earlier, I defined karma as the forming of habitual tendencies, right? The forming of habit. We form habits. Thoughts and emotions need to be released or liberated before the habit is formed, reinforced, and perpetuated.

Another question, from someone who hasn't asked before?

STUDENT: I once heard the example of rigpa being like a needle, innately stable — does that mean that effortless awareness has naturally arisen?

RINPOCHE: We could say that effortless awareness arises by itself, but what that means is that it doesn't happen through effort. Any act of effort or trying or doing is a way to prevent something that already is from being as it is — to prevent what rigpa is, which is our basic state, the ground itself. The basic state gets occupied. Therefore, when not being involved in any deliberate act or effort, whatever already is, is by itself. It is not that it 'arises,' it is what basically *is*. Arise is merely a word. We say also that rigpa lasts longer and longer, that the continuity of rigpa is prolonged or extended, but actually it is not like that at all. Rather, the habitual tendencies and confusion which interrupt the continuity of rigpa become less and less.

STUDENT: I have a question about meditation. Should I leave my eyes open or closed during meditation? What's the difference?

RINPOCHE: If you train in shamatha, meaning peacefulness and calm, that means you try to avoid being disturbed by what you see or hear. You go to a place where there's not too much going on. You don't want to hear a lot of noise or see a lot of stuff because then you'll start thinking about it. Your stillness will be disturbed. In shamatha it's better not to pay too much attention to external things. There's some sense of withdrawing or disengaging from the five senses, and the mind just tries to abide peacefully, in a calm way. Therefore, it's better to close your eyes, or all right, to close your eyes if you practice shamatha.

But if you train in recognizing mind essence, in the context of Dzogchen, then you shouldn't try to change or do anything artificial at all. Closing the eyes is artificial, isn't it? Just as putting in earplugs is. From the Dzogchen perspective it doesn't harm a practitioner to hear sounds or see things. Just leave the five senses as they naturally are, open. One is not bound by what is experienced, as Tilopa said, but by the clinging to the experienced. So in the context of Dzogchen there is no need to close the eyes. Just leave them open.

As you progress further and further, then it is said that the eyes are the 'gates of wisdom,' of original wakefulness. This is a point which is especially important when you get to *Tögal* practice later on. Also, in *Trekchö* there is a practice called 'mingling the threefold sky,' which involves intermingling the outer sky which is the empty space, the inner sky, which is the empty mind, and the innermost sky, which is the empty awareness. When doing that kind of training, not only do you leave the eyes open; you open them a little wider than usual.

So it's up to you. If you practice shamatha you can close your eyes. If you practice Dzogchen, then keep them open. If you practice only shamatha then it's good to close your eyes, put in earplugs, lock your doors, pull the curtains and sit like this. *(Rinpoche covers his head with his shawl)*. Kind of like, "Don't let anything in." Just joking.

A GUIDED MEDITATION ON REFUGE AND GURU YOGA

As a support for and an enhancement of the Dzogchen training, I would like to introduce the practice of taking refuge as well as a traditional guru yoga. As the starting point, keep the pure motivation of the bodhisattva resolve, sit with a straight back, let your breathing flow freely, and for a short while leave your mind without fabrication, utterly uncontrived. First of all we need to improve our motivation by thinking, "For the benefit of all sentient beings, I will practice this meditation session."

Now imagine a lotus tree in the sky before you, with one branch or stem in the center and one in each of the four directions. On the central branch sits Padmasambhava in the form known as Nangzi Silnön, meaning the "glorious subjugator of all that appears and exists," With his right hand holding a vajra. This is the most common way of depicting him. He is surrounded by all the masters of the Dzogchen lineage.

On the branch in front of them are all the yidams, headed by Yangdag Heruka, and surrounded by all the deities of the *Eight Sadhana Teachings*. On the branch to his right is Buddha Shakyamuni, surrounded by an immense gathering of buddhas of the past, present and future. On the branch behind him, imagine the sacred Dharma in the form of scriptures, each resounding with vowels and consonants like a humming beehive. On the branch to his left is Avalokiteshvara surrounded by all the noble Sangha, the sublime beings of both Mahayana and Hinayana. In short, imagine that in the sky before you are all the gurus, the yidams, the dakas and dakinis, the buddhas, the teachings, the enlightened practitioners and all the Dharma protectors in a vast gathering, like cloudbanks assembled vividly in the sky before you.

Towards the external refuge, the Buddha, the Dharma and Sangha, make this supplication: "In this and in all future lives may I be under your protection; please grant your blessings that I may have the opportunity to reach liberation." Let devotion fill your mind, through a sense of deep longing. Then, recite aloud the prayer of going for refuge:

In the Buddha, the Dharma and the supreme assembly,
I take refuge until enlightenment.
By the merit of generosity and so forth, ...
May I attain buddhahood for the welfare of all beings.

The visualization of the Dzogchen lineage over the head of Padmasambhava starts from above with Samantabhadra, then Vajrasattva, Garab Dorje, Vimalamitra, Guru Rinpoche, and so forth. The twenty-five disciples of Padmasambhava, the hundred major tertöns and so forth, are all vividly present around him, as are the yidams headed by Yangdag Heruka and all the other deities of the Eight Sadhana Teachings. In between, filling in all the spaces in the sky, are the dakas and dakinis. The gurus who are the sovereigns of all the buddha families, the yidam-deities who are the source of accomplishments, and the dakinis who dispel all obstacles are vividly present as the inner objects of refuge.

Let your longing and devotion arise from deep within you. Let the sun of devotion rise in the sky, and as it shines on the snow mountain of your heart, the blessings of the lineages will stream down like a river. Devotion is like sunlight that melts the ice, allowing the river of blessings to stream forth. The blessings of the three kayas of the Padmasambhava's essence and the blessings of the Three Roots are transferred into your own body, speech and mind, where they pervade and transform your very being.

After reciting the refuge prayer, imagine that the whole field of refuge dissolves into light, first moving in from the outside, then in a clockwise manner. All the yidams dissolve into Yangdag Heruka, who dissolves into the buddhas; then the buddhas dissolve into Buddha Shakyamuni; he dissolves into the Dharma scriptures; which dissolve into Avalokiteshvara — and finally, all of them dissolve into Padmasambhava, the main figure present in the sky before you, who remains as a single figure.

Address yourself then to Padmasambhava, supplicating him as the single embodiment of the Three Jewels. In essence he is all the awakened ones of the past, all the buddhas of the future and all the buddhas of the present. Thinking of him like this, supplicate him mentally.

Imagine now that from the forehead of Padmasambhava, the white letter OM radiates a brilliant white light that touches your own forehead. Imagine that through this you are conferred the vase empowerment, the empowerment for practicing the development stage of deity yoga. The obscurations and negative karma you created with your body are purified, and the seed for realizing the nirmanakaya level is planted in your being.

From the red letter AH in Padmasambhava's throat, rays of beautiful red light shine forth and touch your own throat. Through this you receive the secret empowerment. Your obscurations and the negative karma created by your voice are purified, and you are empowered to practice the completion stage involving the channels and energies. The seed for realizing the sambhogakaya level is planted in your being.

Now from the blue letter HUNG in Padmasambhava's heart center, azure blue light streams forth and dissolves into your own heart center, purifying all mental obscurations and negative karma from all past lives. You are thus conferred the third empowerment of wisdom knowledge, empowering you to practice consort yoga, follow the *phonya* path and become invested with the fortune to realize the dharmakaya level.

From Padmasambhava's naval center, multi-colored rays of light stream forth and dissolve into your previous three centers as well as your naval center. This light purifies the negative karma created through a combination of body, speech and mind, especially the defilement of habitual tendencies. By being conferred this fourth or precious word empowerment, you're authorized to practice the path of *Trekchö*, the primordial purity of cutting through, and of *Tögal*, the spontaneous presence of the direct crossing. And you are given the fortune to realize the fourth kaya, the essence body.

Now imagine that Guru Rinpoche dissolves into light, which becomes indivisible from yourself so that your body, speech and mind are indivisible from Guru Rinpoche's Body, Speech and Mind.

The essence of your mind is empty, the dharmakaya nature. The cognizant quality of your nature is the sambhogakaya, while your unconfined capacity, the indivisibility of the previous two, is the nirmanakaya. By resting evenly in the state in which your very identity is indivisible from the three kayas of all the buddhas of the past, present and future, you are inseparable from Guru Rinpoche himself. You take the innermost refuge, and again you repeat the refuge prayer.

At this point we should remain evenly for a short while in the very intent that is pointed through the four empowerments, the awareness wisdom. When I ring the bell, let the mere hearing of this sound remind you of self-existing awareness, so that simultaneously with the hearing of the sound you simply lapse into the uninterrupted state of self-existing wakefulness. *(Rinpoche rings the bell.) (Period of silence.)*

You should have some sharpness of presence of awareness. *(Rinpoche rings the bell again.) (Period of silence.)*

STUDENT: Don't we always have to take the support of a teacher to make sure that our practice is correct?

RINPOCHE: Of course we need to follow a spiritual teacher, and of course we need to receive instructions. Of course we need to put those instructions into practice. But if one spends one's whole life trying to follow spiritual teachers, something is wrong there also. We need to supplicate our root guru in order discover the indivisible nature of his mind and our own mind. That is definitely necessary. But it's not good to think, "If I'm not with my teacher I won't know how to practice," or, "If I'm not with my teacher I can't deal with disturbing emotions," or, "If I'm not with my teacher, I am lost, I do not know what to do."

In the old days, people had more opportunities because they were more free, not so busy, not so much work. People had the opportunity to stay with the master for three years, or six years or nine years. These days it is not like that. The teachers themselves are really busy and often have no time, and the disciples have no time also. They may only have four or five days to stay together, like us!

During the five days of our retreat, we should try to understand as much as we can. Whatever we understood we should put into practice, put to actual use. When we leave here, we should leave together with the true teacher, the teacher who is our intrinsic nature. That teacher can be our constant companion.

You know, we are soon going our different ways — I am going to Singapore and Malaysia, some of you are going back to your own countries, or traveling to other places. Maybe we will meet again, maybe not — who knows? There is nothing sure in this world. Everything is impermanent; nothing is fixed or guaranteed. You should try your best to recognize the ground luminosity inside yourselves by means of the path of rigpa.

Somebody who hasn't asked anything?

STUDENT: How do we receive blessings? Is it through faith and devotion?

RINPOCHE: Devotion is the root of blessings, the basis for receiving blessings. Blessings definitely do exist, so we should know what they are, and what the role of devotion is in receiving blessings. Otherwise, there is not much point in devotion.

Blessings are contagious, so to speak, and are transmitted in a fashion that is rather like catching a cold. If somebody has a cold and you are too close, you catch a cold too. Likewise, if you get close to a master who has blessings, they can be transmitted to you. Blessings here mean the sense of some power of realization or power of samadhi, some kind of atmosphere of realization that is naturally present. You move close to him, in the sense of opening up yourself through devotion and making sincere, heart-felt supplications. In other words, you lower your defenses, whatever doubts and suspicions that prevent you from being 'infected' with the blessings. The moment you do that, you catch a cold as well. Devotion is a very deeply felt and sincere emotion, which comes from the bottom of one's heart. It is partly a sense of really rejoicing, rejoicing in the qualities that are embodied in the teacher. At the same time, there is a sense of gratitude for the teacher's incredible kindness. This combination of rejoicing and gratitude is what opens us up, what generates devotion.

Devotion can be towards the Buddha, the Dharma, the Sangha, in terms of truly rejoicing in and appreciating their amazing qualities, of knowledge and compassion, and so forth. To be open towards that and rejoice in those qualities is one aspect of devotion. At the same time, when we understand how it benefits ourselves to train in that the recognition of our basic nature, we feel gratitude, an appreciation of the kindness.

Otherwise, there could be many kinds of devotion. There is the devotion which is simply love, love generated by the thought, "He was nice to me, so I like him." There is devotion which is an admiration, in that you feel in awe of a person or thing. Then there is devotion inspired by some kind of longing to emulate someone — you want to be like that as well. However, in the beginning, devotion is some kind of fabrication. We are trying to feel in a certain way, trying to open up. It is artificial, but it makes us grow closer to understanding the view, in the sense that devotion opens us up to realize emptiness, makes it easier. When some authentic experience of emptiness strengthens devotion even further, at that point it is no longer artificial or contrived. We may begin by trying to feel devotion, and then, later on, actual experience allows it to become totally uncontrived. Uncontrived devotion springs out of the experience of the view. Because when there is some seeing in actuality of what is called rigpa or ordinary mind, the natural mind that really solves or liberates disturbing emotions — when the conceptual frame of mind is opened up by this recognition — *then* we have a personal taste of the value and the worth of the practice. It is that real appreciation which is uncontrived devotion. In this way, devotion and the view of emptiness mutually strengthen one another.

LOSING IT

THE DZOGCHEN TEACHINGS HAVE A FAMOUS SAYING: *If you know how to meditate but not how to dissolve the meditation, what is the difference between you and the meditation gods?* The dhyana gods spend aeons and aeons tied up in meditation. If you don't know how to meditate there's nothing to dissolve, right? Meditation and post-meditation are then the same.

On the other hand, if you know the difference between meditation and post-meditation, you know exactly and precisely what is what. The meditative state is something that is very free, very open. However, some people seem to think that the meditative state is something one sits and keeps, like holding something in your hand. If you're grasping at something, it's very hard to be free at the same time, isn't it?

There are many ways of grasping at the meditative state. Sometimes you might be so blissful that you feel, "Wow, it is so great to feel like this. Even if I were to be pricked with a needle right now, it would probably also be a pleasant sensation. It won't hurt at all." In this kind of state, one feels that there's no suffering at all in this whole world. Everything is bliss. "These people who talk about suffering and problems, what are they talking about? The whole thing is blissful." *(Rinpoche demonstrates, sitting like someone blissed out, smiling and gently nodding.)* You're savoring this bliss. It's the marijuana of bliss! You're stoned on bliss.

This attitude cripples genuine meditation training. It's all right to feel the bliss, but don't cling to it. Sitting and savoring it and getting into this feeling of bliss — many people do this. It doesn't happen quite so often with Buddhists, but lots of Hindus do it. If you believe the bliss is coming from some kind of god or divine influence and you're singing the name of the god, whether you sing "Shri Krishna, Shri Ram" or "OM AH HUNG VAJRA GURU PEMA SIDDHI HUNG" makes no difference. It's clinging to it, tasting it, smacking one's lips over the tastiness of this bliss. *(Rinpoche smacks his lips loudly.)* The object is the god, and you are the subject. The bliss is the connection between subject and object — and you're just drinking it in, gulping it down. That's attachment. Clinging to the bliss plants the seed for future rebirth in the samsaric realms of desire.

Honestly, that clinging to bliss is the cause for rebirth in the realm of desire. Everybody likes bliss. There's nobody who doesn't like to feel good. There's many ways that we try to feel good —singing, laughing, drinking, smoking ganja, the list is endless. We do it in order to evoke some kind of feeling of pleasure or bliss or enjoyment. All these terms are basically identical. And with all of them, there's some attachment to that sense of pleasure.

According to Dzogchen, it's perfectly all right to feel blissful. You don't have to avoid it, but neither should you hold on to it by clinging to or yearn for the feeling of bliss. Instead, recognize that which experiences, and simply allow the bliss to be a reflection in this mirror. Do not fixate upon it at all.

In Dzogchen, there are many ways to generate devotion, like simply remembering your guru, bringing to mind all the wonderful qualities of the buddhas. You may feel so deeply moved and thrilled that tears may come to your eyes and all the hairs on your body may stand up. Experiencing these kinds of sensations does not mean that the state of rigpa is lost. It's possible to continuously recognize the nature of awareness and at the same time be filled with such deep devotion that tears are streaming down your face. It can still be one continuity of rigpa.

The situation is exactly the same regarding compassion. When one is full of almost unbearable compassion for all beings, tears may come to the eyes and the hairs of the body stand on end. Just as with devotion, there doesn't have to be any indulgence in this intense emotion, or of getting sucked into it. It's possible to continue recognizing the natural awareness during the compassion or devotion. Although tears may be rolling down your cheeks, you can still see clearly with your eyes. You don't have to get sucked into the emotion in a sentimental sort of way, like sobbing or bawling. That's how they cry in American movies. Buddhists don't cry like that.

At the same time, one definitely can experience a strong emotion which produces tears. Dzogchen is not about sitting and becoming a vegetable, being so totally spaced out you don't feel a thing. It's not like you sense there is nothing … everything is empty … there is no emotion anymore … and you become totally numb. What's the use of becoming that kind of idiot, someone who sits and gapes and doesn't know anything? It's not like that at all. Actually, in Dzogchen you can feel a lot.

Some people might think, "What's the use of training in rigpa? You don't feel a thing. If you feel something they call it conceptual. If you have pleasure they call it clinging. If you hurt or suffer they call it a thought. You're not even allowed to think! They say, 'Don't hold onto the past, don't hold onto the future, don't dwell on anything in the present.' It sounds really crazy. On the other hand, maybe there's something to it … I don't know. Maybe I should find another teacher who might say it a little better."

Please don't get lost in this kind of confusion. It's really quite simple. Within the empty essence there is still a cognizant quality that notices, feels, experiences, and perceives whatever unfolds. It's not that you don't feel a thing. If you're hurt, physically or emotionally, you feel that you are hurt. If you're happy, you feel that you are happy. It's not that you become totally oblivious through Dzogchen practice, not at all. You simply do not tie knots on your stream of experience. Usually, when people like something, they tie the knot of liking it. When they dislike something, they tie the knot of disliking. Tying the knot of liking being happy or disliking being sad — all the time, knots are being tied, by grasping, by clinging, by fixating. The message in Dzogchen is: experience whatever takes place, but don't tie yourself to it. Don't get tied up in knots.

So, just as you shouldn't get caught up in the experience of bliss, you should not get caught up in the experience of clarity. Although the Tibetan word for clarity and cognizance is both *salwa*, don't mistake their meaning for being the same, however, because they are not.

The experience of clarity is a temporary meditation experience. You think, "This is so clear, so bright, so lucid. I feel completely crystal-clear! Wow, it's so clear and penetrating that I can probably know what another person is feeling and thinking! I can probably see what's going on outside of the house, even though I can't see it with my eyes! Everything is so clear; why are beings confused?" Of course you're very happy to feel like that and have this wonderful experience, which may continue for some time. You may think, "Why bother to meditate?" because it's like this all the time — you are totally clear whether you practice or not.

This kind of temporary experience can go on for a while. While you're in it, you feel that you can indulge in anything. You can eat meat, drink liquor, engage with women, and get involved in all kinds of stuff because you feel so clear, so totally unconfused, that you think you're able to use all sense pleasures as the path. Even if you act frivolously, it doesn't matter, because everything is so clear. But as this clarity is just a temporary experience, it's impermanent and doesn't last. Sooner or later you crash-land, and then you feel really depressed. Maybe you think, "Meditation is no use. I was totally wrong. Maybe I should become a Hindu now, or maybe Taoism is better — anything else! Life seems much more fun for a Hari Krishna!"

The whole problem here is that it wasn't really the view to begin with. One was simply believing that that feeling of clarity was the view. There was no certainty of insight. If one puts one's trust in some temporary experience, there's no stability, because eventually it will fade away. It's like you leaned on the clarity instead of being stable; you leaned on the bliss instead of being stable.

There's a third experience called nonthought, in which one feels, "I'm totally free of thought. I have absolutely no thought whatsoever. I'm totally undistracted. Even if I *try* to think, I don't have any thoughts — not even a hair tip. I'm enlightened!" That type of practitioner sits like this. *(Rinpoche demonstrates an utterly self-satisfied attitude.)* That is the Dharma-drug, the drug of meditation.

So, these experiences of bliss, clarity and nonthought do come. There is nothing wrong with that; just don't hold onto them as being something special. Actually, it's good to have experiences like that, probably some of you already had them, some not. Some of you probably are still staying in what is called 'dry meditation,' meaning there's no juice in it. It's just dried-up meditation. Slowly, with practice, this dry meditation becomes saturated, juicy, so that you feel blissful, clear, and thought-free. Such experiences are okay; they're a sign of practicing. Just don't get caught up in them!

It's like this: when you go to Copenhagen from Gomdé, first you drive on a dirt road, then you come to a small paved road, then further on you get to the highway, then the ferry, then the motorway, and so on. In the same way, you have different feelings as you progress in meditation, as you drive along through your practice. These different experiences are temporary stages or states on the path of meditation, just as along the road there may be a big field of beautiful flowers, or a nice little cafe serving ice-cold beer. You might think, "This is so nice it must be Copenhagen! I'll stay here." But if you mistake this pleasant roadside stop for your final destination, you will never get to Copenhagen. The problem is not that you stopped to admire the flowers and enjoy a beer, but that you liked it so much you felt like staying there. Similarly, the real mistake here is to hold onto that temporary experience as the final result.

It's naturally to feel blissful at times. Just don't cling to it! Simply allow the bliss to be felt. If you feel clear, don't fixate on the clarity. If you're free of thoughts, don't cling to this state of nonthought. Then it's all right. Free of fixation, the bliss, clarity and nonthought become the flavors or expressions of the three kayas.

There are additional pitfalls. For example, I have seen a lot of people who sit and glare into mid-air while meditating. If you give them a little tap on the shoulder, they come right back. If somebody has to come back from somewhere, that proves they are imagining something or constructing something. On the other hand, if someone trains in naturally letting be and being relaxed, there is a constant readiness to respond. They do not have to come back and then respond. If the meditation state falls apart from being disturbed, that is a sign that it was constructed, artificial. Actually, there is nothing to come back to! You are right there to begin with. Only if you imagine something when you meditate do you leave.

Someone who meditates like that, getting absorbed into the 'perceived,' can spend a long time, many years, practicing like that. Later he or she might complain, "I've spent so many years practicing, but I don't seem to be developing any qualities." And he will become anxious, thinking, "What went wrong, what am I doing wrong?" Maybe he will go to a meditation master, who will ask him to describe his practice. The master will tell him, "That's not good enough. You've lost your attention in the outside — now let it come back a little within."

So the meditator will switch over to the opposite procedure; settling down into a peaceful, tranquil state within. He thinks, "Ah, this is nice; now I've got the real thing. It's like there's something to lean back into; ahhhhh, very nice. I'll keep on practicing like this and everything will be okay." As the innate awake quality is increasingly drawn into the all-ground, the *alaya*, the meditator becomes duller and duller. He starts to feel less and less. He doesn't hear or think, he merely dwells. When he practices, an hour seems to pass by quickly — the meditator comes back to normal consciousness, and an hour is gone. He thinks, "Well, it was really hard to meditate before, but now I can keep the meditation state for a really long time. What progress! I have no thoughts, no hope, no fear — this is definitely it." In reality, the active quality of consciousness is withdrawing into the all-ground. "In this state it makes no difference whether my eyes are open or closed, so I might as well close them." In this way we slowly fall asleep. An hour's meditation is an hour's sleep; quite a nice sleep too.

Again our meditator spends five years practicing like that. And then he reads about the qualities that should manifest through meditation training, and notices he hasn't developed any of them still. "Hey," he thinks, "what's happened?" He's becoming suspicious again, so he goes back to the meditation master and describes his practice: "I did just what you said, I settled back and looked inside." The master says, "Well, that is not good enough either. It sounds like you relaxed a little *too* much. Don't do that any more; instead, settle in between. Leave your state of mind somewhere in between inside and outside."

So the meditator says, "Oh, good advice," and he practices by remaining in the present. He rests in the nowness, leaving awareness right in the present. There are no coarse thoughts; he's not looking outwardly and not focusing inwardly, but keeping his attention right in between. There is some quality in this, some peace that feels good. Sometimes this sense of peace permeates his whole body, and his mind feels so elated that nothing can really bother him. This joyful exuberance is such that even if he comes face-to-face with his worst enemy, he would feel, "Actually, that's a nice person, and he doesn't bother me a bit." It doesn't bother him to be in an unpleasant, stinky, dirty place, either — he finds it rather comfortable. He appreciates it, thinking, "This bliss they talk about in the teachings can be quite nice, indeed!"

So he holds on to the bliss. And one day, it fades also. It's replaced by a feeling of sharpness and clarity so strong that he feels he can actually know what is happening on the other side of a wall. It's almost transparent, so sharp and clear. "This is so interesting to feel like this," he thinks. "It must be the unity of emptiness and clarity." So he sits and nurtures that feeling as well, and eventually that also fades. Next, he feels totally empty, free of any thought whatsoever. There is no thought of the past, no thought of the present, no thought of the future. This ongoingness of being completely empty can last for days on end.

So, our meditator is having meditation experiences, 'meditation moods.' His consciousness feels in certain ways, but these sensations all pass. Inevitably, instead of feeling blissful or totally empty and free of thoughts, he's back to feeling uncomfortable. The room smells, he doesn't like where he is, he feels a little upset and unsettled, and he thinks, "What happened? This is not right. Maybe I should go back and see my meditation teacher." And he describes his practice to the teacher, saying "I sat and kept the state in between."

The master replies, "That's not good enough, either. You need to totally let go of any sense of dwelling on something outside, inside or in between. Drop this notion of resting your mind on anything at all, until it's totally free and unimpeded. Do not rest on anything whatsoever; just be completely open." Doing this, the meditator gets a little taste of what the dharmakaya is like. There is some opening.

My point here is not that we have to go spend fifteen years practicing the sidetracks of meditation. It would be much better if we could understand what is wrong with these three different approaches beforehand, and immediately get to the naked state of dharmakaya. It's easy to understand what is known by perceiver and perceived, right? For a beginner, holding on to this dualistic experience of perceiver and something perceived is an obstacle, but it's not so hard to overcome. For an advanced practitioner, the obstacle is more the resting *in* or dwelling *on* something. Do you understand what is meant by resting or dwelling? Like the flower lying atop this rupee note which is resting on the table. That is dualistic fixation. It's like grasping hold of the money, dwelling on the money, and ignoring the direct experience of the table. The present awareness which experiences right now is resting on this moment. Present mind is dwelling on the present moment, but in a fixated sort of way. According to Dzogchen, that becomes an obstacle for meditation practice. From the viewpoint of another vehicle, it may not be an obstacle. There are many spiritual paths in this world, and plenty of instructions that say, "Don't worry, just be here now!" This is basically okay, it can be very helpful — but in the end, you still are stuck with this "Be here now."

Dzogchen maintains that you must transcend that thought construct as well, making way for openness, *unimpededness*, in Tibetan called *sangtal*. This is the point where nowness vanishes, when it is no longer an object remaining. This may sound like it's all a little above our heads; but on the other hand, it is true. First we need to have some sense of nowness, of being present, and to cultivate it, and afterwards dismantle that as well. But if we have no idea at all of nowness, then what it means to be free of nowness is only crazy talk.

I feel like I have to say something about this, because we are only here for five days. If we spend five days cultivating a really nice nowness, we will have no time left to destroy it. On the other hand, some of you may have a very nice feeling of solid, strong nowness in your meditation. If that is the case, now is the time to destroy it! Because it becomes a stumbling block for openness. No matter how the thin the rupee note is, it still blocks something passing through.

The qualities of the awakened state of buddhahood, the enlightened qualities of knowing the nature as it is, and of perceiving all possible existing things, and so forth — the qualities are all blocked by this dwelling on nowness. Free from that fixation, the play of the awakened state can unfold in an unimpeded fashion, freely, like water overflowing from a container. If the water tap is shut by the dwelling on nowness, the water does not come out; so let the water out! Let's say that the awakened state is like a tap that is meant to stay open, but it's temporarily closed by our dualistic fixation on subject and object. Normally it's closed quite tightly. It gets closed more lightly by the dwelling on some experience, and it gets closed very lightly by dwelling on nowness. By letting go of that sense of nowness, the intrinsic — the qualities that are already present — can start to manifest more and more. The devotion and compassion which are nonconceptual start to naturally unfold. And all the other qualities of the awakened state are free to manifest. Certainty itself, in the sense of being totally confident of the innate nature as it is, is found. As long as one is continually caught up in subject-object fixation, it is impossible to be really self-confident. There is no stability in that, and therefore no real confidence. There is no knowing of the innate nature as it is.

In short, don't focus outwardly, don't concentrate inwardly, don't dwell in between. Do you understand? Totally unimpeded, without inside and outside. Totally unimpeded is a phrase that appears a lot in the Tantric texts. Totally unimpeded, without inside and outside. To say that there is no outside, no inside and no in-between doesn't make much sense, right? It sounds a bit like foolish talk. But to summarize, this is what it really means: recognize, and then let go. When distracted, remember to recognize and let go, again and again. That is how to train as a beginner. After a while, one doesn't have to continue doing it like that. Sometimes during distraction, it is enough to simply notice the sense of being awake. In that very moment, one is immediately back in the natural state. You don't have to look here and there for it.

With regard to sustaining the continuity: if you are practicing shamatha, you are keeping continuity of stillness. That which makes the stillness continue is called mindfulness. When sustaining or allowing the continuity of rigpa, then rigpa, the awakened mind, is itself mindfulness. There is no other mindfulness than rigpa itself. At that moment, rigpa is the seeing, rigpa is the training and rigpa is the utilizing of that as well — the view, meditation and conduct.

A few questions?

STUDENT: What if the tendency to be distracted is quite strong?

RINPOCHE: That is due to bad habit which may extend back many lifetimes. It's like a dollar bill that has been folded for a long time. When you open it up it immediately rolls up again, all by itself. That is an example of habit, and karma is habit. We have all different habits in terms of perceiving and holding on. These are karmic inclinations; in fact, they are what is meant by the word karma. We build up habits so that eventually we have this whole construction that forms our world view and our life. But when we look into what this habit is, it is merely a conceptual frame of mind. Through repetition, it becomes reinforced more and more strongly. Habit, karma, and conceptual mind are all interlinked in this fashion.

Rigpa, on the other hand, is free from conceptual attitude. It doesn't solidify an attitude, doesn't create any habits of conceptual mind, and therefore rigpa is free of karma. During the actual moment of rigpa, there is no karmic pattern or habitual attitude present. There is a gap. Not only are karmic patterns not present during the state of rigpa, but they are undermined by the awakened state, and they begin to melt away. It's like the rigpa seeps into old habits and makes it easier for them to be relinquished. Think of oil seeping into paper, spreading into it — it's just like that.

Karma is something formed; habit is something formed. You can think of karma and habitual frames of mind as being like atoms. No matter how tightly packed or dense a piece of matter is, there is still space in between each individual atom. Nothing is ever a solid mass, is it? Now imagine the space of rigpa in between the atoms. However hard or dense the matter is, at a fundamental level it is suffused with or interpenetrated by the space of rigpa. When you view it from this perspective, the conception of a solid mass just falls apart. Likewise, it doesn't matter how uptight the karmic attitude is — it can always be dissolved with rigpa. Regardless of how tight a rosary is strung together, the beads are still separated by a little space. They are not truly joined, not fused together; in fact, nothing is truly joined together. Everything is empty, including karma. That is why karma can be purified.

If karma was something truly real and solid, there would be nothing to do. If karma was ultimate truth, it would be impossible to purify. What to do with a ten-rupee note that won't lie straight no matter what you do? You have to use some method, right? One general method in Dharma is to try again and again to level it out through different ways over an extended period of time. You come back the next day and you flatten it out, and the day after that too. It rolls back up a little bit, but as you continue, it becomes more and more flat, until one day it doesn't curl up again at all. That is one way. The Dzogchen method is like taking a steam iron: make a single pass over it and it stays totally flat. To be able to be like that, just once over and it's done, one has to be of the highest capacity, like King Indrabodhi. His liberation took place simultaneously with his understanding of this nature. Those of us who don't have that capacity have to apply several methods. King Indrabodhi was someone for whom the seeing of mind essence and the dawning of complete and total liberation happened at the same time.

We're not necessarily like King Indrabodhi. We become free for a short while, momentarily, but still we are not totally free. It's like we're holding the paper down a little in our practice. Then we get tired of meditating and we let ourselves get distracted. Still, the more you stretch the paper out, the smoother it becomes, right? We need to get more and more used to this state free of karmic habits.

There's a problem with my analogy of smoothing the paper, because it involves an example of physically doing something. But when we allow the continuity of rigpa, we are not *doing* anything — we are simply allowing it. *(Rinpoche rings the bell.)* We can't stretch or prolong the sound, can we? Superficial examples cannot completely illustrate the real meaning, they can only hint at it.

There is one more point I would like to make. When all objects of distraction dissolve into *dharmata*, into innate nature, there is no more foothold for distraction. At that point the sound continues on in an unbroken fashion. There is no need to hit the bell again; it just rings, ceaselessly. At that point there is no longer any concepts of meditation and post-meditation.

STUDENT: What is the difference between nondistraction and dwelling on nowness?

RINPOCHE: According to the general vehicles, to dwell undistractedly in nowness is to be undistracted. But from the Dzogchen perspective, that is called being distracted. Dwelling on nowness means you are already distracted. Why? Because you are dwelling on something, repeatedly. The awareness is directed towards something which is not rigpa. When there is a split between the rigpa and something other, you are already distracted.

There is some risk of misunderstanding this matter, if you only get half of this message, the nonmeditation part, and you miss the first part, which is to remain undistracted. It would be easy then to simply not meditate! But that wouldn't make any sense. People who are already not meditating are constantly being carried away by the three poisons of attachment, aversion or dullness. That is not meditating at all, so if one is told "don't meditate" in that situation, that makes no sense at all.

On the other hand, if we pay attention only to the first part, 'be undistracted,' it might seem like we have to remain mindful of whatever takes place: "Now I'm walking. Now I'm putting my foot down. Oh, there's a pink flower. The air is touching my skin. I'm breathing in. I'm breathing out. Here is a thought coming. There is the thought going. Now I am angry. Now I have some desire. Now it is leaving again." In the normal sense of the word one is certainly undistracted, but there is no sense of freedom. You are not liberated at all. It's like you're a shepherd totally involved in watching your sheep or goats: "Now they are going up the hill over there ... now they are coming back down ... oh, they shouldn't wander too far ... now they are going up another hill ... now it's five o'clock, I should gather them all together and go home." That type of practice is called "maintaining the meditation." You are herding the meditation, keeping constant watch. Dzogchen practice is not like that. Instead, meditate without being distracted at all, and without "keeping" a meditation.

If we aren't able to maintain a free and easy attitude, we will never have good meditations. During these few days up here at Nagi Gompa, give up any anxieties, hopes, fears or worries. Just leave them all behind. There is nothing you need to do. There is no office you need to go to, no long-distance phone calls to make, no faxes to reply to. Let go of the whole thing. Let go, let go and let go, until there is nothing more to let go of. Let go until that point.

STUDENT: What should I do when I fall into dullness?

RINPOCHE: There are two ways of dealing with this problem. One can either apply some kind of mental activity, or work on sharpening or strengthening the quality of *awakeness*. The first technique involves shamatha, in which the attention is focused on a particular object, be it internal or external. Through keeping that focus, it becomes more and more steady. Then we kind of relax, because it is okay. We kind of lean back, slow down — eventually, we fall asleep. That is one way. The other is the case of vipashyana, which is in this case the training in rigpa. First there is this awake quality, but gradually, after a while, it becomes the *concept* of that awake quality — "it's empty, it's clear, the two are indivisible." We sit and nurture that idea of rigpa; the rigpa imitation. Feeling quite comfortable with that idea, we slowly settle into that, and eventually we fall asleep.

If we are practicing alone rather than with a group, it's a little easier to deal with dullness, because we can get up and move around. Even when we're sitting with others, we can mentally get up, instead of remaining in the state we are in. That dullness is something that is entirely maintained by us. Drop it, and start fresh, start from scratch. Whatever meditation we had before, just drop it and start all over again. If you can't let go of your meditation state, then perhaps you should think of something else, maybe something interesting that you've done in the past. This kind of thought wakes us up. Upon awaking, immediately recognize the essence.

It's really best to totally destroy the meditation state, but sometimes it's a little hard to let go of it, and we need to try something else. That is what is meant by the statement: "knowing how to meditate, but knowing how to be free." If our training is in genuine rigpa, there is no habit being formed there at all. But if we're training in a conceptual 'make-believe rigpa,' we are creating or strengthening the habit of keeping that imitation. We make up something in our minds as rigpa, and we sit and keep that as the meditation. Because we are occupied in or involved with that, it takes a few seconds, perhaps longer, to get out of that habit we just sat and created.

We need to get woken up in order to get back. It could take a little while. If you are alone, you can suddenly stand up and continue the practice while standing up. Or you can do twenty or fifty prostrations, bowing down quickly. Tire yourself out, sit down and continue. If you are training in Trekchö, you can exclaim PHAT so forcefully and abruptly that you even scare yourself. This sharp sound interrupts whatever thought you were involved in. Stay with that interruption. We need to do something. If we abandon the methods before reaching perfect realization, we are being stupid. But if we hold onto the methods after being fully realized, we are being stupid again in a different way. We should not be stupid both before and after!

We need to have some sense of being awake and clear, some sense of wide-awakeness. There is a vivid or vibrant quality that is actually visible in people's eyes — whether they are really awake, or whether they are feeling really comfortable, leaning into the meditation and falling asleep. One needs to sit and be wide awake, but not in a glaring way, sitting and staring out into space. If we do this, our attention is occupied with what is seen outside. After a while it's quite hard to come back and be present and unoccupied.

We need to be resting on nothing, like a bird soaring in the sky. There is space above, there is space below, there is space in front, behind, and to both sides, and the bird is not dwelling on anything whatsoever. It is soaring in mid-air. That is the way to sit. Do not lean forward into something, do not lean back into something that you rest on, do not settle down on your seat either. Be suspended in mid-air, with space above, below and on all sides. As a matter of fact, your very being is space as well; it is no different from space.

If a sound is heard, let it be heard. If a dog is barking, let it bark. You don't have to fix your mind on that. Anything seen around you, let it be seen. Whatever is experienced, let it be experienced. It doesn't have to be an obstacle for the essence. It's possible to be too particular about our ideas of meditation. If we think, "I need to be in a cute little retreat hut on the mountain. It must have a shower and a little kitchen, so I can make tasty food. I will sit down on a very comfortable seat, with a big window right in front of me. Whatever I need to use is within reach, I don't have to stand up to get it. *Then* I can meditate, and my meditation will be nice and beautiful." So later you sit in your cute little retreat hut, and you think "How nice it is now!" You're looking out the big window ... there's another small window on the other side for ventilation ... you think, "This is a real meditation hut. This is what they describe in the books. Now I can enjoy myself doing this meditation." But when you are not in that situation, maybe in a place with a lot of people around, you feel bothered and uncomfortable. "I can't practice like this, I'll go home to my own place in the mountains. The food isn't good here, there is no good place to sleep, it's not nice at all, and the people are irritating too." You feel constricted and crowded, and you want to escape back up to the mountains.

Really, it won't do to be like that. According to Dzogchen teachings, one should be able to be anywhere, even a place or a situation with the maximum amount of disturbing emotions, of turmoil and chaos, and still be free. That is the main reason to practice, to provide training that's of use when we are in the bardo later on. Remember, there is no retreat hut in the bardo! There is no chance to be cozy. We need to be free in that situation.

Someone who hasn't asked questions before, please ask a question.

STUDENT: How do we know the difference between a rigpa likeness and the true rigpa?

RINPOCHE: Through experiencing the authentic rigpa. Imagine that you are someone who has never seen an apple in your whole life, although you've been told about it. People have made drawings of apples and explained to you what they look like, their round shape, how thin the skin is, and what it tastes like — it's sweet and juicy and so forth. But you haven't seen one or tasted one yet. Then one day you see a display of fruit that includes some apples, and you look at it and think, "Hmm, this looks like the apple that they've talked about." You take it and you put it in your mouth, you bite and you taste and swallow. You think, "Yes, this is exactly what they told me about. Now I know."

It's like that. If someone then says, "This is an apple" and points to an orange, you won't believe them, because you've tasted the real thing. In the same way, first we hear about rigpa, then we think about it, and then we meditate. At some point we experience with certainty how it really is. There is no other way to do this. One way of understanding it is conceptual; the other is free of concepts. If you haven't tasted the absence of concepts, you can hear about or understand what it's like, but you still haven't experienced the real thing. First we need to recognize and resolve on one point. With the resolution, one feels really sure.

Right now you're hearing a lot of talk about the qualities and characteristics of rigpa. But when it becomes part of your own experience, you *know*. For that to happen, you need to train day and night, like Milarepa, to the point where your buttocks become callused from sitting so much. Train further and further until realization dawns within your stream of being.

Nowadays you don't have to sit on bare rock like Milarepa — it's really all right to sit on a comfortable seat. Likewise, you no longer have to make your own food — you can hire a servant to cook for you. But you need to save up some money first, when you are young. If you want to do good practice, you need a yogi credit card! In the past you could beg and people would support religious practitioners, but nowadays it's not so easy. In the past people were happy with simple food; nowadays they need rich food. And when you go to a big shopping center, there are so many things. There is a lot of stuff we don't even know about, and we have to decide what to pick. We don't buy just one or two things; we need to be completely stocked up with a lot of items. That all takes money.

First you need to accumulate some wealth when you are young. When you have the money, you can practice Dharma. I'm not joking! Honestly, without money we can't really practice, because there is no time, we have to go to work everyday. Of course, if you get a good sponsor, it is better. We need to be a little intelligent about how we use our life. It's not a good idea to totally occupy ourselves with Dharma, and find that after a while we haven't gotten anywhere with spiritual practice, and we don't have any career either. We need to be skillful and think ahead. Otherwise, when we are fifty or so, we start to panic. "I have no money, what should I do now? I'm getting old, and I must practice, I must meditate. But I've no money." Think well about this while you are young. It's good to practice, of course, but we need to think from both sides. Dharma doesn't only mean religion, it means something that you can depend on, something that can help you throughout your entire life. So, work to improve your life — not merely this life but throughout the future as well. When we say 'life,' it doesn't just mean being alive in this body, but rather the continuation of mind which moves from incarnation to incarnation. That is what life really is.

In Tibet, although there were four schools of Buddhism, they didn't use the word 'religion.' That was applied only after Tibetans came down to Nepal and India. Instead, they used a word for the 'way of Dharma,' *chölug*, which carries the sense of what is real, what is true, what is genuine, what is ultimately beneficial, both now and in the long run. The meaning is more referring to something that is in tune with how things really are, something that is helpful, that can improve us. So *chölug* means 'spiritual way of life' — not a confused or deluded life, but a way of being genuine and true. That is what we train ourselves in. We should be without any confusion about how we approach this, how we involve ourselves in spirituality, for this entire life.

In any case, be happy. Don't entertain a lot of pointless worries, re-peating the same words over and over again in your mind. A lot of our thoughts are repetitions, 30 or 35 times the same thought. And we play and replay the same ten themes: one, two, three, four, five, six, seven, eight, nine, ten. Then we start all over again, thinking about the same ten things again. It doesn't actually help that much, does it? If you could have something different to worry about — say, the eleventh, twelfth and thirteenth things — it would be a little more interesting! But if it's the same ten things over and over again, it's just habit. We are caught up in the same habits, the same re-making of karma, the same way of deluding ourselves. All this makes our minds the opposite of open. Don't be like that. Be clever about yourself. Smile, and continue practicing. You don't have to show your teeth while smiling; smile from within, with a nice radiance.

Right now we have very a good opportunity. Even though it may seem a little crowded and stuffy in this room, there is a reason for why we sit down together and practice. Yes, it can be boring, but sitting down and being bored can also be quite a good foundation for progress.

VAJRASATTVA MEDITATION

TODAY WE WILL TOGETHER DO A MEDITATION on Buddha Vajrasattva. Keep the body straight but relaxed. Remain loose, and leave your breath and mind free, without conceptualizing anything. The mind should be vivid and wide-awake. Don't follow any thought about the past, don't invite any thought of the future, and don't think about the present. Leave your mind open and empty, like a blank piece of paper. Within this state, you can keep your eyes either open or closed, as you like.

Now imagine in the sky before you a white lotus flower with eight petals. Upon this sits our teacher, Buddha Shakyamuni, with a body that is golden, as radiant as pure gold. His left hand is in the gesture of equanimity, his right hand in the earth-touching mudra, and he is smiling. He looks upon all sentient beings with the same love that a mother has for her only child. Bring to mind the fact that the Buddha is endowed with inconceivable qualities of enlightened body, enlightened speech and enlightened mind. Imagining that this remarkable being is present in person, form this resolve: "From now until complete enlightenment, I will rely upon you. I take refuge in you until my view, meditation and conduct is equal to yours."

The form of the Buddha is insubstantial and transparent, visible yet devoid of any solid substance. He is not made of stone or clay, but is rather like a rainbow. Remind yourself, "From now on until attaining supreme enlightenment, I accept you as my teacher, my guide. I will put the words you have spoken, the Dharma, into practice; I will take the two levels of truth as my path." Until we have fully realized ultimate truth, we will take refuge in the Dharma. Similarly, we take refuge in those who are following in the Buddha's footsteps — the shravakas, the pratyekabuddhas, and all the bodhisattvas — we take refuge with them as our companions.

After that, imagine that rays of light stream forth from the body of the Buddha and dissolve into yourself. Through this, boundless obscurations and negative karma are purified and removed. Imagine that you accomplish the vajra body. Now imagine that from the throat of the Buddha, boundless rays of light shine forth and dissolve into your own throat. Through this, all the negative karma and obscurations created through your past words are purified, and you accomplish the vajra speech. Now imagine that from the Buddha's heart countless rays of light shine forth and dissolve into your own heart. They purify all negative frames of mind, ill-will, wrong view, craving, ignorance, and dullness. Not only that, but the qualities of the enlightened mind — the knowledge that sees the nature as it is, and the knowledge that perceives all possible existing things — are fully developed and perfected.

Now imagine that the Buddha melts into light and that this light mingles indivisibly with yourself. The Buddha's body, speech and mind and your own body, speech and mind are of 'one taste.' Without following any thought about the past, or thinking about the future, and even letting go of the thought, "I am the Buddha;" remain in the state of primordial purity which is unconstructed. *(Rinpoche rings the bell. Period of silence.)*

Don't focus on anything as the meditation. But don't let your attention wander either. Whatever is experienced, all the various different contents — don't hold any of that. Do not conceptualize anything perceived, not a single thing. Like Paltrül Rinpoche said in his *Tsigsum Nedek, The three Words Striking the Vital Point*:

Nothing whatsoever — totally disengaged.
Disengaged, yet utterly open.
A total openness which is indescribable.
Recognize this as the dharmakaya awareness.

Or like Milarepa sang:

In the gap between two thoughts,

Thought-free wakefulness manifests unceasingly.

Now we will chant the refuge three times:

Namo⁚
Dagsok semchen dugngel dröldön du⁚
Jangchub bardu kyabsu zungwey ney⁚
Lama dorje sempa könchok sum⁚
Yidam khandrö tsokla kyabsu chi⁚

NAMO⁚
In order to liberate myself and all sentient beings from suffering,⁚
I take refuge in Guru Vajrasattva, the Three Jewels, ⁚
The yidams and all the dakinis;⁚
Until enlightenment, I will regard you as my refuge.⁚

Remain free and completely at ease. Within this open state of mind, remind yourself that all sentient beings possess this awake openness as their basic nature. Everyone has buddha nature, yet, unaware of this, they suffer in all sorts of terrible samsaric states. Contemplate how utterly sad this is, and form this resolve: "Through the method of this training, I will remove the delusion of all sentient beings. I will do away with this temporary delusion of seeing things as they are not." Develop that confidence, that courage. Remind yourself that all the confusion of samsara, all deluded experience comes about through clinging to the notion of me and mine. It all originates from cherishing oneself. Breath out deeply and slowly, a long deep breath, and imagine the exhalation carries all your virtue, positive karma and merit to all sentient beings. Gently breathing in again, gather all their negative karma, obscurations and suffering. Take it into yourself, and again send them your positive merit. Practice like this for a while. *(Period of silence.)*

Now imagine that all the suffering of sentient beings really does dissolve into yourself, that you really do take it on yourself. When their suffering enters you, it vanishes completely, melting into the state of primordial purity, like snow on water. Imagine that your positive karma, virtues and merit are truly given away to all sentient beings, and that they receive it and it dispels all their suffering.

Let's chant the bodhisattva vow in both Tibetan and English, three times.

Dagni ngöngyi gyalwey dzepa zhin⁞
Semchen kün-gyi dönrab tsönpar ja⁞
Semchen magal draldang madröl dröl⁞
Semchen ug-yung nyangen deygö jug⁞

Like the deeds of the Victorious Ones of the past, ⁞
I will endeavor in the ultimate goal of all beings⁞
To take those across who have not crossed, and liberate those who have not been liberated. ⁞
I will give assurance to beings, and establish them in nirvana. ⁞

Dronam deden dugnel drelwa dang⁞
Pakpey detob tangnyom laney shog⁞

May all beings have happiness and be free from suffering. ⁞
May they achieve the sublime happiness and dwell in equanimity. ⁞

(Once again Rinpoche rings bell. Period of silence.)

Now remain in equanimity without sending out, without taking in, without accepting, and without rejecting. Remember the statement: "Seen by merely looking, free by merely seeing." What is seen? The absence of concreteness and all attributes. No center and no edge. Without past, present or future. Empty, awake mind.

(Period of silence.)

You don't need to be afraid that a thought may arise. You don't need to be afraid that rigpa will slip away, or that you will become distracted. If you nevertheless do think this, simply look into the thinker. When seeing no thinker there, rest evenly in the seeing of this absence. This vivid emptiness, free of center and edge, is the primordially pure dharmakaya. At the same time, we are not oblivious or knocked out. There is a sense of being wide awake. That is the sambhogakaya quality. Within this, any perception can unfold, and while perceiving, nothing is held or fixated upon, it is utterly empty, and yet perceiving — there is no barrier between being empty and perceiving. That is the nirmanakaya quality, the seed of nirmanakaya. In this way, in one moment of rigpa, the basic substance, the seed, of dharmakaya, of sambhogakaya, and of nirmanakaya is fully present. We recognize that simultaneously, our essence is empty, our nature is cognizant, and its capacity is unconfined. That is rigpa. Now, remain evenly like that. *(Rinpoche rings the bell. Period of silence.)*

Remain without even an atom of a focus being mediated upon, and without being distracted for even an instant. Undistracted nonmeditation. Your mind is doing nothing, there is nothing you need to do. However it is, leave it like that, without modifying. However mind is right now, leave it be exactly like that. You don't need to improve it or correct it in any way. The five senses are wide-open and clear. You don't need to block that. And you don't confine your attention to only one of the senses. *(Period of silence.)*

This kind of rigpa, this kind of awareness is the ultimate and real guru. The mind of the guru is dharmakaya, by nature. When recognizing that our own nature is dharmakaya, then without supplicating, without effort, but spontaneously and naturally, our minds are indivisible from that of the guru.

(Period of silence.)

Now destroy your meditation. Move a little bit around. You don't need to stand up. Now continue the training, immediately. *(Rinpoche rings the bell. Period of silence.)*

Now destroy the meditation, immediately. Now continue. *(Rinpoche rings the bell. Period of silence.)*

Now destroy your meditative state totally, so that nothing remains. Now get angry. Recognize the essence in that. *(Rinpoche rings the bell. Period of silence.)*

Now continue the training. There is no need to block anything. It is nothing exciting. However it is, leave it naturally as it is. Within this state, remind yourself of the thought, "I am Vajrasattva," without losing the essence. You can see the painting of Vajrasattva on the wall over there. In that picture he happens to be single, but you can also imagine him with consort. The Vajrasattva with consort symbolizes experience and emptiness together. It is not that Vajrasattva needs a consort. Rather, it symbolizes the indivisibility of experience and emptiness.

Now, let's chant the Vajrasattva practice.

Our meditation got a little distracted, but that's okay. If you don't feel like imagining yourself as Vajrasattva, you can imagine Vajrasattva in the sky before you. Vajrasattva is an extraordinary deity, the embodiment of all buddhas in a single figure who has the power and ability to remove all negative karma and obscurations.

Imagine that Vajrasattva is seated on a multi-colored lotus flower, alive and vibrant, fully present. He has a very awesome presence. He is very beautiful, very handsome, very compassionate. First imagine this radiant form, then recite the hundred-syllable mantra of Vajrasattva. This mantra is unique in that purifies broken commitments, failings and conceptual obscurations. Also, it is the *dharani-mantra*, the syllables that are the life-force of the hundred peaceful and wrathful deities, the hundred families of the victorious ones. These deities are present right now within our own bodies, and will fully manifest at the time of the bardo. In order to prepare ourselves to realize that the hundred peaceful and wrathful deities experienced in the bardo are nothing other than our own display, we chant this mantra. For these two reasons, the hundred-syllable mantra is extremely profound.

Chanting the hundred syllables gently and slowly, we imagine that countless rays of light radiate from the form of Vajrasattva into all directions. The stream of nectar flows from his body down into the crown of our head, totally purifying our body, like a stream of white milk slowly filling up a hollow crystal ball. All impurities, karmic and otherwise, leave our body from the lower openings. This does not only apply to ourselves. Imagine that a Vajrasattva also sits at the crown of the head of every other sentient being. We are the main chanter, and all sentient beings chant along with us, all of us together. It's like we are all taking a special shower that washes away all impurities. It is best if we can remain in the state of rigpa while imagining that this takes place; if not, simply consider it as being like a magical show, visible and yet empty.

> **Om bendza sato samaya, manu palaya, bendza sato tenopa, tita dridho mebhava, sutokayo mebhava, supokayo mebhava, anu rakto mebhava, sarva siddhi mem trayatsa, sarva karma sutsamey, tsittam shiri yam kuru hung, ha ha ha ha hoh, bhagaven sarva tathagata bendza mame müntsa bendzi bhava maha samaya sato ah॰**

OM VAJRA SATVA SAMAYA. MANU PALAYA. VAJRA SATVA TVENOPA. TISHTHA DRIDHO MEBHAVA. SUTOSHYO MEBHAVA. SUPOSHYO MEBHAVA. ANU RAKTO MEBHAVA. SARVA SIDDHI MEM PRAYACCHA. SARVA KARMA SUCHAME. CHITTAM SHRE YAM KURU HUNG. HA HA HA HA HOH. BHAGAVAN SARVA TATHAGATA VAJRA MAME MUNCHA VAJRI BHAVA MAHA SAMAYA SATVA AH.॰

(Vajrasattva mantra continues.)

Now imagine that Vajrasattva melts into light — the Vajrasattva above you as well as the Vajrasattva above everybody else — and dissolves into each of you, so that everyone becomes indivisible from the body, speech and mind of glorious Vajrasattva. One's whole experience becomes the buddha field of Vajrasattva, so that whatever is seen is divine, all sounds are the hundred-syllable mantra, and all movements of mind is the mind of Vajrasattva. Now we will chant the short version of the Vajrasattva mantra. While being indivisible from Vajrasattva, our form is Vajrasattva, everything perceived is divine, all sound is mantra, and all mind, all thoughts and memories, are the play of luminous wakefulness.

Om benza satto ah⁝

OM VAJRA SATVA AH⁝

Finally, we dedicate the roots of virtue, taking all the goodness that has been created through the meditation and recitation of Vajrasattva and dedicating it to the enlightenment of all beings. On the exhalation, keep this attitude: "Through this, may the age of strife, famine and warfare be pacified. May all sickness may be relieved. May there be peace in the world, may all beings have happiness. And I as well, may I in all future lives always take rebirth in a precious human body, connect with qualified masters, and quickly progress to liberation and complete enlightenment. In all future lives, may I be a male or female bodhisattva endowed with the noble frame of mind of benevolence, acting for the welfare of all sentient beings." Let's do the dedication chant.

Hoh,
Lamey yeshe leyjung wey⁝
Sönam taye dampa dey⁝
Kha-nyam semchen malü kün⁝
Dorje sempa tobpar shog⁝

HOH⁝
Through the pure and endless merit⁝
Arising from unexcelled wisdom,⁝
May all beings equal to the sky⁝
Attain the state of Vajrasattva.⁝

Gyurwa meypa rang-gi shi⁝
Tagching tenpa dorjei ney⁝
Rang-rig yeshe yermey par⁝
Ngönsang gyepey tashi shog⁝

May there be the auspiciousness of true awakening,⁝
Indivisible from the spontaneous awareness-wisdom,⁝
The permanent and firm vajra abode⁝
Of the changeless innate nature.⁝

(Period of silence.)

RINPOCHE: Now it is all right to arise from the meditation state.

What we just did here is traditionally considered how one should engage in Vajrayana practice. We start with taking refuge, forming the bodhisattva resolve, and developing the four immeasurables of boundless love, compassion, joy and impartiality. But each of these has a relative and an ultimate aspect. Relative refuge involves visualizing the object of refuge in the sky before us, with the attitude of placing our complete trust in it. Ultimate refuge involves resting in the state of mind in which we are indivisible from the objects of refuge. Bodhichitta as well has two aspects, relative and ultimate. To send out one's goodness and take upon oneself the suffering and obscurations of others, that is the basis for relative bodhichitta. The ultimate bodhichitta is simply remaining without any mental constructs, without anything whatsoever formed in one's mind.

After that comes the yidam practice, in this case, Vajrasattva. The foremost way to practice is to imagine that we ourselves are the deity, having the form of Vajrasattva, and at the same time to recognize the nature of mind. The development and completion stages are thus simultaneous and indivisible. This is the unity of means and knowledge. While chanting the mantra, we accomplish the welfare of all beings by means of the four activities with the emanating and reabsorbing of the rays of light. Finally, we experience all sights as the divine deity, all sounds as mantra, and all movements of mind as the play of original, luminous wakefulness. We remain in samadhi like this for some time.

We can also practice by alternating these, reciting the mantra for a while and then resting in equanimity, in the view, and continuing like this. When we get tired of chanting then we simply let be into equanimity. When we get tired of letting be into equanimity, we continue reciting the mantra. At the end, dedicate the merit, make good aspirations, good wishes, and then rest in equanimity as the unconditioned dedication.

This is the traditional way, and if you can practice one session with this structure it is excellent. Once a day is very good. If you do it quickly, it doesn't take longer than half an hour. If we speed it up we can do it in five minutes! Practicing very gently and slowly, we can easily spend two or three hours. In general, two or three hours is a good duration for a session. If we do four three-hour sessions a day, that is called staying in retreat. If in a three-year retreat the three-hour sessions are too short, we can do sessions lasting three-and-a-half or four hours. In a normal retreat, three-hour sessions are long enough.

We need to be diligent in the beginning. If you are in doubt about this, read the life stories describing how other practitioners acted in the past, how they trained and what difficulties they undertook. And especially explore how the masters in the Dzogchen transmission practiced. We can learn from the lives of the Kagyü and Nyingma lamas.

There are two ways to deal with spiritual practice. If you are interested in being totally free, completely liberated, and attaining full enlightenment, you have better hurry up and practice with great diligence. The other approach is to take spiritual practice as a sort of vitamin, or dietary supplement. When you feel a little low on energy, or a little upset, you sit down and practice a little in order to feel better. We try to balance ourselves through practice, then later we return into activity. This approach advocates a little dose of spiritual practice once in a while.

Which of these particular ways we want to follow is up to us. I personally feel that it would be better to eliminate confusion from its very root, so that we no longer have to powerlessly take rebirth within the three realms of samsara. On the other hand, if we want to get through life without hurting too much, if we feel that doing business and getting rich or being successful in a career is not quite enough, and we need a little meditative stability to embellish our life or make it a little more beautiful, that is all right too. If we choose to use spiritual practice in that way, it's entirely up to ourselves. It's like giving our life the Dharma-polish!

Some people have this attitude, believe me! We tell ourselves that we need some spirituality in our lives, that we can't be totally materialistic. So we give ourselves a little dose in the morning and evening to

‚ive the gloss of spirituality to our normal life. This is also a particular solution or style, and certain teachers — not masters, but teachers — teach in this way. They instruct their students in five-minute meditation sessions. They are trying to make spiritual practice more easy, more appetizing or palatable; trying to bend the Dharma to fit people's attitudes. That is not the true Dharma. It is possible that we could encounter this type of 'convenience-Dharma' when we go back to our own countries. Don't make the mistake of confusing this type of practice for the real thing.

We *can* practice only five minutes, and do it in a genuine, true way, in which we establish a sincere attitude, and then train in the main part with genuine focus, then dedicate in a genuine way afterwards. In this case, even five minutes becomes something authentic. Otherwise, you could also just give it up altogether. There are a lot of other things on which we can spend a life. If we try to practice the Dharma but don't really practice it, we do a disservice to the Buddha's teachings. We become an embarrassment to the Dharma, and we waste our lives as well.

Even if you practice just a little bit, try to do it in a genuine way, with genuine view, genuine meditation, genuine conduct. Even if it is for a short while, let it be real. Otherwise, it is better to give it up all together, because not only are we caught up in confusion, but we use the Dharma to tie ourselves up with as well. That is really a wrong road, a wrong attitude. To pretend to be a spiritual person and wear a rosary in one hand is useless if it's false. If it happens naturally, it is okay — no problem if we are really that way. But if our intention is to be respected by others, to be regarded by others more highly because we meditate or are spiritual, that is a fake or wrong attitude.

Regardless of whether we are new or advanced students, we should always be certain not to fool ourselves. If somebody else fools us, there's not much we can do about it. But to fool ourselves is much worse, isn't it? So try not to do that. Make use of spiritual books that teach authentic practice, not Dharma-polish. The former cuts through confusion and clears up delusion; the other glosses over the confused state. The latter type of spiritual practice can make our deluded state appear more pretty, more pleasant. One can advertise the value of spiritual practice, like advertising an exciting machine: "Use it two times a day for three weeks, and it's guaranteed you'll have a flat abdomen and lose five kilos!" In the same way, "Use this practice daily, only five minutes a day, and your confusion is guaranteed to clear up!" It sounds nice, but does it really work? We need to think about this. Let's not fool ourselves.

We need to exert ourselves and persevere. When you get bored, just be bored, but continue the training. I feel that being bored is very good. The more bored one is, the more opportunity there is for progress. Meditation practice is not meant to cater to short attention spans, like TV ads where every twenty seconds there is a new and exciting thing to catch our attention. Something interesting does not happen every twenty seconds in meditation!

You can see this tendency in movies also. Old movies are long, with long conversations and not so much happening. Nowadays the scene changes every few seconds, and there is so much action. People's expectations have become like that. It's a combination of what movie producers believe people need and want, and also that people expect something exciting all the time. It's a kind of mutual confusion, mutually reinforced confusion.

People can also be deluded by the movies they see. A lot of young Nepalese, both boys and girls, are really influenced by the role models presented in Indian and American movies. They try to act like that, they try to be like that, dress like that, and so forth. They become imitations. This type of delusion is like mutual dependency, a coincidence of factors from both sides.

What we need is to have a natural mind: unconfused, unmistaken, undeluded. We need a natural, fresh, original state of wakefulness to cut through the stream of confusion. Original wakefulness cuts deluded experience into pieces, so that it becomes insubstantial. You can also think of confusion as a knot fashioned of burned rope — something totally insubstantial.

The basis for realization is a happy mind, along with diligence. When we are unhappy at root, uneasy, and we try to be diligent on top of that, we might go a little crazy. Don't do that. On the other hand, if we go astray into feeling happy, feeling good, we can become stuck in blissing out. We become like a Hari Krishna practitioner! We get caught up in the emotion of feeling good, being happy and blissed out, singing "Hari Krishna." True spirituality is not a training in being overtaken by bliss, allowing ourselves to get caught up. On the other hand, as long as we retain the innate stability of wakefulness, it's all right to look like we're a Hari Krishna devotee, to sing loudly and have tears of devotion rolling down our cheeks. As long as the stability of wakefulness within is not lost, it's perfectly okay to behave like that, because one is not getting caught up in the emotion.

Questions?

STUDENT: Could you explain more about this Vajrasattva practice we are doing? It seems quite unelaborate.

RINPOCHE: This Vajrasattva practice is one of the utmost simplicity. There are not that many words, but if one personally wants to fill in more of the meaning, one can. In itself, however, it is complete, sufficient. One takes refuge and bodhichitta; then for the main part, beyond concept, you can either see yourself as the yidam, or else imagine Vajrasattva in the sky before you. At the end, when you chant OM BENZA SATTO AH, imagine yourself as Vajrasattva, and feel that whatever is seen has the nature of Vajrasattva, all sounds have the nature of mantra, and so forth. "All sights are the deity" doesn't mean that we literally see Vajrasattva everywhere, holding vajra and bell. It's more that all sights possess the quality of the unobstructed — visible emptiness is itself the form of Vajrasattva.

Among the traditional three samadhis of deity practice — the samadhi of suchness, the samadhi of illumination and the seed-samadhi — what evolves out of the seed-samadhi is insubstantial and transparent, with a sort of see-through quality. It is not something solid or concrete, like solid matter. Nor is it like imagining that everything else we normally see becomes empty and disappears, and that only Vajrasattva's real, concrete form is left behind. The whole development stage has that insubstantial quality, and that is the form of Vajrasattva.

DEVELOPMENT AND COMPLETION UNIFIED

THERE ARE TWO WAYS to carry out the development stage: to either imagine ourselves in the form of the deity in a single instant of recollection, or to gradually build up the visualization. In the beginning especially, building up the visualization can be a gradual process, proceeding through first one detail, then the next. It doesn't always have to be done like that, however. In one instant you can remind yourself of being the deity. In fact, if it's not done like that, it is only conceptual, meaning with conceptual attributes. It is then known as "development stage with conceptual attributes."

When for example we who live in Nepal hear the name "Boudha Stupa," we immediately have a picture in our mind of the stupa. It's not like we first have to remind ourselves that there is the ground underneath, and on top of that is the stupa; that it's surrounded by a wall, that people are walking around it, and so on. Rather than thinking all these thoughts one by one, our image of the stupa arises in a single moment.

The development stage should be like that, so that in one instant I visualize myself as the physical presence of the Buddha Vajrasattva. This can occur because our minds are not only empty essence. There is also some sense of knowing, a natural cognizance, out of which the visualization takes place.

Of course there are a lot of details to a visualization in the traditional development stage, as when one 'unfolds the structure of the three samadhis' – the samadhi of suchness, the samadhi of illumination, and the samadhi of the seed syllable. These three are a necessary part of the right framework for the practice. The samadhi of suchness is a sense of complete quiet. In certain seasons when there is no wind at all, the prayer flags at Nagi Gompa hang there completely calm and quiet. This is a good image for the samadhi of suchness. When we experience this, we are completely open to the fact that the nature of all things is emptiness.

From this total quiet, a subtle breeze starts to move, and the prayer flags begin to gently wave. This is the image for the samadhi of illumination, which is a compassionate frame of mind towards all sentient beings. The samadhi of suchness becomes compassionate, like a gentle breeze starting to move the prayer flags. The third, the samadhi of the seed syllable, is when the wind blows more strongly, and all the different-colored prayer flags flap in the breeze, creating a sort of spectacle, a drama. All forms seen are the divine forms of the deity, all sounds are mantra, and all movements of mind are the play of original wakefulness.

All of that is activated out of the first, the samadhi of suchness. Without departing from that arises the samadhi of illumination, with its compassionate breeze. Finally, the stronger wind of the seed samadhi gives rise to all the different details of the visualization. This process is called unfolding the structure of the three samadhis.

Another way of explaining it involves three aspects, called identity, power and display — in Tibetan, *ngowo*, *tsal* and *rölpa*. The first, identity, is like a horse, a beautiful, strong, well-trained thoroughbred horse. So a strong, fully-developed horse is the identity, the horse *itself.* The expression is the capability or the strength of the horse. Its prowess or capacity, its strength and ability to race, is the second aspect. The third, display, is when the horse actually uses its power for racing. A television camera can show a horse running in slow motion, revealing how it actually puts its strength to use and makes a display of its power. So, all phenomena have these three aspects of ngowo, tsal and rölpa — identity, power and display. Power and display can have an impure and a pure aspect, but the identity is simply what it is in itself.

Development stage is simply training in the pure aspect of tsal and rölpa, the pure aspect of the strength and the display — the form of the deity, the palace and so forth. All of what unfolds or takes place is a way in which rigpa as identity shows its capacity to be cognizant, to manifest, and to take on all different forms. It is a way of displaying the capacity of rigpa without leaving its identity, itself. It does not leave behind the unbroken continuity of rigpa, the samadhi of suchness; nor is it interrupted by thoughts of the past, future, or present.

Within this continuity, there is a natural knowing which is unobstructed and which can unfold itself. This is the samadhi of illumination, the compassionate energy, a capability that is not separate from the essence itself. Without leaving behind the continuous state of rigpa, which is empty in essence and cognizant by nature, the unobstructed display can manifest as all the other manifold details of the visualization. All phenomena, whatever takes place as arising and ceasing, actually unfolds without really arising and without really ceasing within a backdrop or continuity which doesn't arise or cease. All feelings of joy and sorrow, whatever appears, are all seen as a display of this state.

This description makes it sound like we have three aspects, but actually, all three are embodied within rigpa itself. Rigpa is empty in identity, yet has a power, a strength of natural knowing, which can manifest unobstructedly, display in all different ways. The three samadhis that give rise to all the various details are part of one single identity of rigpa.

Remember, rigpa is empty in essence, cognizant by nature and unconfined in its capacity. From the perspective of *instantaneousness,* the quality of rigpa is the single, sufficient king that is all-embodying. Of course, in the beginning one starts out by practicing these different aspects in a sequential order, but we shouldn't let it remain like that always. At some point, all of it becomes different ways of expressing one identical nature of rigpa.

What I am speaking of here is the best type of development and completion stage. In essence the two are indivisible. Within the state of rigpa, the development and completion stage are fully present. It is not like you always have to first invoke one, then the other, after which they have to be fused together and united as one. As a matter of fact, they are a natural unity. In addition, the two accumulations of merit and wisdom can be perfected within the single continuity of rigpa. Remaining in the samadhi of suchness, never leaving that behind; forming no concept or constructs in mind whatsoever, perfects the accumulation of wisdom. In the same way, the power and the display of rigpa can be allowed to unfold to unhindered in any way, without leaving behind the state of suchness. All of that display perfects the accumulation of merit. In this way, within the continuity of rigpa as indivisibly embodying the three samadhis, we can perfect the two accumulations of merit and wisdom.

Through the realization of empty essence, we perfect the dharmakaya and realize it fully. Through the training in the power and display of the cognizant nature and unconfined capacity, we perfect the *rupakaya*, the form body which includes both sambhogakaya and nirmanakaya. In this way both dharmakaya and rupakaya are perfected within the state of the continuity of rigpa. Within the genuine, authentic practice of rigpa, of Trekchö, both development stage and completion stage are fully contained. To be absolutely truthful, we can realize the dharmakaya of all buddhas in this very lifetime exclusively through the training in rigpa.

Rigpa here means the rigpa in completeness, not a fragmentary version of what rigpa is. It is not training in a little aspect or corner or facet of rigpa, but rigpa as it really is, in actuality — all-embodying, complete and full. Training in that type of authentic rigpa is enough in itself. Rigpa is endowed with natural strength, natural sharpness, an intrinsic steadiness. One is continually getting caught up in something other, the attention will always stray whenever an object is perceived, unless there is some innate steadiness, some real stability.

When a strong wind comes, a piece of straw bends towards where the wind is blowing, regardless of how thick it might be. A needle on the other hand may be extremely thin, but no matter how strong the wind is, it remains exactly as it is. In the same way, any act of deliberate paying attention in some direction, no matter how virtuous or good it is, is easily influenced and bent in some direction. The effortless moment of awareness that is rigpa is always innately stable; it doesn't bend in any direction.

For example, when practicing shamatha, your attention is quietly fixed on one particular object. Even if you feel like you are utterly undistracted and totally focused on the nowness, still, when something bad happens, the apparent concentration falls apart and you get carried away. Rigpa is not focused on anything. It is like wide-open space. Anything can move through space freely, without hurting or harming the space in any way. Thus, authentic rigpa is unassailable by distraction.

You can compare the focused attention of shamatha to a pillar of concrete reinforced with iron. It may appear quite sturdy, but a bomb can cause it to fracture and fall apart. On the other hand, rigpa is like unformed space, not made out of anything whatsoever. No matter how many bombs you blow up in mid-air, it doesn't ruin or change the space in any way whatsoever. Bombs only explode themselves, they don't explode space. In this way, rigpa is more like the basic space within which everything can unfold and vanish again, arise and cease, come and go. Rigpa itself is not subject to any of that.

That is why when I started out showing us how to train in rigpa, I said "be free of reference point." Rigpa is not a thing that we can focus our attention *on*; it is not an object to be held in mind. That explains the 'not-meditating' part. In addition to that, we need to not be distracted. Not being distracted by itself is not enough, because willing oneself not to let one's attention wander involves holding a focus in mind. It becomes just another deliberate thought, which is not good enough. Remain without meditating on something, and yet without being distracted.

Any questions?

STUDENT: How does visualization fit into this context?

RINPOCHE: There are two ways of practicing visualization or development stage as the means, and completion stage or knowing rigpa as the knowledge aspect. The first way is that you don't combine or unify the two. You practice the development stage, and then at some point you give it the stamp of the completion stage. In other words, you try to adorn or embellish development stage with completion stage during the session. The other way is when you allow the visualization or development stage to unfold out of the completion stage indivisibly, without separating means and knowledge. Whether one practices the first way or the second depends entirely on the individual.

For instance, at the beginning of a sadhana you recite "OM SVABHAVA ..." and so on, and you imagine that all phenomena dissolve into a state of emptiness. From within this state of emptiness something manifests. That is called 'giving the seal of emptiness at the beginning.' After a lot of visualization you may say HUNG HUNG HUNG, and the celestial palace and the surrounding deities dissolve into the chief figure, the chief figure dissolves into the seed syllable in the heart center, the syllable dissolves from the bottom up, and finally everything is the state of emptiness. You remain like that for a while, and hereby conclude by giving another 'stamp of emptiness' onto the visualization. Then, you may say AH AH AH, and from this state of emptiness you again manifest in the form of the yidam deity.

There's also a way to combine Ati Yoga with the development stage, with the visualization. Within the framework of the three samadhis, first comes the samadhi of suchness, which means recognizing rigpa and remaining like that. The second is the samadhi of illumination, which means the radiance of rigpa is allowed to unfold as compassion. The third samadhi is the samadhi of the seed syllable, which is in fact the indivisible unity of being empty and compassionate. This unity is allowed to manifest in the form of a seed syllable from which the deity and the palace and so forth all manifest.

Basically, there are two ways of practicing development stage: through gradual, progressive visualization, and through instantaneous recollection, in which everything is brought to mind in one instant.

What happens if I ask you to think of your room back home? Your room and your house comes to mind in a single instant, don't they? It's not a gradual thing. You could visualize being Vajra Kilaya, for example, in the same way. Without losing that presence of being the deity, you don't have to stray from the continuity of rigpa, either.

When we're chanting the text, we recite from the state of emptiness: "I appear in the form of Vajra Kilaya standing on such-and-such seat. In my three right hands I hold three vajras, and in the three left hands I hold such-and-such." You can say all these things aloud, without losing the vivid presence of the deity, and without straying from the state of rigpa. It's perfectly all right if, from the first moment of the emptiness mantra, you appear spontaneously as the form of the deity. Even though you chant all the details, it doesn't have to be itemized piece-by-piece in your experience. You can be the deity fully perfected from the beginning.

If you're practicing the visualization using dualistic mind, then when a new thought arises the previous one is replaced. The thought of the left hand replaces the thought of the right hand, and when thinking of the head, the body is then gone.

When you think of home, you don't have to think of all the details one by one, do you? It all comes to mind at once. You don't have to first imagine the front door, then the hallway, then the living room, then the bathroom and so forth. Instead, 'my home' is immediately and vividly present in the mind.

It's quite helpful to combine development stage and completion stage and you can use the yidam practice as the structure. If you for instance are using the *Trinley Nyingpo* sadhana as the framework, vividly imagine yourself as Padmasambhava, and, in all the directions, imagine the twelve manifestations and so forth. The whole environment is the buddhafield of Padmasambhava. You chant the mantra of Padmasambhava. If you are unable to practice the unity of development and completion, simply practice the development stage, chanting the mantra 108 times or 200 times. Then take a break and recognize rigpa. Remain like that. After a while it gets a little boring; you get a little tired. So again you imagine yourself as Padmasambhava, and recite the mantra OM AH HUNG BENZA GURU PEMA SIDDHI HUNG. When you get tired of that, remain in rigpa. You can alternate, shift from one to the other.

COMPASSION

In the ground itself, there is no real confusion. Confusion arises when something seemingly is, but actually isn't, like mistaking a rope for a snake. That is a clear mistake, because in reality the rope is not a snake, no way.

There are many kinds of or levels of view: the view of shamatha practice, vipashyana, Mahamudra, Dzogchen and so forth. But the true, real view is the indivisible unity of emptiness and compassion. This view should be actualized in your present mind.

How do we do this? We have a lot of thoughts, one after the other, involving the duality of subject and object. When the subject latches onto or grasps the object, that is what is normally called mind, the thinking mind. When there is this subject-object clinging, that creates karma. When karma is created, there is confusion.

What is this thinker that always grasps onto an object? That is what we need to discover. What is it, really? Identify what it is that thinks, clearly and directly. Let your mind recognize itself, in an awake way. Try that. It's as simple and immediate as switching on a light. Instead of thinking of this and that, one thing after the other, let your mind recognize itself in a single moment. When the mind recognizes itself, there is no thing to see there. It's just wide open. All of a sudden, it's wide open. There's no thing at all. That's because the essence of mind is empty. It's wide open and free.

This busy, grasping mind,
Always latching onto things,
Let it be given a break to recognize itself instead.
In that very moment of recognition,
This mind becomes wide open,

Free, and unconfined.
That's called empty essence.
At the same time, there is a certain knowing that it is empty.
That's called cognizant nature.
Your mind's empty essence and cognizant nature function simultaneously.
They are not two separate things, not at all.
In fact, they are indivisible.
That's called unconfined capacity.
Know these three simultaneously —
Empty essence, cognizant nature, and unconfined capacity —
That's called the view.

In this way, to actualize the view, to realize or understand the view, is to know that our minds are empty in essence and cognizant by nature simultaneously.

Essence is like the sun itself. The sun's nature is to shine, to be warm and to illuminate. The capacity of the sun is that makes things grow and brings forth life. In the same way, you should distinguish between mind and mind essence. Mind essence has all three of these qualities. It is the *essence* of this mind essence which is empty, the *nature* of this mind essence which is cognizant, and the *capacity* of this mind essence which is unconfined. Please try to learn these words and understand their meaning, because without knowing the words, it's hard to get the meaning.

Do you understand the words here?

Do you understand them a little bit?

The ground is buddha nature, which is unmistaken in nature, the basic state of all things. It is the natural state which is not made by the Buddha, and not created by any ordinary being either. It's naturally so, all by itself. That is the ultimate truth. Whether a buddha comes into this world or not, the nature of things is still the nature of things. The Buddha is someone who realizes what is true, what actually exists. If we want to become enlightened, we needn't try to create something where it doesn't exist. We simply have to acknowledge or recognize what *is*.

An enlightened buddha is someone who has simply awakened to what is, to what is real and true.

What is the basic state, the ground? Through training on the path, we realize the ground as the fruition. We contact what was there to begin with. At the moment, while we are deluded and on the path, we are somehow missing the pure ground, not seeing it as it is. We are mistaking it for something else, just like mistaking a rope for a snake. We need to abandon that state of temporary confusion.

The path is the state of confusion. To remove confusion we need view, meditation and conduct. When we have a glimpse of natural mind, it's like we see a piece of the ground. Again we recognize a moment of natural mind, and we see a little more. The more we get used to it, the more we see, until we finally realize the ground as it is in its entirety.

That's why, in the context of path, there are three aspects: recognizing, perfecting the training of that recognition, and attaining stability. We need to dissolve confusion. At the moment of the view, dissolve the confusion. When meditating, dissolve the confusion. When applying the conduct, dissolve the confusion. All we need to do is to let the confusion dissolve. When all confusion has been totally removed or dissolved, then you can call that the fruition.

We can know emptiness. We can know compassion. But if we don't know or experience the indivisibility of emptiness and compassion, it's hard to get through life smoothly. Imagine a man and a woman who live together happily and love each other very deeply. One day the wife hears some teachings, and she becomes interested in the Dharma. She listens a lot and she understands emptiness; she realizes that nothing in this life has lasting substance. Everything is impermanent. There's no real core or substance to anything.

Then she thinks, "My husband and I, we go to lots of parties and dance and enjoy ourselves. We go shopping together and we buy all sorts of things. But actually, none of that really matters to me anymore. There's no real point to it." And she starts to close herself up, to shut herself off from her past activities. From one point of view, what she thinks is actually true. Everything is in fact insubstantial, there's no real point to it. The husband is puzzled: he looks at her and thinks, "My wife is changing. Maybe I did something wrong? Maybe she has a new boyfriend?" But he is patient, and he lets it slide for a while.

Then she starts going into a room, closing the door and doing prostrations, which he can hear the noises from outside — 'boom, boom, boom' — and he thinks, "Hey, my wife is going a little crazy." Sometimes she sits in a really strange way, holding a string of beads in one hand. The husband thinks, "This is really weird!" So he says, "Tonight, let's go out and enjoy ourselves. Let's go dancing and have some fun." She says, "That doesn't mean anything to me any more. I like just sitting here; I'm happier like that. Besides, why waste the money?"

And he thinks, "Before, she was very active. She'd cook us delicious meals, clean the house, water the garden and do all sorts of things. But nowadays she's doing less and less."

She thinks, "What's the use of watering the garden? You have to do it again tomorrow anyway, it's never enough. And if I clean now, it just gets dirty later. What's the point? I'll just sit and practice."

Now the husband is beginning to get unhappy. They start to growl and argue back and forth. In a while, perhaps, they will separate.

What's wrong with that woman? She understands emptiness but not compassion. If there was more compassion in her, then she would realize that although certain things may be pointless, it's not necessary to avoid doing them just because they don't mean anything for oneself. They may be important to others, so why not just do them? Actually, if the woman truly understood openness and compassion she would be happy to do something meaningless if it made others happy. She would be even more eager to do it than before, when it was merely her own enjoyment she was pursuing! This is the Mahayana style.

Vajrayana is even better, because you can do anything, enjoy anything, without attachment or clinging. Please understand that the indivisibility of emptiness and compassion means they should be a unity. It's not enough to just understand emptiness and the general pointlessness of things, because then we may become selfish and apathetic. If we understand emptiness in a one-sided way, thinking "Things are point-less and nothing really matters to *me*," then we don't really care about what matters for others, either. Our understanding of emptiness can actually become very selfish, very ego-oriented. We might end up say-ing, "I'll just sit here and meditate because then I'm happy. I don't care about the children, my husband, or anything else." This kind of attitude is actually quite selfish.

The point I'm trying to make here is that there's a danger in not understanding the unity of emptiness and compassion. Do you under-stand?

TRANSLATOR: Could you please say something about understanding compassion without emptiness?

RINPOCHE: Without understanding emptiness, compassion can never be authentic. There's a very high chance we will confuse compassion with downright attachment and desire. One thinks that one's passion is compassion, that one's attachment to others and caring for others is true compassion. Actually our ordinary version of compassion and affection is selfish in a way, because it's *my* family, *my* children, *I* care for them, *we* should enjoy ourselves together, because *I* love them. It is compassion in a sense, but without the understanding of emptiness it becomes very narrow, very limited. Compassion is not that kind of attachment. It is not passion for or attraction towards something that one loves or likes. Compassion is called the 'great passion,' but it is not the passion of latching onto something and not wanting to let go. True compassion is a very open and free atmosphere.

Compassion without the understanding of emptiness easily becomes selfish attachment, while understanding emptiness without compassion can also becomes selfish, one-sided, and limited. In order to avoid these dangers, it's very important to understand the unity of emptiness and compassion. Your naked, present ordinary mind is the door to this unity of compassionate emptiness. Recognize that, and you've opened the door. The more we grow used to this, the easier it becomes.

Right now this door is closed by our preoccupation with an almost uninterrupted string of thoughts. But if we allow just one gap between one thought and the next, we may glimpse the naked ordinary mind, self-existing awareness. Then the door is opened right there, to reveal compassion and emptiness united. It is a timeless moment.

The great wisdom qualities of the buddha mind — the wisdom that sees the innate nature as it is and the wisdom that perceives all possible things — are blocked again and again, almost continuously, by the concepts that we form. These concepts are actually temporally based; they are, in essence, time. The moment we start to allow gaps in this flow of concepts, the innate qualities of the awakened state begin to shine through.

Any questions?

STUDENT: Rinpoche, sometimes it's difficult for me to tell the difference between wishing to help someone and feeling responsible for their happiness. Can you say something about that?

RINPOCHE: It's probably a matter of intensity or strength. When you take responsibility for something, you feel more strongly about it. If you just try to help, then you don't feel so strongly about whether it happens or not.

To help others without feeling responsible for their happiness is good. But it's better to take it upon oneself and make it one's responsibility that other people are happy. However, you'll suffer more yourself if you do this. We need to be a little careful here, because it gets dangerous if you try to force on others your particular idea of how they should be happy. That is not really what is meant by taking responsibility for others' happiness. You have to be wise about it, and sensitive too.

It's easy to be wrong about what others need. We need to be flexible and open, rather than a certain predetermined shape. We shouldn't be square or triangular! To be a really good person, I feel you need three qualities. First, good heart. Second, a clever mind — intelligence. Third, diligence. Without these three, it won't happen. I've met a lot of people already in this world; clever people, good-hearted people, all kinds. But they don't do much of significant value. There are many people like that, right? Some know exactly what other people should do to solve their problems, and they can explain it quite succinctly if they are asked. But they don't really do anything; they just lean back and relax and stay lazy.

Some other people are very kind-hearted and concerned about others, and also very diligent. They expend a lot of effort, but everything they do is wrong! They try to help, but it becomes harmful, due to their lack of wisdom. A lot of people are like that — they want to help other people, but it goes wrong, because they lack the know-how.

Still other people are really intelligent and very diligent, but they are nasty. In fact, most people are like that these days. Their attitude is, "I want to get what *I* want, and I'll do whatever it takes to get it." Pushing hard to get something takes a lot of effort, so they're actually very diligent. And because they are smart, they know how to get it. But everything comes to them, because they are intrinsically selfish. Maybe they even harm other people on the way. With intelligence and diligence, one can make an atom bomb, but the end result is extremely harmful.

Therefore, you need to be all three — intelligent, kind, and with the initiative to do something, to exert yourself in ways that are helpful to others. This is something we should check out within ourselves. Are we smart enough, are we kind enough, do we really do something for others? If the answer is yes to all three, we should rejoice. If not, we should try and change that.

Honestly, isn't it quite rare nowadays to be kind, intelligent and also work hard for others? I hear a lot of people say, "The world is so bad. I really want to do something." But these people are not so smart. Maybe they have good hearts, but they're not really smart. They might even have time to do something to help, to set up a project, but they really don't know how to do it. They simply have good thoughts, good daydreams: "I want to do this." It's a good fantasy, but not good enough. It needs to be applied; you need to carry it out.

STUDENT: How can I tell the difference between pity and real compassion?

RINPOCHE: This is a very good question, because compassion is of vital importance in Buddhism. First of all, compassion motivates us to practice. Second, it forms the main body of practice as well. Finally, it's out of compassion that we can act for the welfare of others. Thus, it's good to know exactly what compassion is, and how it differs from pity.

In Buddhism there is the phrase "to first have formed the resolve towards supreme enlightenment." The teachings differ about when exactly the Buddha first developed this resolve of compassion to benefit others. One tradition maintains it was when he was born into one of the hell realms he saw a terrible person torturing all the others unbearably. The Buddha made the wish," If he could just torture me instead of the others, they would be free." It is said that in that moment the Buddha first engendered the root cause of enlightenment. Afterwards he gathered the accumulations for three incalculable aeons, but this was the first cause.

The attitude of compassion is extremely important to understand. Compassionate motivation is essential in any level of practice, beginning with the *ngöndro* — the preliminary practices for Vajrayana — and extending all the way up to complete enlightenment. If we practice a spiritual path not really for the welfare of others but only for ourselves, just trying to subdue our own disturbing emotions, we never really get the best result. Therefore, every practice starts with motivating ourselves with compassion. "I will engage in this training in order to be able to liberate countless sentient beings" — that kind of attitude is extremely important.

Ultimately, that which ensures we will act for the welfare of others, that after having obtained true and complete enlightenment we will manifest the form bodies — the rupakayas, consisting of sambhogakaya, and nirmanakaya — for the welfare of others, comes out of the compassionate attitude not to abandon or exclude even one single sentient being. "I will teach everyone, guide everyone" — that is the feeling of compassion. That kind of attitude which springs out of compassion is the driving force behind the ability to act for the welfare of beings after enlightenment. That's why it's said that, in the beginning, the compassion is like a seed. In the middle, compassion is like the moisture and warmth necessary for growth. And finally, compassion is like the fully ripened crop. Those are its qualities.

There are different kinds of compassion mentioned in Buddhism, but the true compassion manifests only after we realize the nature of emptiness, after realizing egolessness. After fixation on the concept of self dissolves, the expression of that realization manifests as compassion. One could say that the "atmosphere" of realizing emptiness is compassionate. The true compassion is *undirected,* and holds no conceptual focus. That kind of genuine, true compassion is only possible after realizing emptiness.

Of course, we feel compassionate now as well. However, that kind of compassion is not the true and genuine, compassion, because it's always mixed with a conceptual frame of mind. Often mixed with our compassion we feel some distance between ourselves and others. Our attitude is, "I am here, and sentient beings are over there. I am higher than they are. They are pitiful. They need help, so I should help them." That kind of compassion is not true compassion either.

This may sound a little bit crazy, but honestly it really isn't. Think well about it. Right now we think that being compassionate requires an object towards which we feel compassion. Without this object, what are we feeling compassion for? Think well about this.

When we realize emptiness, this all makes perfect sense. Realizing emptiness doesn't mean we have attained the tenth bhumi and are really close to being a buddha. There is some realization of emptiness at any point of the path. We are not talking about the full realization of emptiness, but rather any point of knowing emptiness, even to a small degree. A certain kind of authentic compassionate atmosphere comes with that.

Some of you here may have already recognized the state of rigpa and perhaps have some familiarity of experience. When we simply settle into the state of equanimity of the nature of mind, at that moment we can't really say that there is an object held in mind because there is no act of conceptualizing, no fixating of attention on any particular object.

But on the other hand we can't say there is no object at all because we have not fallen into a deep sleep; we are not oblivious or unconscious. There is still a vivid display of experience; our five senses are wide open. We can't say that there is no object, but it's not really the same as a usual moment when the mind is fixating upon something in a gross way.

There is a clarity of mind, a natural awake quality, from which compassion can arise. It does not center on someone in particular whom we feel sorry for. During this moment there is not a conceptualizing of 'another being,' but still in this tenderness there is some way of directing one's attention to other beings who have not yet recognized the nature of mind. And there is a feeling of sorrow for sentient beings who don't know that their nature is self-existing wakefulness and therefore are deluded in samsara. This way of reaching out is not really formulated, but we can call it nonconceptual compassion, genuine compassion.

Compassion free from concepts is an expression of self-existing wakefulness. That compassion is not necessarily the same as the completely awakened state of a buddha. It is a sign of a yogi on the path, a genuine practitioner. You can't say that the compassionate feeling which is naturally present in the experience of the nature of mind is exactly the same as fully awakened compassion.

On the other hand, if we are someone who hasn't yet recognized the nature of mind, it doesn't mean that we can't be genuinely compassionate. There is a way also to be conceptually compassionate, which is different from the compassion that I just described. That is the frame of mind in which we regard ourselves less important than others. Usually beings regard themselves as more important than others. When we have the attitude that others are more important than *me*, we call that genuine, although still conceptual, compassion.

As for the difference between compassion and pity: if a beggar feels sorry for a king, that is compassion. But if a king feels sorry for a beggar, then that is pity.

Of course it is good to hear this, it is good to think about what compassion is, but the real compassion is the actuality of it in our own experience. Here's an analogy: if the experience of emptiness is wet, then that wetness or moisture is compassion. You need to experience that. You need to personalize this, and not examine compassion from the outside. If you are studying philosophy, it's sufficient to just get the definition of compassion. But if we want to be enlightened, we need to recognize our nature. We need to make it an actual experience; we need to live it, to *be* the compassion.

STUDENT: Why does recognizing mind nature give rise to compassion?

RINPOCHE: I'll explain this gradually. Three things are taught: to recognize, to train and to attain stability. When recognizing, what is it that is recognized? The nature that is present in oneself. When is it recognized? For a beginner in this practice, in the first moment we notice that we are carried away, that we are distracted. The second moment is to remind oneself to recognize the essence. In the third moment one arrives back in the innate nature. That is the moment of recognizing.

Sometimes it is possible to arrive in the state of rigpa while walking, sometimes while eating. All of a sudden we are wide awake, in the state of rigpa. Nowhere is it written that you can only recognize the nature of your mind while sitting on your meditation cushion! For some people it may be easier to recognize mind essence while walking. Rigpa is something which is possible to acknowledge at any moment, in any situation. How can it happen at any time, at any situation? When there's a gap between two thoughts, the intrinsic nature is revealed as self-existing awareness. When the past thought has ceased and a future thought hasn't occurred yet there's a gap, and in that gap you can discover your intrinsic nature. But this gap is not necessarily very long.

That's why it is said "short moments, many times." From this angle, then, within one meditation session it's fine to repeat the recognition of mind essence many times — twenty times, thirty times, whatever. First you recognize mind essence. You let be. You allow it to last a while. Then you lose track, you get distracted. Then again at some point you remind yourself. Again, let the meditation state last for a while. In this way you alternate between meditating and being distracted. You meditate, the meditation gets destroyed, you try again, it gets destroyed, you try again. Like that.

Getting really good at this meditation involves growing used to, getting accustomed to, rather than *doing*, because it's not a meditation on some "thing." As a matter of fact, recognizing self-existing awareness totally destroys the act of meditating. Just let it be. Immediately. Be sharp. Direct. Let be.

During this training, you may feel more and more open from within. More and more vast. And within this openness, compassion just unfolds. There are two kinds of compassion: superficial or conceptualized, and true. The former is compassion made by thought, while true compassion, ultimate compassion, is simply the way our nature is.

What is the experience of true compassion? While recognizing mind essence, there's some sense of being wide awake and free. As I mentioned before, at the same time there's some tenderness that arises without any cause or condition. There is a deep-felt sense of being tender. Not sad in a depressed in a hurting way, but tender, and somewhat delighted at the same time. There's a mixture; that is the true compassion. It's slightly joyful and slightly sad. There's no sadness for oneself, nothing selfish about it. Nor is there sadness for anyone in particular either. It's like being saturated with juice, just like an apple is full of juice.

In the same way, the empty openness is saturated with the juice of compassion. Why is this? Because a lot of qualities are present here. Knowing our empty nature clearly creates an immediate sense of certainty. This certainty has a taste. Through this taste, which is kind of joyful, kind of tender, there's a compassionate atmosphere.

There's a certain time of day, when the sun is setting in the west, when, if we go outside and sit and face the sunset, a feeling of compassion arises easily, spontaneously. It's kind of free and a little joyful, a little tender, a little sad. It comes all by itself. If you're not totally open or free from within, then this sadness is not really felt, or even noticed.

If there is any sadness without the openness, notice that it's always for someone in particular, be it me or him or her. When we simply let ourselves be in that open way, there's some sense of tenderness which is a little bit joyful, a little bit sad, a little bit detached. There is a feeling of renunciation, not in the sense of giving up something, but more like letting go of ambition. More like being content.

Sometime go outside and sit,
In the evening at sunset,
When there's a slight breeze that touches your body,
And makes the leaves and the trees move gently.
You're not trying to do anything, really.
You're simply allowing yourself to be,
Very open from deep within,
Without holding onto anything whatsoever.
Don't bring something back from the past, from a memory.
Don't plan that something should happen.
Don't hold onto anything in the present.
Nothing you perceive needs to be nailed down.
Simply let experience take place, very freely,
So that your empty, open heart
Is suffused with the tenderness of true compassion.

CAREFREE

It's actually fine to be happy, carefree. The more carefree you are from deep within, the better your practice is. Carefree means being wide open from within, not constricted. Carefree doesn't mean careless, that you are sloppy or that you don't care about others. It's not like you don't have compassion or are unfriendly. Carefree is being really simple, from the inside.

You need to be relaxed, yet without stupidity. Sometimes people relax like this: *(Rinpoche lies back limply with eyes half-closed and a vacant expression)*. Especially around the swimming pool! You have a swim, then you climb out of the pool and lay down with your hat, sunglasses and maybe a cold beer. You're very relaxed, but you're relaxing into stupidity. You've relaxed peacefully into a very dull state. The point is to be relaxed and yet very clear. There is no need to create something by meditating; no need to achieve something — simply be very clear. Relaxed and bright.

You need to be in charge of yourself. Check yourself out, and if you find you're missing some qualities, then work to develop them. It doesn't help to go about with your hands outstretched, trying to obtain good qualities from others. Take charge of yourself. Be happy. Even when it's not funny, still smile.

Think about how much time we put into washing ourselves, freshening up, brushing our teeth, putting on make-up, and so on. It's just as important to fix up your mind. If your mind is down, pull it up. If you're flying too high, ground it. Take charge of yourself. Of course you can't literally wash your mind or comb it. You can't cut your mind's nails when they're too long. But you can be in charge of your attitude; you can take responsibility for your mental and emotional state.

In fact, that's the main point of the Buddhist teachings. Be aware of your own mind. Let it be undisturbed and free of confusion, because only then can you be of help to others. Otherwise you just remain confused, confusing yourself, and there's no way to really be of help to anyone else. Don't get too overexcited about this, either. Just relax, sit upright, and be open — wide open and carefree. The view in the Great Perfection, is to be totally open and carefree.

If we act a little *too* carefree, that is not so good either. That is called losing the conduct in the view. A lot of people do that. They revolt against a particular culture, against the system, against the establishment — against the fixed habits of this world. They shave off half their hair, or half their beard, or they dress funny, or they wear no clothes at all. It's all a reaction against cultural mores. Sometimes they take drugs, all kinds of drugs, and they try to be free in that way. Actually, that's not being free at all. That is losing the conduct in the view.

Once I met a man who wore all his hair pushed up atop his head, had painted it blue, and had half his beard shaved off. I am not saying that he was a bad person; not at all. His behavior was his way of reacting against stereotypes of how we should look. But if you're carefree and open from within, you can fit in anywhere, anyway, without having to go to dramatic extremes or make shocking statements. If you're not open or carefree from within, you'll find you always get bumped up against things. Your life gets so narrow, so tight, so claustrophobic. The point is to be free, not to be crazy.

Be carefree and open, and feel free. Train in being free. Tonight when you lie down, try to fall asleep in a very carefree, very free state of mind, and try your best to recognize that your dreaming is actually dreaming. Make up your mind to practice during the dream state, to first of all to become aware that a dream is a dream. Then, try to remember the practice, or maybe remember your guru and the teachings, the instructions. Maybe try to do your practice, a yidam practice if you have one, during the sleep state, bringing the vivid presence of that to mind. If you don't know how to do any of these, then just sleep happily and don't worry about it.

It is said that when the Dharma is not practiced correctly, practice could become a cause for rebirth in the lower realms. We're supposed to practice in order to become free, to liberate ourselves. But if our practice only makes us more stuck, then what? What if we get stuck in the method? When you take the ferry; the ferry is the method. Once you get to the other shore you leave the ferry behind and go on. There's no point in dragging the ferryboat back to your house. Nor is not good to stay on the ferry, for twenty-four hours a day, forever.

The state of rigpa I mentioned before is not bound by any method. It's not stuck at all. It's naturally free. If that's the case, what's the point of sitting and making up ideas in meditation? The situation becomes completely claustrophobic — why try to accustom yourself to that?

If your hands are very dirty, you wash them with soap. Once you're finished rubbing in the soap, you don't keep it on your hands. You rinse it off, because you don't need it any longer. The soap is used to get rid of the dirt. Once the dirt is loosened from your hands, why keep the soap? Likewise, don't hold on to the method; don't hold onto the meditation technique. Just let be and relax. This is called nonmeditation, undistracted nonmeditation. Don't be distracted. Don't meditate. Undistracted nonmeditation. If you meditate, it's conceptual. If you get distracted, you're just a normal person. So, don't mediate; and don't get distracted.

The next point is don't harm others, but help others. Liberate yourself, and after liberating yourself, help to liberate others. When this retreat is over, we need to go home, because that is where we live and where we make our living. We can take something with us, however. Even if it is only this much, we can remember, "I will not harm others, I will try to be helpful. I will try to be unconfused, and help others be free."

If we have gotten some smell of that undeluded state, if we've inhaled it even once and we take it home with us, that's good. On the other hand, if we make ourselves believe that we have a high view and just sit and space out, and if we practice the development stage fixating on concreteness, we become no more than a hard lump of conceit. We are inflated with the view, and the whole thing has no point. If you compare a self-professed Dzogchen practitioner with a wrong view to an ordinary good-hearted person, who is better? The one with a good heart is better, because he or she will at least not harm others. It is quite okay if this person is not a Buddhist. As long as she has a good heart, she's in a much better situation than the so-called Dzogchen practitioner.

Someone who is really full of himself might think, "I am practicing something that is special. In fact, my practice is Ati Yoga, the highest form of Tibetan Buddhism. Hey, I am really something!" If one has that type of attitude about oneself, really, what is the use? It doesn't help anyone. Far better to run away and give up practicing. Because if spiritual practice really doesn't help oneself, why bother? It's much better to be genuine and real about how things are. Take the truth of impermanence more and more to heart, in a very sincere way. Be more loving, more kind, more compassionate, and have more trust, more devotion. Be increasingly able to apply yourself to the six paramitas. If you find that this is happening, then the Dharma is really taking effect. To have less craving and more contentment — that is the point.

It's quite okay also to not be very educated; in fact, to be simple-minded is fine. It's far preferable to being egotistical. Much better to be simple about oneself, and not get into a lot of details about 'what is good for me.' It's all right to get into a lot of details and make a lot of fuss when it comes to being helpful, to helping others. But if we complicate our own lives and focus too much on ourselves, we forget how to be simple, and we are never happy.

Any questions?

TIBETAN NUN: How does one know the difference between really progressing in meditation and Dharma practice, and just looking like it from the outside?

RINPOCHE: First of all, when one's being is liberated from within through realization, through this practice, one knows it personally. It is like fire is naturally hot and water is naturally wet. The atmosphere or feeling also seeps out in a way and is felt by others.

One of the qualities of recognizing emptiness is that the thought 'I' or 'me' has no longer any basis, and thus it dissolves. There is no self-identity present. Through recognizing and realizing the empty essence, instead of being selfish and self-centered, one feels very open and free. It feels like everything is possible; one could just go anywhere; it is all okay. One is not really fixated or tied down. Realizing the cognizant nature has many qualities. In fact, it is the basis from which the immense enlightened qualities manifest: clairvoyant powers, wisdom, and so forth, all of which become ever-deepening. The third quality is not really a separate third entity at all, but is rather the indivisible unity of the first two.

In short, the bottom line during the meditation state is whether or not your delusion falls to pieces. By letting be in rigpa, the string of thought which ties confusion together is suddenly no longer tying anything together, and it naturally falls apart. When there is no pursuit of past thought and no inviting of future thought, that gap means that the whole delusory process vanishes. The effect of that — the after-glow of that, you can say — shows itself in the post-meditation. In daily life one has much less craving and compulsion to chase after things. One is much more content and at ease, and possesses much more devotion, appreciation, and compassion. That is how it shows itself outwardly, naturally.

This is the sign that is shown at the time of the path. There's really no need to go into the signs shown at the time of fruition or complete enlightenment, because we will know that for ourselves. All confusion will be cleared up.

This is actually a good question, because we need to take care that there is real progress in our practice, and every so often, we may have to look back and assess: "What has happened with me? Is there any improvement in my personality, in my character? Am I more or less attached to things? Do I have more or less craving, more or less aggression? Am I more or less dull than before? In which direction am I really going; am I improving or not improving?" We may think, "Now I have been meditating for five years ... ten years ... fifteen years. But what has really happened? Can I discern any real improvement when I compare how I used to be with how I am now?" It's very good to scrutinize oneself that way, to check oneself and see if there is any progress. Of course, this checking is something we do in post-meditation, not during the state of meditative equanimity.

It may sound a little strange to say this, but when one practices in a place where there is no external support for Dharma practice — a place where people don't necessesarily respect and praise the fact that you are a spiritual practitioner — maybe it is more possible to be a really genuine practitioner in such a place. In fact, maybe it is much easier. Who knows? Conversely, in a place where there is a lot of support for practice, there may be plenty of people who are not really practicing genuinely.

This might sound upside down, like backwards logic, but think about it. If we are in a place where spiritual practice is popular, others will honor and respect us for acting like a practitioner — they may even take care of us, giving us certain provisions and privileges. We don't even have to do too much to succeed in getting through life this way; we just have to look like a practitioner from outside. But in a place where there is no support for the Dharma, we don't get any of those perks. Perhaps we are forced to assess our progress in a more genuine and honest way. It might be less easy to fool ourselves in this situation.

We should be really concerned with these questions: Am I really practicing in a genuine way? Am I really progressing? We need to check ourselves, again and again. As we practice more and more, the basic guideline is: are our disturbing emotions diminishing? Is wisdom developing and increasing? Yes or no? We should examine ourselves honestly in this way.

PROGRESSIVE PATH

For a person to awaken to true and complete enlightenment, he or she needs to proceed by means of two factors: means and knowledge. We have all entered the teachings of the Buddha of our own free will. Nobody forced us to do so; and neither have we blindly stumbled into this situation. Embracing Buddhism is our own choice. We were searching for a good path, we thought about it a lot, and we chose to seek out the instructions belonging to the tradition of the Buddha.

The term Buddha refers to someone who is totally purified and fully perfected — totally purified of ignorance, dualistic fixation, all obscurations, and the habitual tendencies for these. The state of buddhahood is having complete mastery over all that is and exists. The Buddha was not always enlightened. For three incalculable aeons he perfected the *accumulations*; then he undertook various hardships for six years. Finally, he completely saw through the falsehood of the delusion that covers the intrinsic nature and awakened to fully realizing this nature. That is why he is called the Enlightened One. The Buddha first trained in shamatha, in tranquillity. Discovering that that in itself is not enough to transcend the three realms of samsara, he went beyond subject-and-object meditation. Transcending all conceptual constructs, he realized the state that is called the true enlightenment.

The word *buddha* means 'purified and perfected.' The original wakefulness is brought to full blossoming or perfection, and delusion as well as its causes are purified. In short, a buddha realizes exactly as it is the intrinsic nature that we all have. The innate nature of the Buddha and of our own basic state are identical. Buddha nature is not specific to the Buddha; it is the nature of everything. That is why the Buddha said,

"Whether a buddha appears in the world or not, whether a buddha teaches the Dharma or not, whether it is awakened to or not, the nature of all things, the basic state, is utterly and originally pure." This is really very profound, a very significant statement. The basic state, the natural condition, is not of anyone's making. It is simply what is, already. It is also called suchness, or ultimate truth.

The different vehicles use different words for it. The full realization of this basic nature, exactly as it is, is called buddhahood. The method that shows how to realize it is called the Dharma. The Buddha also said, "I will teach you the path of how to be enlightened, but whether you follow or not is up to you; it is in your own hands." That means it is the Buddha's responsibility or duty to show us how to be enlightened, how to discover what he himself discovered. But he is not forcing anyone to realize what he realized. This is totally up the individual.

There are two aspects of the Dharma: the Dharma as what has been told or stated, and the Dharma as what has been realized. These two aspects are embodied in those that uphold the teachings, the noble Sangha. The Dharma of realization is something which a teacher may or may not have talked about. We may or may not have understood it, listened to it, or tasted it personally in our own experience. Regardless of all this, it is something which called a special name — rigpa. Rigpa is your present, fresh wakefulness, unspoiled by the thoughts of the three times. It is uncorrupted, unpolluted and possesses the three qualities of being empty, cognizant, and unconfined. That is the Dharma of realization. Anyone who embodies this, or is experiencing this as their nature, belongs to the noble Sangha.

All of us here have, either directly, in actuality, or indirectly, already taken refuge in the three precious ones, the Buddha, Dharma and Sangha. Because we take some delight in what the Buddha represents, we are interested in the awakened state, and that shows we have a sincere interest in or devotion to what enlightenment is, what the Buddha is. That means we have automatically taken refuge in the Buddha. Moreover, we are interested in the teachings, the instructions on how we ourselves can become enlightened. There is some sense of taking delight in finding out what the awakened state is, which means we have naturally taken refuge in the Dharma. In addition, we haven't wandered off by ourselves in order to find these things out, but have been happy to have company to learn from, to discuss with, and so forth. That means we have automatically taken refuge in the Sangha.

The phrase 'taking refuge' in Tibetan is traditionally used to indicate a commitment. Please understand that it's not some kind of en-slavement. It's not like we change from being free to being bound by something, that we fall under someone else's power by coming under their protection or refuge. Rather, taking refuge is a personal choice. It is our free will expressing itself as, "I would like to be like the Buddha. I want to realize what the Buddha has realized. I want to understand what he taught about how to awaken, and I will listen to whoever knows this, whoever embodies these qualities, and has authentic un-derstanding and is willing to speak about it. I want to follow in those footsteps. I want to be like the Buddha myself as well." That is a per-sonal choice, and that kind of choice is what taking refuge is all about.

To place one's trust in something external like the Buddha Shakya-muni and take refuge in some outer object, could be a superficial act. The real significance of it, however, is the recognition that we ourselves actually do possess the same awakened qualities that the Buddha has. It is in order to fully awaken these, in order to fully realize what is our true nature, that we take refuge in the Buddha. That is the real refuge. Most of us have already formalized that attitude through a ceremony. We have gone in front of a Buddhist teacher and with that teacher as witness, we have formally said with our own voice, "I take refuge in the Buddha, the Dharma and the Sangha." That makes it kind of official to ourselves and to others that we have taken refuge. On the other hand, some of you have perhaps not done this, but still in your innermost heart have some admiration for and interest in what the Buddha, Dharma and Sangha represent. Because of this sincerity, we can say that you have actually taken refuge as well.

There are many people who consider themselves very intelligent — in fact, so exceptional that they don't want to belong to some group called 'Buddhist.' At the same time, inside, they agree wholeheartedly with what the Buddha represents. Within themselves, they are already Buddhist. Actually, to be a Buddhist means one understands the way things really are. One knows how it really is; one understands the actual state of affairs, the real condition. Everyone wants to have this kind of true understanding. Nobody wants to be deluded and to misunderstand how things are. Nobody wants to have the wrong idea.

In terms of the three vehicles in Buddhism, as soon as someone has genuinely and sincerely taken refuge in the Three Jewels, in the core of his or her heart, that person has entered the first of the three vehicles, the *shravaka-yana*. After doing this, we need to make up our mind to avoid causing harm to any other sentient being. It is a vow that we take. The first aspect of taking refuge, is rejoicing in what the Three Jewels are, having a sense of admiration and liking for what the Three Jewels are. We all have that. We all have taken refuge on that level. The second part involves forming the resolve, "From now on, I will avoid causing harm to a single sentient being." We need to form that pledge in our minds, but whether we are successful in living up to it or not is another matter.

I would like to encourage you to form that resolve. It is not enough to like the Three Jewels, to be fond of them or have some admiration, thinking, "How nice the Buddha, Dharma and Sangha are!" We need to apply that feeling of appreciation, and the way to do so is to train ourselves in the attitude of, "I will not cause harm to any other sentient being."

If we wish to move forward from this point in a progressive way, the next step is to be a bodhisattva. A bodhisattva's path encompasses both emptiness and compassion. We must understand emptiness and be compassionate at the same time. Many of us may have already taken the formal bodhisattva vow. Some of us may not have done so, but we may nonetheless already possess the attitude of a bodhisattva.

The bodhisattva's attitude is something in addition to the aspiration to never to cause harm to others. It is a shift in attitude where we start to regard all other beings as our guests, as someone we have the responsibility to take care of. If you invite a guest to your house, it is your responsibility to provide for them, to make sure that they are comfortable, have food and drink and so forth. That is the attitude the bodhisattva assumes with regard to all other beings. A bodhisattva acts as a host for all other sentient beings, treating them as his or her guests. He or she makes sure that they are comfortable, and works to guide them in the right direction. This bodhisattva attitude can be expressed directly or indirectly.

We may perhaps already have this attitude and yet not be able to fully carry it out. In order to fully express it in a complete way, we need to train in knowing emptiness. The bodhisattva path has two aspects which are inseparable: emptiness and compassion. We may have already taken on the compassionate attitude in front of a guru, or a Mahayana teacher, by vowing, "Not only will I not harm others, but from now on I will try my best to lead all sentient beings in the right direction, towards liberation and enlightenment." This is a somewhat conceptual attitude which grows out of compassion and this attitude of compassion is something which is resolved either in front of a teacher, or perhaps formed as something we spontaneously express, a habit from the past.

However, in order to be able to apply it in actuality, there is something more which is necessary, and that is the training in emptiness. Training in emptiness makes it possible to actually carry out the compassionate attitude, to live it. Emptiness is extremely important, extremely profound. Emptiness is the *prajnaparamita*, transcendent knowledge, the mother of all Buddhas. It is because of realizing emptiness that all buddhas of the past awakened to true and complete enlightenment, and it is because of realizing emptiness that all buddhas of the present and the future awaken or will awaken to complete enlightenment.

Emptiness is the direct remedy against egotism, the holding on to the idea of *me*. Many other methods can reduce ego-clinging, but when it comes to the actual battle of defeating ego-clinging, the only truly effective method is the understanding of emptiness. If emptiness is what cuts the tree, all the other methods are more like buying a piece of iron, giving it to the blacksmith, having it heated up and beaten and sharpened into the shape of an ax. All these activities produce a very fine ax with a sharp cutting edge, but they are not what actually cuts the tree. The act that connects the edge of the ax with the wood and cuts through, the actual wielding of the ax, the decisive moment, can be compared to the moment of insight into emptiness.

Other practices may all contribute to the cutting through of ego-clinging, but it is only emptiness, in the sense of the knowledge that realizes egolessness, that actually cuts through ego-clinging. All other virtuous activities, all forms of accumulating merit, are like creating a beautiful ax and putting it on one's table. If the ax on the table is not put to use, it doesn't help you at all. It is the actual using of the tool that is most important.

When we say emptiness, we are actually referring to *knowledge of emptiness*. Emptiness means the insight that phenomena are not arising out of themselves, are not arising out from anything other, and not arising from some combination of these. It is the understanding that all phenomena are beyond arising; that they are actually the nature of *non-*arising. It doesn't help to comprehend this and hold onto some idea that confines oneself to the idea of emptiness as non-arising. Non-arising also has to be realized as being non-arising. In this way, emptiness is realized to be totally beyond the 'four limits and eight constructs.' You can call that the emptiness of emptiness.

Teachings on emptiness are meant to refute the notion of a self, to eliminate the erroneous concept of an independent and permanent identity. At the time of the Buddha in India, this type of absolute identity, in terms of a divine self, an absolute, supreme godhead, or the great oneness of a god, was crucial to most religious systems. This idea was very strongly held onto. Through the teaching on emptiness, the basis for holding onto the idea of a self was taken away. This teaching on emptiness is primarily embodied in what is called the second turning of the Wheel of Dharma, also known as the 'intermediate set of teachings.' The first turning of the Wheel of Dharma focuses on the Four Noble Truths. Within the second turning which focuses on the absence of characteristics, we find the teachings of prajnaparamita and emptiness.

In terms of the three vehicles we have already entered the first, the vehicle of shravakas, because we have taken refuge in, placed our trust in, the Buddha, Dharma and Sangha. As part of this, we have turned away from wanting to cause harm to others, and have formed that resolve in our minds. The next step is what most of us have already done: taken the bodhisattva vow. Based on a desire to not harm others, in addition we have the wish to help others, to bring benefit to others. In order to really be able to do so, we need to be free from selfishness, holding onto the idea of 'me.' That concept is a stumbling block for the full implementation of compassion, and that is why the knowledge of emptiness is so important. That is the main principle of the bodhisattva vehicle.

Before we came up here, we all also received the empowerments for the Three Roots from Tsikey Chokling Rinpoche. By taking these empowerment, we have entered the gate of Vajrayana. We received the empowerments, which were transmissions for *termas* revealed by Chokgyur Lingpa, from someone who himself is the reincarnation of Chokgyur Lingpa. Through receiving empowerments for the Three Roots, the seeds or the potential for the ability to realize the three vajras that are intrinsic to our buddha nature in this very lifetime, or within three lifetimes, or seven lifetimes, have been implanted in our stream of being. As long as we don't turn against or break the *samaya*, the link to Vajrayana practice, we are assured of awakening very quickly, and of not having to undergo three incalculable aeons of accumulating merit and purifying obscurations. These empowerments guarantee that very quickly, within one, three or seven lifetimes, we can awaken to true enlightenment.

Empowerment is like being implanted with a seed. We can imagine our three doors — body, speech and mind — as being like a fertile field. The seeds being planted in this field will certainly grow and produce grain. When a qualified master confers empowerment on a ready, open, and devoted disciple, it is like the soil has been loosened up so that it's no longer hard and infertile, but receptive, ready to accept the seed. The openness of devotion assures that the seed being planted will be able to grow and produce. The four empowerments, beginning with the vase empowerment, are given in order to bring to full maturity the seeds that we already have the potential for.

The empowerments we have received authorized us to begin the Vajrayana practices contained in Mahayoga, Anu Yoga and Ati Yoga. Through Mahayoga we practice the development stage and realize the vajra body of the yidam deity. Through Anu Yoga we focus on the key points of the channels, energies and essences of this vajra body in order to actualize the unconditioned state of original wakefulness. Through the practices connected with Ati Yoga — Trekchö and Tögal, cutting through and direct crossing — we are in this very lifetime authorized to fully realize the original state of purity, culminating as the realization of the rainbow body. By receiving these empowerments, we have been infused with or implanted with the basis for these practices. In other words, the potentials for all these practices are included within the empowerments.

The reason I am laying the vehicles out like this is to show where the view we have been presented during the previous days fits into the Buddhist path. We lay the basis by taking refuge and by avoiding causing harm to others. Next, we form the bodhisattva attitude of compassionate emptiness. In addition to this, there is the Vajrayana path. I feel it is a very good idea, very beneficial, if we adopt a yidam and use it as our practice. Through this combination of Dzogchen view and yidam practice, one mutually assists the other. By combining means and knowledge through the yidam practice, we can awaken to complete enlightenment within this very lifetime.

There is a certain link between our past karma, the wishes and aspirations we have made in the past, and the form of the yidam deity that we feel inclined towards and want to practice right now. That is one way. Another way is through the aspirations that have been made by other practitioners in the past. Way back, for example, the being who is now Arya Tara made the aspiration, "Through the outcome of my spiritual practice, after attaining enlightenment, may I manifest a form that can alleviate the eight kinds of fears." Avalokiteshvara's aspiration was "May I benefit beings through a form that inspires the compassionate attitude in all other beings," while Manjushri's was "Through intelligence, may I benefit other beings." The connection to a yidam can also be a result of strong aspirations made by other practitioners in the past.

We cannot say that we have now met the Dharma for the first time. It is very likely that we have been in contact with spiritual practice in past lives. By this I mean someone who in the past formed the attitude to avoid harming others, and also to help others look into the absence of self and to some extent realize egolessness. Someone who has that habitual frame of mind naturally becomes a spiritual practitioner in the next life.

Let's say as an example that someone has in a past life been a teacher of children, telling them what to do and what not to do, showing them a way of knowing what is right and wrong. One did this out of a good heart, not just for business reasons. This kind of person already has a connection with the essence of Manjushri, because Manjushri embodies the activity of knowledge that is carried out for the benefit of others. The attitudes formed in the past thus create a present link with Manjushri practice, and by using Manjushri as the yidam, one can make very quick progress.

Sometimes a realized master with clairvoyant powers will tell the disciple which yidam deity to practice. In other situations one might just notice an inner feeling, some kind of attraction when hearing the name or seeing the form of a certain deity. This kind of natural liking shows a previous connection that we have formed with the deity, due to karma and the power of past aspirations. We can use the yidam practice as a support for our further development.

If the yidam practice is the equivalent of the foundation of a house, the development stage is the interior decoration, so to speak — picking out the furniture and curtains, arranging beautiful objects. Next, there are the inner practices of the channels, the energies and the essences connected with Anu Yoga; involving sitting upright, breathing naturally, and keeping the vase-shaped breath. These can continue into the traditional practice of *tummo,* inner heat, which is a way of melting away and dissolving the *karma-pranas* into the central channel; and thus purifying the habitual grasping at duality.

These inner practices are like cleaning up one's interior. Often people complain, "It hurts here, it hurts there, my back hurts, my front hurts," and so forth. This is because there is no real balance or free flow of the inner energies. Through such practices, all this can be cleared up. It's like arranging the interior of the house very nicely and beautifully. When you have a comfortable house with a good seat, a nice toilet, and a good kitchen, everything is ready to live a comfortable life. This kind of interior cleanup is very beneficial when it comes to real meditation.

So, those are all methods. Development stage is a method and the completion stage with attributes, involving the channels and energies, is also a method. Next is Dzogchen, or Ati Yoga, which has three aspects: mind section, space section and instruction section. If we continue our analogy of the house with its foundation and interior decoration, Dzogchen is like the actual person living in the house, which is the main thing. After all, the house is built for the person, and not the other way around. In order to realize the self-existing awareness directly introduced in Dzogchen, however, the development and completion stage practices are all necessary and beneficial.

Any questions?

STUDENT: Is it best to first visualize step-by-step, and then recognize rigpa?

RINPOCHE: Not necessarily. It's really an individual matter. The best situation is when the visualization takes place within rigpa, without one obstructing or hindering the other. On the other hand, it is all right to first start by imagining something like a Vajrasattva with the different attributes and properties and so forth. Afterwards, you can infuse it with rigpa. This is like giving it a stamp of rigpa on top, so that there is both visualization as well as recognition of the awakened state of rigpa. That way is also all right.

STUDENT: What does it mean to ask questions to Manjushri? Does one actually meet him?

RINPOCHE: Manjushri is the embodiment of knowledge and wisdom, the principle that explains or gives knowledge when there is ignorance. He shows a way, a method, in order to dispel unknowing. Whenever there is something that we are not clear about or don't know, there is an opportunity to ask a question in order to clear it up. That is what is meant by asking questions to Manjushri. We do it in order to find out what is real.

With regard to having a vision and seeing Manjushri: one shouldn't think that deities are totally non-existent and nothing other than one's projection. It is not like that, either. The deity definitely exists, although not necessarily in a way that is separate from one's own perception. One shouldn't think that there are no deities at all. However, in order to progress on the path, one does visualize the deity as being apart from oneself, for example seated in the sky in front of one. We do this in order to, at a later point, realize the indivisible nature of our self and the deity.

Sometimes it is possible that Manjushri will literally show his face before you by appearing and giving answers to your questions. At another time you might just be remaining in equanimity, and an answer to your question arises from within yourself. That could also be said to be the blessing or inspiration of Manjushri.

For example, We often heard the word 'primordial purity,' and perhaps we don't understand what is really meant by it. It may not be so obvious to us. At some point, we may be sitting all by ourselves, and suddenly the comprehension of primordial purity dawns on us. We experience it. You could say that this kind of experience has that quality of knowledge which is actually Manjushri.

The blessing of Manjushri may involve giving yourself the answer. Or it could be that you hear the answer as words spoken from outside yourself. What we perceive, what we experience, is not permanent, fixed or predictable. Actually, it's some kind of magic. It's not easy to lay down a rule for how our experience is going to be in the future. The reality of what is being experienced isn't fixed; it is not something solid, permanent, and concrete. When speaking about seeing a vision or hearing a voice that gives replies from Manjushri, this involves something perceived, right? We cannot necessarily have a fixed program, a schedule, for how this blessing of Manjushri will appear to us.

In a way, we can say that whenever we have some insight — whenever something unknown or not understood becomes known or understood — that that is the blessing of Manjushri. Manjushri is not separate from your own intelligence, your own capacity to understand. As a matter of fact, one could say the very nature of knowing is Manjushri.

STUDENT: If our thoughts are insubstantial and possess the nature of emptiness, then what is there to rely on?

RINPOCHE: It is perfectly all right not to trust in or lean on anything that is conditioned, because it is ultimately unreliable. When one doesn't rely on or trust in anything whatsoever, there is some kind of confidence that comes from within. This kind of self-assurance is a natural property or natural quality of emptiness. As a matter of fact, everything in deluded experience is unreliable, and whatever you put your trust in eventually lets you down. It becomes so tiring, exhausting. Eventually, at some point in discovering the falsehood of all deluded experience, one grows weary of chasing after something to lean on. Finally we realize it's perfectly all right not to place one's trust in anything whatsoever. We can just be free. This confidence opens up some kind of self-assurance that you can do whatever, and you will not be harmed. You can go in any direction — forward or backward, up or down — and nothing bad happens, it's not harmful in any way. That kind of assurance is real trust; because it's not dependent on anything.

Conceptual involvement, trying to be safe and sure in a conceptual way, is always unreliable. If one tries to trust in emptiness, that emptiness is only one's idea. What is the use of that? It's not real emptiness. One day the idea will change, so it is perfectly all right not to hold onto emptiness for dear life. Holding onto emptiness, thinking "Emptiness will never let me down!" One's idea of emptiness will definitely let one down. It will change one day, because ideas always change.

There is another way of relating to the matter of trust, and that is to simply let go. Whenever you have the need to hold onto some idea because it's comforting and feels secure, it's really only another thought. Drop it, just let it go, and it vanishes. All of these attempts to attach oneself to different things that we can rely on become increasingly transparent. You let one thing go, then you let another thing go, letting go more and more, until finally there is no need to hold onto anything whatsoever. At that point you experience a self-assurance, a natural certainty that is anchored in yourself. It is totally fearless, not afraid that any harm is going to happen. It can't go bad by being further deluded, because there is no room for further delusion. Neither is there any idea that you are somehow going to be more safe by being enlightened, because there is no further enlightenment than the natural state. It is really possible to experience that kind of fearless self-assurance.

There is no need to use some kind of patchwork of concepts to try to make oneself feel safe and secure. "Emptiness is there, it will watch out for me, I will be all right as long as I have the idea of emptiness." This isn't necessary at all. It's similar to what you could call crutch therapy, where you try to convince yourself of a particular wholesome idea, and whenever you remember that good idea you feel okay with yourself. If we use emptiness like some kind of conceptual patch that we hold onto, we will never discover true confidence in the Buddhist sense. Confidence in the Buddhist sense means the total absence of fear, of anxiety, and of any expectations. It is like a fearless warrior. If you have been victorious in every fight, in every battle, then you have absolutely no fear of any enemy or opponent, do you? You don't even have the thought of fear.

After recognizing one's nature and training in that recognition, after developing the strength of that recognition, one becomes stable in it. When attaining stability, there is a point at which all objects of distraction dissolve into the innate nature. There is no object of distraction; there is nothing to sidetrack you or carry you away from this stability any longer. That is like having already conquered all opponents. There is nobody left who can rise up and fight with you. You have already won, you are victorious in all directions. Therefore there is no fear, no anxiety, and no dread in any way whatsoever. That kind of confidence comes after we've gone beyond any kind of object of distraction, after we've attained total stability.

STUDENT: Can't we fall into nihilism with this practice?

RINPOCHE: You are concerned about not falling into nihilism, into the view of nothingness, right? You feel there is some need for a support, for help, and that is all right. There are two ways to deal with this. One way is the reason why the Buddha taught that there is buddha nature, there is wisdom, there are the kayas, there is wakefulness. That is one support for avoiding the nihilistic view. The other is actual experience. If you apply the key points of training exactly as I've described them, you will avoid falling into the limitation of nihilistic view.

By recognizing that the essence is empty, we are freed from the limitation of eternalism. When recognizing that by nature we are cognizant, awake, we are automatically freed from the limitation of the nihilistic view. When there is this sense of being wide awake, totally clear, and not void, vacant, or oblivious, you are naturally not falling into the nihilistic view. It is already avoided. How do you understand the nihilistic view?

STUDENT: Isn't the view of nihilism like an abyss? If there is no eternalism, then one attains only nihilism.

RINPOCHE: No, it's not like that! What you've said sounds more like logic, like when one argues in a debate: either there is or there isn't, there is no alternative. In the past, we've always had a permanent idea that there is a self, there is a me, that "I am." All the time, we are thinking "I am." That is the view of eternalism. When we hear that there is the possibility that this could be untrue or unfounded, that such a self actually can't be found, we get scared. We think, "Oh no! If there isn't this 'me' that I've been thinking of all the time, I'll fall into the view of nihilism!" But we haven't fallen into the view of nihilism at all.

Instead, we are still in the view of eternalism, thinking, "I am afraid to fall into the view of nihilism!"

You haven't fallen into nihilistic view yet, you are still in the view of eternalism. But it feels like you could fall into it. It's just another thought. How will you go beyond the view of eternalism? Are you going to jump out of it? Will you destroy it? What are you afraid of?

STUDENT: I feel as if empty means empty of anything, totally void.

RINPOCHE: This is a cultural problem. Your feeling about emptiness is simply a an idea. You need to drop that idea. Actually, you don't have to be worried at all, because rigpa is not nihilistic at all. Rigpa is totally wide open and empty. That is what is called empty essence. It is how it is in itself, which is not an *ism*. But it is not only like that. There is also some sense of being awake and present, alive and cognizant, all by itself. It is not an either/or situation. It is not that you are either empty or cognizant; the two exist simultaneously. We perceive while mind is empty. At the same time mind is empty, it is perceiving. There is no barrier or obstruction between the two; you are not confined to one or the other.

When you naturally let yourself be like that, you haven't fallen into any extreme. You haven't chosen either emptiness or cognizance. But it is naturally the unity or middle way, and therefore the two extremes are automatically excluded. It's true that we could sit and try to be totally absent-minded and not know a thing. We could totally close off to everything, but we are not really trying to do that, are we? Or we could sit and really get into the feeling of how nice it is, how blissful, how clear, how free. If we sit and nurture that experience for a long time, if we sit and get really cozy with the feeling, that could turn into the view of eternalism. But we are not really doing that, either. So you needn't fear falling into either extreme.

Most people don't fall into the view of nihilism. Most people fall into the view of eternalism. Actually, it would be good if we could fall into a little bit of nihilism, but it rarely happens! The very fear, "I may fall into the view of nihilism" expresses an eternalistic view!

STUDENT: Isn't the object we take refuge in conceptual?

RINPOCHE: There are two ways of taking refuge: the relative or superficial way, and the ultimate, real way. When we have a relative attitude, we need a relative support as a method. We shouldn't mistake that relative method for the ultimate, however. This kind of mistake comes from not knowing where one is. We need to know at exactly what point we are at. Here I'm not talking about our basic nature, which is always the same, but simply who we are right now, where we are experientially. For example, even though there is no real 'I,' we still feel like there is, don't we? That feeling is what I'm talking about. We need to check whether this feeling is anchored in something superficial or whether it is the ultimate. Whether we are at the ultimate state or not.

If this identity of what one is right now is relative or superficial, one can take refuge in a relative or superficial way and will obtain some benefit. The extent of this benefit depends on how one takes refuge. I am not questioning whether the object of refuge actually gives benefit or not. It's like the sun shining. The sun most definitely shines, I have no doubt about that. But whether the sun shines into oneself depends on if one faces the right direction. The sun doesn't shine inside a north-facing cave.

So, exactly how we take refuge makes a big difference. If we are in a relative state and make relative prayers asking for help or guidance or blessings, we will be given relative blessings. There is certainly some relative attainment in that. It's all like magic. Making the prayer is like magic, and receiving the blessings is also a kind of magic. It is perfectly all right on that level. If one is on the relative level, you can take refuge in a relative way. To have relative trust is perfectly all right.

However, that belongs to post-mediation. In the meditative state, the state of equanimity, various concepts of here and there, up and down and so forth are not appropriate. They don't belong. The meditative state should be more like an unshakable presence of wakefulness. That of course doesn't exclude taking refuge at the beginning of the session. One can still take refuge, but in a way that acknowledges the play of the magic, acknowledging that everything is just an expression or a display. Within the vajra-like samadhi, one can take refuge like that. To sum up, let me say that we need to become more familiar with the principles of what is relative and ultimate, the conditioned and the unconditioned.

STUDENT: When trying to recognize mind essence, visual forms totally distract me. What should I do?

RINPOCHE: How about you wear really dark glasses! It's okay to close your eyes a little bit sometimes. But if one sits with closed eyes all the time there is some danger that the attention will subside or dissolve back into the all-ground, the *alaya*, which basically means that you fall asleep. It's also possible to be wide-awake with closed eyes. Rigpa is not dependent on whether the eyes are closed or open, because rigpa is not dependent on any of the five sense objects at all. It doesn't matter that much. Therefore, when training in rigpa it's good to alternate your environment, sometimes staying in bright light, sometimes in darkness. Sometimes sitting with open eyes, sometimes with closed eyes. Sometimes you train in rigpa while lying down, sometimes while standing up. Practice in all different ways, so that you don't become reliant on any particular technique. Sometimes you can put your head down on the cushion and your bottom up in the air! As a matter of fact, rigpa has no head and tail; there is no top and bottom. It is only the habits we are used to that determines what we think is up and down. In rigpa there is no up and down.

Right now, in this present human incarnation, we don't have eyes in the back of our heads. We have eyes in the front of our heads. Thus, we are not necessarily disturbed by anything going on behind us. It is usually only what is in front, right? Rigpa, on the other hand, has no front and back. Our present experience is dictated by our habit of being occupied by what is seen in front of ourselves. We should develop more sense of space, an awareness not only of what is in front of us, but all around, behind and on the sides. If we think that space is only the area in front of our faces, then instead of focusing our attention on rigpa, we are focusing the attention on what is in front of us. That's just like leaning on what we perceive. Just imagine how much trouble we would be in if we had a third eye!

STUDENT: As we engage in this practice of seeing the essence more and more, do we somehow draw closer to rigpa?

RINPOCHE: When a good cook is making a really nice meal, you can't help but notice the delicious aroma as you draw closer and closer. Even if you're hungry, when you get really close, just inhaling some of that delicious smell can make you feel satisfied to some extent. In the same way, as you get closer and closer to rigpa, you feel more and more open, relaxed and at ease. Being close to rigpa means it is not really rigpa — it is a rigpa imitation that one is training in. That is actually very good in some ways, in that it reduces one's normal attachment, anger and dullness.

However, when it comes to actual, real rigpa, we can verify whether it is the genuine thing or not through our own sense of knowing. Genuine rigpa is accompanied by a sense of certainty. The other sign is that by training in real rigpa, our disturbing emotions grow less and less, and we experience less attachment, less anger, less dullness. Devotion and compassion both grow as well. These are not only signs of rigpa, of course; they are the signs of any true spiritual practice.

What if the more we practice the more attached we become to all sorts of different things? What if we become more conceited, more aggressive, more competitive, more dull, more sleepy, and so forth?. That is a sure sign that we are not practicing in the right way. What should we do? Either we give up that kind of "Dharma practice," give it up totally, or we clear up the problem by finding out what is wrong and changing it. Otherwise, it is like the famous statement: if one doesn't know how to practice the Dharma correctly, that incorrect practice becomes a cause for rebirth in the lower realms.

Any other questions?

TRANSLATOR: I was wondering if there is some relationship between genuine training in the visualization during the development stage and what you mentioned about the objects of distraction dissolving into the innate nature.

RINPOCHE: Yes, there is a definite relationship! When we no longer have to imagine that things possess divine nature, but when we vividly see and experience the actual purity of everything as it is, then the perfection of the development stage is that the entire environment, whatever is perceived, is seen as it is really is, a pure land, a buddhafield. There is no impurity, no concreteness, apprehended anywhere. In actuality, your experience is in such a way that whatever used to be an object of distraction have now become a play of the innate nature. There is no longer any distraction to be found anywhere.

BARDO

ALL THE DIFFERENT PHENOMENA, all things, whether we call them pure or impure, samsaric or belonging to nirvana, are not something fixed at all. They depend upon our thoughts. In fact, they are created by our own thoughts, our own ideas. It's just like ice on the ocean. In the winter the ocean can freeze into a solid mass, like the rigid, solid reality that we usually perceive. In this kind of reality, all things are real and concrete. I am here, you are there, and over there's the world. This is nice and that is bad, and so forth. All these concepts have frozen our experience into a solid reality.

However, it doesn't have to be that way. As we experience the innate nature, these concepts begin to melt or dissolve. It's just like when the heat and warmth of spring comes, and the ice begins to melt. It breaks up the ice, and slowly it melts completely, becoming indivisible from the ocean itself. By the time you walk down to the beach in summer, there's no ice to be seen anywhere, is there? It has all dissolved, completely dissolved.

In the same way, the more we train, the more stable we become, and all conditioned phenomena slowly dissolve into the vastness of basic space, into our innate nature. Finally, all phenomena are of one taste, which is to say they are of one nature with the basic space of dharmakaya.

This total melting away of all conditioned phenomena is the attainment of the final fruition, the end result of practice. At the time of the path, it's like things have frozen over. The ice of confusion is fixating concepts. When we start to apply the warmth of the view, meditation and conduct then the frozen states of confusion start to dissolve, until finally they melt away. The ocean that was never frozen over to begin with and the ocean that all the ice has melted into is the same ocean. There's no difference whatsoever. That is what is called the 'indivisibility of ground and fruition.' That is the final result. This is the realization of dharmakaya.

The three kayas are called dharmakaya, sambhogakaya, and nirmanakaya. Out of dharmakaya the form bodies, the sambhogakaya and the nirmanakaya, manifest unobstructedly. From the purity of the dharmakaya, it becomes possible to manifest in order to influence countless sentient beings. The dharmakaya buddha Samantabhadra sends out countless sambhogakaya and nirmanakaya emanations, like Buddha Shakyamuni, who actively work for the welfare of all beings.

If we have sharp intelligence and deep devotion, it's possible to realize dharmakaya within this very lifetime. Only a few people manage to do this, but it's not impossible. In the past there have been many who have attained complete liberation, true enlightenment within a single lifetime: Garab Dorje, Manjushrimitra, Sri Singha, and Padmasambhava; Milarepa and Longchenpa, and so forth. Over the centuries, thousands and thousands and thousands have attained true accomplishment within a single lifetime. Many of them also left this life in what is called the rainbow body.

Rainbow body means the realization of dharmakaya. The nature of dharmakaya is that every experience is indivisible from dharmakaya itself. All experience: all sights, sounds, smells, tastes, textures — everything is the sway of dharmakaya.

This can indeed happen within our lifetime; but if not, we still have the opportunity to be liberated during the four bardos, the four intermediate states. These are the bardo of this life, the bardo of dying, the bardo of dharmata, and the bardo of becoming. Each of these offers the opportunity for being liberated.

The bardo of this life actually means the bardo between birth and death. It lasts from the moment you come out of your mother's womb until you catch a fatal sickness or begin to die in some other way. Everything in between these two points is called the bardo or the intermediate state of this life.

The bardo of dying begins the moment we contract an incurable sickness. It lasts from the moment we start to die until the exhalation of our last breath. During this period the body slowly disintegrates. This process involves different stages of dissolution, but they form a gradual progression towards the final moments of death.

At the very end of life, the white element obtained from the father descends from the crown of our head, while the red element from our mother rises from below our navel. The moment they meet together at the heart level, the inner circulation of energy ceases. One's consciousness experiences a temporary blackout, and the bardo of dharmata begins.

From the end of the bardo of dharmata until the moment we take a new rebirth is called the bardo of becoming. This last of the four bardos, involving the state between death and the next rebirth, is what is usually meant when you hear the term *bardo*. Generally speaking, it lasts for an average of forty-nine days or seven weeks. But the length of time is not certain or fixed, just as a human lifespan might average 70 or 80 years but is not fixed.

If we don't succeed in being fully liberated during the bardo of this life by attaining stability in self-existing wakefulness; and if we don't attain rainbow body, we go through the bardo of dying. While it's a bit difficult, practitioners who have trained to some extent have the chance to be liberated during the bardo of dying and of dharmata.

When the red and white element meet together at the heart center, all thought states dissolve, and we arrive at an experience of our basic nature. This is the mother luminosity, which is our basic state. The child luminosity is our experience of the nature of mind during this lifetime. If we don't lose the continuity of that recognition, that which we have trained in on the path, then, at that very moment of dying, it's said that mother and child unite. In other words, we merge fully with the basic nature and become liberated right there. For such a person no bardo of becoming arises afterwards, because he or she is already liberated into dharmakaya.

For a practitioner, the bardo of dying and dharmata are the opportunities to really show off. If a practitioner has some guts, this is the time to show it, just like some people show off their courage by getting into fistfights.

It's hard to become liberated right now, because our mind is connected very strongly to this body. It's like gravity, in a way. The body anchors the mind so that it's actually quite difficult to dissolve this body into the pure essences. Sooner or later the body does however disintegrate anyway, and at death is when it starts to fall apart. At the point of actual death, the mind and body part, and at that moment we are only consciousness by itself. Since the mind at that point is all alone, if it's able to recognize and simply be its own nature, that is the moment to be totally liberated.

But if you fail to be liberated at that point, the experiences of the bardo of becoming begin. Most people at this point experience what is called 'the collapse of heaven and earth.' It's like heaven and earth clash together, and one just faints or blacks out. This period of blacking out is said to last about three or four days, then all of a sudden you wake up again.

At this point, most people are unable to acknowledge the fact that they've died. They go to their own house, but they are only a ghost. You move around and search for the things you used to value: "Where are my children? Where's my spouse? Where's my house?" You can see others, but they can't see you, so you start to get worried. "Why don't they respond to me? They don't seem to do anything for me." You start to feel really sad, rejected.

In this stage one is just a spirit by itself, with no body to anchor it. Thus, it moves like a feather in the wind. If you think of New York you're immediately in New York, and perhaps the next moment in Paris. If you think of Århus, you arrive in Århus. Think of Gomdé, and all of a sudden you're in Gomdé. It's very difficult actually to just remain in one place, because you move with the movement of your thinking mind.

You see and experience things from this life, this reality, but there is also a lot of additional turmoil, in terms of sounds and colors and lights. In actuality these are all manifestations of one's own nature, of dharmata. The whole buddha mandala of one's body start to manifest as the 100 peaceful and wrathful deities. If one doesn't recognize them as manifestations of one's own nature, the wrathful deities look like devils, and these male and female hell beings start to haunt and chase you. If you don't recognize them as your projections, it can be very scary.

At this point it would be very helpful if you could acknowledge that you are actually dead, because then there is something to do. You can remember that during your lifetime you went to Denmark, to a place called Gomdé, where you heard a Tibetan lama talking. Remember he said, "At some point you will arrive in the bardo, and at that time try to remember that it's all illusory. It's not real. It's your personal experience. There is nothing that you need to be attached to or afraid of. Remember to recognize the nature of your mind."

If you can remember this and apply this, then your fear will subside to an extent. Let's say thirty percent of this anxiety disappears, and you feel more at ease. Often we get scared there's nothing to actually fear, but our own panic makes the cause of fear seem much bigger than it really is. In the same way, if at this moment we could relax a little bit we will find the situation is not so bad after all.

If we have trained somewhat in this lifetime and we are somehow familiar with recognizing this naked state of natural awareness, then becoming liberated in the bardo of dharmata is not so difficult, because at that time there's no body. The moment you recognize, all the deluded experiences fade away; they vanish, dissolve. Immediately you're liberated. Right now, because our mind is attached to our body, we don't get liberated by recognizing mind essence one single time. In the bardo state, on the other hand, one recognition may be enough to be totally freed.

To recognize the bardo state as the bardo is very much connected with the ability to recognize that dreaming is a dream. If we practice in recognizing the dream state for what it is, and in addition to that remember to recognize the nature of our mind and let be in that, we are developing our ability to do the same in the bardo.

The enlightened ones, out of skillful means and great compassion, try their best to teach beings methods for liberation which are useful and practical. They examine every opportunity. "Where will it be possible for these beings to be liberated? Where can they be helped? We teach certain methods that can be used in this life, but if they aren't liberated and they arrive at death, they could use these other methods. The moment of death presents another opportunity, and so does the bardo state, where one can use these practices." The end result is that we've been given many methods to use at different times.

The thing to always remember is that the bardo is your personal experience. That's why you can be freed within it upon recognition. If it was truly an external place that one was dwelling in, then it would be very hard.

There's an old story told by the Buddha in one of the sutras which illustrates the relativity of one's personal experience. Long ago in India there lived a famous magician, who was expert at conjuring up magical apparitions. His skill was so great that his reputation spread far and wide. Far away in another part of the country lived a young man who thought, "I want to learn magic. I want to be a magician myself." He walked for many days to reach the great magician.

When he arrived, he found the magician sitting like this, beside a very hot fire, with one foot up like that. *(Rinpoche poses in the Indian way of sitting.)* Many seats were laid out around him, and his beautiful wife sat beside him. The man approached him, joined together the palms of his hands in salutation, and said, "Please teach me how to do magic."

The magician said, "You must be tired, traveling so far to get here. Why don't you sit down for a while right there." He called his wife and said, "Dechen, come here and pour some wine for this new guest." Dechen gave the man a cup and began to pour wine into it. At this moment, a big earthquake began to shake the surrounding countryside.

The house they were in had animals stabled in the lower section. The magician said, Hurry! We need to grab some horses, and ride off quickly, because the house is about to collapse." So the three of them jumped on horses and galloped out of the valley, with the entire landscape trembling violently.

As they rode off at full speed, they separated. The young guy was riding off all by himself. He came out into a desert, where he didn't know which way to turn. He had no idea which direction was east or west, because clouds blocked the sun, and there were no compasses in those days. So he just rode and rode without stopping for five or six days. He wanted to return to the magician's house, but he was totally lost, as well as thirsty and exhausted. Finally he came to a pass and looked down into an unknown valley.

In the distance he saw a huge tent, with smoke rising up from it. He was really happy at the sight, because he thought "There must be somebody there who will give me some food." He led the horse down the steep slope, and eventually he arrived at the nomad tent. Inside was a family consisting of a father, a mother and a girl, all of whom were very surprised to see this starving, exhausted stranger. They said, "We really thought we were the only ones in the world, and all of a sudden you show up!" They took care of him, and gave him tsampa to eat, so he stayed and relaxed for a few days.

Then the father said, "I have an idea. Maybe you should stay here and marry my daughter." The man was exhausted from his long journey, and he had no idea where he was or how to return to where he came from. He looked at the girl, noticed she was quite pretty, and said, "All right!" So he settled there, and seven years went by. At this point he and his wife had a five-year-old son.

Every day, the father had the habit of leaving the tent, crossing a small bridge over a river and heading up to a nearby forest to collect firewood. One day when he was crossing the river, a sudden strong gust of wind came up and knocked him off his feet. He fell into the river and drowned. His wife and daughter were extremely sad, especially his wife. She thought, "There were only three people in this whole world, and now my husband has died." She felt so depressed she would sometimes walk up and stand on the bridge and look down at the water, thinking "This is where he fell in and drowned. It's so terrible, so awful! Maybe it's better I die, too. There's no point in me living any longer without my husband." So one day she jumped in and drowned as well.

Now only the daughter and her husband were left. She thought, "The only real people in this world were my parents and me. This guy here is a newcomer, and I don't really know him that well. Since the two of them have died, there's no real meaning for me anymore." So she as well jumped into the river and drowned.

Unfortunately, her five-year-old son saw the whole thing. "My grandmother and grandfather have died," he thought, "and now my mother has also died. It's too much." His father tried to take care of him, but he couldn't give him the same kind of affection that his mother used to give. The little boy became increasingly depressed, more and more sad, and after a few days he ran up to the bridge, jumped in the river, and also drowned.

The man was now left all alone. He was quite sad, but to begin with, things weren't that bad. He had food to eat and water to drink, but as the days went by there was less and less food, until finally it was finished. He stayed for a few days, getting more and more hungry. He thought, "I'm not that successful, am I? I originally set out to learn magic. That didn't go very well. I ended up in this place, I got married and had a child, but now my wife and child are both dead. And there's nothing left to eat or drink! This is really unfortunate." So he also went to the bridge and jumped into the river.

The moment he touched the water, it splashed up into his face. At that moment he saw that the magician's wife was still pouring wine into his cup. He was still sitting by the fire, back at the original place. Yet within that split second, it seemed like seven years had gone by. The magician looked at him and said, "That's magic!"

For that particular man, his relative personal experience truly felt like it lasted that long, that so much had happened during those seven years. Actually, it was a magical illusion. That's one reason why time is not something that really exists. It's simply created by our own thoughts.

Imagine there are two people, one sleeping and one awake. The sleeper may be dreaming about all sorts of things. Perhaps he dreams he's getting married and a child is born, or maybe he won a million in the lottery. He sleeps for a few hours, and in his experience it feels like a long, long time has gone by. The other guy, the one who's awake, looks at his watch and sees that actually only five minutes have gone by. This illustrates that our feeling of time is not something fixed; it's not an absolute. Rather, it's a personal experience created by and modulated by our own concepts.

The real importance is to understand what the Buddha taught: that everything is like a dream. Everything is like a magical illusion; nothing is real; nothing has real substance. If we train ourselves right now in understanding this, that kind of practice will prove to be very beneficial when we arrive in the bardo.

STUDENT: When letting be into the state of rigpa, it is said that the six sense objects are liberated or set free. Since the six senses are also liberated at the time of death, is that the same as being enlightened?

RINPOCHE: We cannot really equate the liberation of the six senses with complete enlightenment, because true enlightenment, buddhahood, is something much more than that. In the state of an Arhat, all imprints obtained through the six senses [the five physical senses plus mental cognition] are brought to a halt for a very long time. It's called the cessation of the six senses. Still, this is not the same as buddhahood.

Complete enlightenment, buddhahood, involves something extra, something superior to the interruption of the six senses. The wisdom quality of the awakened state is something a hundred or a thousand times greater. There is something called the 'boundless gates of wakefulness,' in which countless wisdom doors all open. This involves something much further than the six senses temporarily being brought to a halt. We can also talk about the cessation of form aggregates, the cessation of sensations, conceptions, formations and cognitions, and so forth, but none of these in themselves are buddhahood. Buddhahood is much more grand, something tremendously greater than that. Buddhahood involves the boundless opening of the doors of wakefulness.

We need to experience both the purification of the disturbing emotions of the sense doors, as well as the unfolding or the perfection of wisdom. Normally, when we have a feeling or sensation, we notice it through our senses. Our mind is conditioned by sense objects and the attention which is directed through the senses. But the awakened state of a buddha is not confined in that way. Instead, it is totally and utterly wide open. The mind of a buddha experiences everything, without having to go through any of the senses. There are no sense doors in the awakened state, yet everything is perceived, unimpededly. The buddha's mind can see, hear, taste, smell, and feel texture without having to operate through sense organs. And it can do a lot more than that as well!

STUDENT: How does a being experience without going through the sense organs?

RINPOCHE: In the same way as when you see, hear, smell taste or feel something while dreaming. How do you do that? Maybe we're just lying peacefully in our bedroom sleeping, but we dream of all kinds of things — of huge elephants, of flying in airplanes, of going to all kinds of different places. We may dream that we get married and have children, and that our children grow up and also get married. There is no limit to what we could be dreaming. And all this takes place while we are asleep in a small room. To your friends, it appears you are asleep and snoring. You're not actually hearing or seeing anything, and yet you experience it vividly without the intervention of the sense organs. When you wake up in the morning, you can remember what you dreamt — who you met with, what you saw, and even the conversation you had while dreaming. So who or what heard the words said in the conversation? And who remembers it?

That's what bardo experiences are like, and that's why it's called personal experience. Delusion, in short. If we closely examine our delusion, we realize we are really deluded. If we look even more closely, we realize it is pure magic.

STUDENT: How can we practice during the dream state?

RINPOCHE: If you want to make use of dream time, here is how to do so. When you lie down, first of all relax yourself and make yourself at ease. Make a prayer, a supplication to your root teacher, and the masters of the lineage, receive the blessings, and mingle your mind indivisibly with them. Make the wish to be able to recognize the dream state as dreams. Do this gently, in a very loose and free way. If you do it too forcefully, you won't be able to sleep!

So, make the wish to be able to recognize the dream state as dream. If we are able to do that and can maintain our presence of mind while dreaming, we can remember to practice meditation during that time. That would be very good. To practice mediation while dreaming doesn't mean that we wake up from sleeping. We still look like we're sleeping, but we are awake to the fact that this is the dream state, and we are practicing during it. I am not asking you to actually wake up at one in the morning and sit up and practice; I'm not saying that.

If an awake person views a sleeper, he may think that person is totally, completely asleep. But who knows? The sleeper could be recognizing the dream state, recognizing rigpa within that, and training in this way. That would be very good.

To simply recognize that a dream is a dream is not that useful; it doesn't help that much. Conscious or lucid dreaming is like being a gatekeeper, in that you keep taking notice of what is going on. Now a car has arrived, so you write down the number; a car has departed, so you write down the number. In the same way, you note that now it is a nice dream, now it is a bad dream, and so forth. None of this helps that much.

What is necessary is to be able to remember one's guru, to remember the instructions and to apply them, and especially to remember how to mingle our mind with the guru's mind and remain in the state of rigpa.

To be able to do that seven times in a row is described having the assurance, the certainty of being liberated in the bardo. Tibetan masters don't really like to give such assurance, or such guarantee, but there is this one, that if during the life you can recognize and remain in rigpa seven times during the dream state, you can be sure of being free in the bardo. Even if you are not liberated in the bardo of dying, into dharmakaya, in the bardo of becoming, you will be liberated.

There is a very strong connection between the dream state and bardo. It's not only that, also the waking state experience is very closely related to dreaming. Dream state is like magical illusion, it is unreal, it doesn't really exist. For some reason, we believe that during the waking state, that everything is real, strange enough. But honestly, who knows, maybe the dream state is real and the waking state is unreal! It's not sure.

STUDENT: Could you say more about the bardo and training in rigpa?

RINPOCHE: If one has some training in rigpa, at the moment of death, at the end of the bardo of dying, the last moment we have in this life, if we at that moment recognize the nakedness of rigpa, this body is discarded, like a snake shedding its' skin and we are liberated.

This is after the white essence from the father and the red from the mother have descended and ascended and meet together in the heart center. In most beings, at that moment, they black out, lose consciousness. But if someone has some familiarity with this, it is possible to recognize self-existing rigpa at that moment. It is said that no matter how much negative deeds and karma one has accumulated, one can awaken to complete enlightenment at the dharmakaya level, at the moment of death in the bardo of dying.

This is called the meeting of the mother and child luminosities. Mother which is the ground luminosity or basic state, and the path luminosity, what we have recognized as the path, meet together. The path luminosity is a piece of dharmakaya. The rigpa as path is a piece of dharmakaya. It is like the sun passing behind a gap in the clouds. When it comes to the gap we see the whole sun for a short while, it passes by again it gets obscured by clouds. But, at the moment of death when the mother and child luminosities mingle, it is like going through that gap in the clouds, becoming one with the wide open sunlit sky, it is more like that. That is an example. Don't confuse the example with the meaning.

Recognition of rigpa is called the 'single sufficient king,' meaning that itself is enough in any situation. Rigpa is sufficient for dealing with whichever of the 84,000 types of disturbing emotions that we might meet or are about to be occupied by. Someone familiar with this recognition doesn't need to try any other method. If we are angry or irritated, we don't need to try to be kind and compassionate, thinking "How sad for that person, I should be more kind," and so on. Simply recognizing rigpa is enough to immediately dissolve the disturbing emotion, whether it be anger or anything else. Rigpa is the single sufficient method to deal with any situation.

There are, of course, other methods in Buddhism to counteract desire. For example, to subdue the desire for another's body, one visualizes a rotting corpse or a skeleton, imagining in detail the decomposition of the bodily parts. Sometimes a practitioner may even hang up a skeleton in front of him and use it as a meditation object. All these techniques involve rejecting something and trying to accept something else instead. While this does work, it takes a really long time, and we don't really know how much time we have. Many of us have already gone through half of our lives, or maybe more. We may think we have a lot of time left, but we don't really know.

Then there's the issue of how we use the time we do have. If we are sixty years old, we probably spent around twenty-five years of our life sleeping. That leaves us with thirty-five years out of the sixty. We spent a lot of those years being educated, probably eighteen or nineteen years, maybe more. When students graduate from college, they're often unsure of the direction of their life, and might spend three or four years finding out what they really want to do.

People often think that they are being very intelligent and capable by postponing decisions on what they will do. They might think, "I don't want to be stupid about how I use my life; I want to try out all sorts of different things first. I don't want to get caught up in a career I don't really like." So one tries different things for two years, three years, six years — some people are trying different things their whole life! And in the middle of this trying, they die.

It is true that we don't have that much life to waste, so we need to be intelligent about how we use it. It's good to be intelligent, but if the intelligence is not wise, it becomes an obstacle as well. We need to be not just intelligent, but also wise. So, as the saying goes, don't grab for the twigs and small branches, but take hold of the trunk at the root. Try, if you can, to get to the Great Perfection, the view that can cut through the very root of any disturbing emotion. Only this has the capacity to cut any type of confusion into bits.

STUDENT: What state should the mind be in during sleep?

RINPOCHE: As a basis, it's best to fall asleep undisturbed, in a peaceful way. Not too dull, not too angry, and not too attached to anything, like a clean piece of paper.

In addition to that, I feel it is really helpful to remind yourself before falling asleep, "When dreaming, may I be aware of the fact it's just a dream state. May I recognize that the dreaming is just a dream, and when doing so, may I remember the practice so that I'm able to train further in meditation. While training, may I be able to recognize mind essence."

Making that kind of wish or resolve is very helpful, because everything depends on the inclinations that we form. For example, if we fall asleep really angry about something, we're still angry in a subtle way in our sleep, and the whole dream state is suffused with the tendency to be angry.

I have had some personal experience with this. Six months before, I went to Tibet to see one of my gurus, Adhi Rinpoche. We flew together up to Lhasa and stayed together for ten days there. Then I had to fly back to Nepal.

Now, the standard time in Tibet is Beijing time, which is three hours different from Nepal time. To catch the morning plane you have to get up really early, at four o'clock, in order to make it to the airport in time. I was staying in a hotel, and of course I stayed up so late the night before that I was unable to ask anyone to wake me up the next morning at four a.m. There was no alarm clock, either. "What am I going to do now?," I thought. I was getting a little anxious about it.

I decided I was simply going to wake up at four o'clock by myself. Normally I'm a very good sleeper; I can lie down and immediately go to sleep. I was worried about sleeping too late, but I managed to go to sleep with the thought of four o'clock in my mind.

I didn't wake up once the whole night, but at exactly four o'clock my eyes opened. I didn't have any dreams about waking up at four o'clock; in fact, I didn't have any dreams about anything like that at all. But still I woke up at exactly four o'clock. This kind of thing indicates the force of the inclination or the habitual tendencies we form. You may have experienced something like this yourself.

It's also said that it is good to fall asleep not only peacefully, but with a really good heart. One way is to think of all sentient beings with love and compassion. Maybe you feel some devotion towards the Buddha. If you simply fall asleep in that state, then the whole night will be wholesome.

If you don't become aware of that the dreams are just dreams, there's nothing you can do. One just gets sucked around in the turmoil. But if you become aware that the dream is a dream, a lot of things can be done in the dream state. According to the general Vajrayana system, you can transform or multiply all different things. According to the Dzogchen system, you remember your guru, his instructions, and the yidam, and most especially you remember to recognize mind essence. To be able to do that is quite good enough. Most important is to be free of confusion, to recognize natural mind.

FRUITION

IN THE DRUKPA KAGYÜ LINEAGE there was a master with a disciple called Lingje Repa. The master told Lingje Repa to remain in retreat for three years. "Seal up the opening to your room with mud, and leave only a small window for some food," he said. He told him to eat only a little bit, and to mainly practice living off essences, a practice called *rasayana*.

The master had another disciple by the name Taklungpa, who was a monk, while Lingje Repa was a *ngakpa*, a tantrika. One day, the master said to Taklungpa, "At a particular place about two day's walk from here a dakini is passing away in two days. Go there right away, and as soon as you find the corpse, chop open the kapala [skull] and quickly eat whatever you find inside. Hurry up because by doing so, you will attain supreme accomplishment."

Lingje Repa, who was sealed up in retreat at the time, had developed clairvoyant knowledge. In his mind's eye he saw that the day after tomorrow a special dakini was passing away, and that whoever ate the brains from the skull would attain supreme accomplishment. So he broke open his door and went very fast and got there way before Taklungpa. Lingje Repa chopped off the skull and was walking back with it, eating from it. On the way, he met Taklungpa, still heading for his destination. Taklungpa saw Lingje Repa eating quite happily from the skull cup. Lingje Repa said, "Friend, if you want to eat, have some," and gave Taklungpa a spoonful. So Taklungpa got a little bit and proceeded further. When he got to the corpse, he found out that there wasn't anything to get, because Lingje Repa had already taken the whole thing.

The two of them returned to their master, who was sitting on a throne teaching Mahamudra to a group of people. Lingje Repa was wearing a white *chuba*, and to tell the truth, his behavior wasn't that dignified. He was eating from the skull cup and singing a song that could be heard by the entire assembly:

> *The original nature which the Guru explained*
> *I have trained in and trained in again.*
> *Now that the meditator and the meditation object both are lost,*
> *And there is no division between sessions and breaks,*
> *What is there left for me to do?*

At that point, the master knew that his disciple Lingje Repa had reached the same level as himself, at which there is no difference between meditating and not meditating. It soon become a widespread saying that "On the opposite side of the river Ganges, Saraha had the highest realization, but on this side of the river Ganges, Lingje Repa had the highest realization." He was said to be of the instantaneous type. He was someone for whom the object of distraction dissolved into the dharmata, into the innate nature, so that even when trying to be distracted, it was impossible for him to be distracted from the innate nature. Like arriving on an island of pure gold — you don't find any ordinary stones. On such an island, everything you see, everything you pick up in your hand, is gold.

When we are like Lingje Repa, it really doesn't matter whether we keep sessions or not. But until that point it surely does make a difference if we actually set off time to practice.

The Dzogchen tradition teaches the 'three-fold motionless.' The first of these three is an unmoving body, as stable and steady as a lofty mountain. The second is unmoving senses. Whatever is perceived is reflected clearly, crisply, and distinctly, like the planets and stars reflected on the clear and undisturbed surface of a lake. The last is unmoving mind, unmoving rigpa, like space.

> *Allow your present wakefulness to simply be;*
> *Totally without fabrication.*

Don't try to improve upon its freshness,
Remain unoccupied
By any memory of the past,
Any plan about the future;
Involved in any dualistic appreciation of the present.
Don't dwell upon anything as the object of meditation.
Remain totally free,
Vividly clear,
Wide awake.

This state we can call rigpa. It needs to be acknowledged, recognized, in one single instant, like flicking on a light switch and illuminating a room.

Rigpa is empty in essence, cognizant by nature, and unconfined in capacity. When these three qualities are simultaneously present, we can call this rigpa, or nature of mind. The basic state, the natural state — whatever we call it, we should train in it, sustain the continuity of this recognition.

In terms of time, this type of recognition is often described as 'four parts without three.' The three here refers to the time of past, time of present, and time of future. When you take those three away from the four parts, what is left is the time of rigpa. What time *is* rigpa? Is it the past? Is it the present? Is it the future? No, it's none of these three. If you want to call rigpa a time, it is actually timelessness. Timelessness is rigpa.

We say that rigpa is what should be realized. Is it an object which is empty? Is it that sometimes it is cognizant and other times unconfined? If we have one of these qualities, do we need to have the other two also? When all three are complete, have we got it? Is it something like that? No, it's not.

In the beginning of training in the awakened state of mind, it is said that liberation is like meeting a person you already know. This means that when we get occupied with a thought and are thinking of something, at some point a certain presence of mind arises to remind us to recognize the essence again. In the beginning we rely on mindfulness.

At that moment of mindfulness the thought is liberated. Thus, it's like meeting an old acquaintance.

Recognizing the essence of mind is not a recognition of something which is seen, something that we experience, something that we can perceive and dwell on or rest in. It is not like that at all. If we regard the essence or the state of rigpa as some state that we are liberated into and we remain there, kind of relaxing into that, there is still no real freedom. We are not free from this comfort of dwelling on or appreciating or being fond of this experience.

In the beginning, the main obstacle in meditation is the holding of duality. Later on, what becomes the obstacle is more the dwelling *on* an experience, the dwelling *in* the meditation state. The clinging to the resting, the clinging to the feeling of being in meditation, is very subtle. In the beginning, we are mostly disturbed by the perceived. If something is unpleasant, it disturbs us, of course. If it is pleasant it also disturbs us, because we get attracted. We feel either aversion or attraction, and that kind of disturbance is based on what we perceive.

Later on, we reach some kind of balance where we are not so easily influenced by whether something is pleasant or unpleasant. Still, there is some obstacle, which is our own attachment to the feeling of meditation, of equanimity, to the resting or dwelling upon some object of attention. This is why Naropa said, "Son, you're not bound by perceiving, but by clinging. So cut your clinging, Naropa." This is a very important statement. You are not fettered by the perceived objects, you are fettered by clinging to them— so cut your clinging.

The point is to be free, to be liberated, right? That is why we train; we train in order to be free. But if the training makes us unfree, we are caught up in the method. First of all, we need to use the method to be free; next, we need to free of the method. If we have ink or dye on our hands, it's not enough to rinse our hands in water. We need to use a special soap or cleaning liquid, but we can't stop there — we have to rinse the soap away with water. Then the water has to be wiped off so that everything is gone, right? If we say, "I want to be free of the dirt, but I'll leave on the soap," that wouldn't be good enough. We need to be free of the soap as well. If we don't clean off the soap, that's just like having dirt on our hands.

Similarly, once we let be into the state of emptiness of rigpa, to keep holding onto this emptiness or to rigpa becomes a stumbling block as well. We need to be completely free, free like a knot tied on a snake, which is liberated by itself. The snake unties itself; it doesn't need someone else, some other agent to do it for it. In the same way, rigpa becomes free by itself, without using some extra technique, some extra method. By simply letting rigpa be as it is, then whatever covers it falls away, vanishes.

When you have a rosary and there is no knot on it, if you pull the string all the way out from the beads, everything falls apart. In the same way, when the fixating attitude of mind that holds onto the concept of 'me' is relinquished, everything dissolves. All the mental events, as well as the eighty innate states, or the 84,000 types of disturbing emotions, simultaneously fall apart. It's like chopping the trunk at the root so all the hundreds of thousands of twigs and leaves simultaneously wither. This is why rigpa is pointed out as the main method, the direct way to deal with any kind of disturbing emotions — because it has the ability to immediately dissolve that state. All the great masters, like Garab Dorje and Manjushrimitra, Shri Singha, Jnanasutra, and Padmasambhava, knew all the teachings of the buddhas. If there was some superior method, some more direct way, they would surely have given it.

We should also understand this teaching as an aspect of the naked state of dharmakaya. We say naked rigpa, naked awareness — why is it called naked? Because it is not covered by any kind of cover of conceptual mind. Conceptual mind or conceptual attitude is something that is formed, retained, and repeated many times. That is what we need to be free of; that is what we should learn how to relinquish.

Right now I am speaking as if we are all advanced meditators. Whether we are new to this or whether we are old hands at this doesn't matter right now. During this retreat there is no extra time left to get into all the details of the more materialistic or coarse states of mind. What we are dealing with now is the main point, the most subtle point.

Our natural state is covered by or occupied by a conceptual attitude, even though we call that meditation practice. That conceptual covering is what needs to be dissolved. Regardless of whether we practice sitting down or moving around, or whether we call it meditation or not, if we retain some conceptual focus that we are doing something in the meditation, that we are holding something in mind or dwelling on something, we possess a conceptual attitude. It is that attitude which obscures the nakedness of rigpa.

The main obstacle for rigpa is actually a 'rigpa imitation,' something that seems like, feels like and looks like rigpa, but isn't. The more similar it is to actual rigpa, the easier it is to be a hindrance. A state that is totally different from rigpa is more obvious and thus easier to get rid of. But if one uses a state that looks like rigpa to cover up rigpa, that is definitely an obstacle. We need to be free of clinging, free of attachment, free of reference point. It is said that this reference point or holding of a focus poisons the view. Here we are speaking in the context of Dzogchen, and not in terms of shamatha practice. In shamatha training one needs a focus. But shamatha is conceptual. Shamatha involves time, present time. One dwells on the present, on the nowness.

In recognizing rigpa we are jumping into the abyss, into the scary bottomlessness of timelessness — like hang-gliding through space. Immediately and totally let be, without focus, without reference point, without meditation object, without any concept held in mind. That's like jumping over the brink.

This teaching of the Great Perfection is very precious and profound, but whether the person who puts it into practice is also Dzogchen is not for sure. There are two types of Great Perfection; the Great Perfection as the natural state and the Great Perfection of the person, which is something personal, individual. The person him or herself needs to be the Great Perfection; the person needs to be Dzogchen.

It is not enough that the teaching is Dzogchen, because it already is! The teachings describe how the basic condition of everything already is. This is not our business, or rather, it does not require our meddling with that, because it is already perfect. Dzogchen exists totally independent as to whether we believe or don't believe, or whether we do something to it or not. The very basic nature of all things is already the Great Perfection, and that is independent of whether it is being spoken of or not spoken of, of whether I spend hours or days teaching it or not teaching it, of whether I quote from the *Tripitaka* or other scriptures, or not. None of this makes any difference whatsoever.

What makes a difference for us individually is whether we *are* the Great Perfection. That is what we have to be concerned with. This is our task. Do you understand this? To be the Great Perfection, we need to be free. We need to be free of dualistic fixation. We need to be free of ignorance. We need to free of confusion. We need to be free of perceiving something to be what it isn't. We need to be free of all that. But also, we need to be free of any view which is being used as a method to be free.

That is a very important point, which is why I'm repeating this. Many people are not free of that. They may be free from the coarser states of duality or holding onto objects, or free from holding on tightly to the five poisons. Other people are free to some extent from holding onto a perceiver. But still, the method of the view is something that is rarely let go of, totally. Most meditators are holding on for dear life to the view. That is why I have to repeat this. To kill someone with a sword of gold or a sword of copper makes no difference to the person whose head is chopped off. He still dies.

What is necessary is to attain freedom. People regard different states as being freedom. Some say the state of the meditation gods, the concentration levels of the *dhyanas*, is liberation. Beyond there are the four formless meditative states, which some people regard as liberation. Beyond that is the cessation of concepts, which is also regarded as liberation by some people. Still, all these states are still tied up in a method. It's like putting a cloth over the confusion — the subtle confusion is still retained.

To summarize, you need to be totally free of any clinging, like an utterly pure and cloudless sky. To be like that just for a second is very pleasant. Imagine this room in total, pitch-black darkness. If the light is switched on for just one second, that single second of illumination totally dispels the darkness, doesn't it? Or, imagine a cave in the depths of a mountain where not even a single sunbeam has ever penetrated for a hundred thousand years. If you go in there and switch on a torch, it doesn't matter how long that darkness has lasted — it is still dispelled in one instant.

> *No matter how long ego-clinging and obscurations,*
> *Negative karma and disturbing emotions,*
> *Have covered our nature,*
> *They are totally gone in that one instant*
> *Of genuinely recognizing the naked state of dharmakaya,*
> *Rigpa in actuality.*
> *Once you have some training in this,*
> *And if at the moment of death you recognize naked awareness,*
> *This body is discarded like a snake shedding its skin,*
> *And you are liberated.*

Do you understand about ground, path and fruition? Do you understand what is meant by path? What is path? It's okay to repeat what I said before.

STUDENT: Path is confusion.

RINPOCHE: What's the way to clear up this confusion? How many ways are there to clear up confusion?

STUDENT: Training. Meditation training. Conduct.

RINPOCHE: And? I mentioned these steps. Repeat them. It's okay.

STUDENT: Confidence.

RINPOCHE: Where does confidence come from?

STUDENT: From within.

RINPOCHE: How? From within what? From within the house?

STUDENT: From freedom.

RINPOCHE: Where does the freedom come from? Does it come from being confused? Does it come from being without confusion?

STUDENT: From seeing one's own nature.

RINPOCHE: Right. How is this nature?

STUDENT: It is rigpa.

RINPOCHE: What is rigpa?

STUDENT: Self-existing awareness.

RINPOCHE: What is self-existing awareness? It has three qualities. What are those three?

STUDENT: Empty, cognizant, and endowed with capacity.

RINPOCHE: Is there any sequence in those three?

STUDENT: No there is no sequence.

RINPOCHE: When I talk about them I seem to talk about them one after another. Why is that? What is meant by empty essence? What does the emptiness feel like when experiencing? I mentioned before no center, no edge. What was the second?

STUDENT: Cognizant nature.

RINPOCHE: What is that like? Just use baby talk, normal words.

STUDENT: All five sense doors wide are open, and everything is clearly known.

RINPOCHE: Knowing what? Knowing that the five senses are wide open, or knowing what? Knowing that the consciousness is clear, awake? Knowing what?

STUDENT: Knowing that there is no subject.

RINPOCHE: It sounds good. The words sound good. The third quality, what's the third?

STUDENT: Unimpeded.

RINPOCHE: What does that mean?

STUDENT: All appearances, perceptions, and experiences are unimpeded.

RINPOCHE: What's the connection between this unimpededness and the first two qualities? Is there a connection?

STUDENT: The emptiness and the cognizance are united.

RINPOCHE: And how does that feel like?

STUDENT: Anything can arise.

RINPOCHE: What does that feel like in experience? Actually, there is no separate third quality. It's simply the unity of the first two, because the first two are indivisible. That indivisibility is described as a third quality, but it's not something separate at all. Honestly, the third is not a third. In fact, there are no two either. All three are simply one quality. What is that called?

STUDENT: Panoramic awareness, like wide-screen awareness.

RINPOCHE: Could you come up with a Tibetan word for it?

STUDENT: I don't know Tibetan.

TRANSLATOR: I believe we have used one particular Tibetan word quite a lot.

STUDENT: Rigpa.

RINPOCHE: Rigpa is good enough. You're not to blame if you don't know Tibetan and you're new to this. How many qualities does rigpa have? It's all right to say the three qualities just mentioned. [Laughter.] What about these three qualities? In the moment of recognizing, do we recognize them one by one, or what?

STUDENT: No.

RINPOCHE: But in terms of time?

STUDENT: Simultaneously.

RINPOCHE: That's true. That's what we should know. When the three qualities are present simultaneously, at once, that can be called rigpa. Do you understand this? They are present at the same time, which is not really a time, but we can call it timelessness. Really, it's timeless time. It can be called by another word also.

STUDENT: View.

RINPOCHE: View of what? Or by what? What knows this view? Rigpa knows. What is rigpa? Rigpa is something that has three qualities. Knowing these three qualities at once simultaneously is called rigpa. That we can also call the view. The view is used in all the different vehicles. But what is the Dzogchen view? The view in Dzogchen is rigpa, which is the simultaneous knowing that your essence is empty, your nature is cognizant, and your capacity is unconfined. Do you understand this? Is this clear? So, what is the training or meditation?

STUDENT: Sustaining the continuity.

RINPOCHE: What needs to be sustained?

STUDENT: Unfabricated naturalness.

RINPOCHE: What is that?

STUDENT: Thought-free.

RINPOCHE: What's that? What about rigpa? Wouldn't it be okay to sustain rigpa? Don't you like the word sustain?

STUDENT: It seems like there is some effort in sustaining.

RINPOCHE: What about effortless sustaining? Would that be okay?

STUDENT: Yes, that's okay.

RINPOCHE: The continuity of that needs to be sustained. This is the continuity. *(Rinpoche rings the bell.)*

First, by some effort, there's a hitting together. There's sound. That means you've arrived in rigpa. The three qualities are continually present, and that is called sustaining. After all, you have to use some word to describe it. That sustaining is what we call meditation. *(Rinpoche rings the bell again.)*

After hitting you, leave it. Right? You're not continuing to keep, you're not holding on, right? This is the sustaining of the undistracted nonmeditation. Now, what is meant by conduct, or putting to use? Earlier I mentioned view, meditation and conduct, quite a few times. What do you understand by conduct? When is it needed? What is it?

STUDENT: Post-meditation.

RINPOCHE: Can somebody else answer? You don't have to say more than two words, really, but if you need to, say as much as you want to say.

STUDENT: As soon as one is distracted, to arrive back in awareness effortlessly.

RINPOCHE: That sounds really good. If you can arrive back in rigpa without effort, that's first-class. I didn't expect that much. If you said something like, "To deliberately remind yourself to arrive back in rigpa," that would be good enough. Even that would be first-class. But someone training in the way that you expressed means that you're almost at the point of stability in rigpa. All objects of distraction have dissolved into the innate nature.

CONFIDENCE

THE DZOGCHEN VIEW IS ESTABLISHED through three steps: recognizing, developing the strength of that recognition, and finally attaining stability in it. The great knowledge-holder Garab Dorje expressed how to become grounded in this recognition in three brief sentences:

Recognize your own nature.
Decide on one point.
Gain confidence in liberation.

When we are really familiar with these three points, we can say we have truly recognized. That is the basis for the view in Dzogchen.

The first point, recognize your own nature, means recognize what you already are, what you already have — *dharmata*. Recognizing in the sense of acknowledging that that which knows is placeless, objectless and rootless. Seeing this in actuality is what is meant by recognizing your own nature. As we grow more familiar with this recognition through our own training, a conviction grows out of our experience, that this actually works, this is what solves the problem, this is what dissolves the confusion. When this certainty comes from within, we can feel sure, and this is the second step, deciding or resolving on one point.

The third point is being confident. No matter what we do there is a moment, a time when we become self-confident. We have some natural assurance that what we are doing actually is working. For example, if we are doing business, this self-confidence arises when we are successful, when we make a profit from our investment. When we know that we are doing good business, and something is actually coming out of it, we can relax in ourselves and feel confident that the effort we have put out actually worked in the way we intended.

Where does this self-confidence come about in meditation? It comes from within oneself. We find that we can be free by simply resting in natural awareness, by simply letting be. That is how to liberate any disturbing emotion, any thought, any habitual tendency. Just like a drawing upon water which vanishes as soon as it is made, we discover that a thought can be liberated simultaneously with its arising. It is free without anything gained or lost, and there is no anxiety about that. When this kind of confidence grows from within, then we have reached the third point, gaining confidence in liberation.

This freedom in which we feel such confidence consists in knowing that everything in samsara — all situations and all states — are nothing other than a conceptual frame of mind. Habitual tendencies, disturbing emotions, the three realms, the lower realms, and even the hells are nothing other than habitual ways of perceiving. When we feel confident that any kind of disturbing emotion, conceptual state or habitual tendency can be liberated through this practice, we gain immense self-confidence, both temporarily and ultimately.

A yogi, meaning a real practitioner, needs to have this kind of confidence, the confidence of being able to free himself or herself in all possible situations that might arise during this lifetime, as well as at the time of death and through any of the bardo experiences. If we can do that, then when we face the bardo we will not be deluded by our own perceptions. Having that kind of guts or natural courage, being totally fearless, not intimidated by anything whatsoever, that kind of self-confidence is necessary. You can call it guts, you can call it courage, you can call it certainty, you can call it confidence, self-confidence, but what it means is something which is natural, which comes about from within. It is not the kind of artificial courage from having some support to back us up, because we line up something all around us so that we can feel safe and secure.

The Khampas of eastern Tibet are known as people who are ready to fight, warriors who have guts. But there are different kinds of courage.

Some people who are not really that brave make a big show by carrying all kinds of weaponry — rifles and swords and long knives and short knives — and wearing them all on the outside for everyone to see. But honestly, those kind of props are only a show. Someone who needs all that pomp is not really that brave.

A truly brave warrior may only have a small knife in his sleeve, but if it comes to a fight, his attitude is clear: "I have no hesitation, I will set straight what needs to be set straight." That kind of self-confidence does not have to make any show of itself. The other person is busy taking out the rifles and long knives, polishing and oiling them, pushing his chest out and squaring his shoulders, and so forth. This kind of outward display of courage is only necessary if one doesn't really feel it from within.

In the same way, a genuine meditator, a yogi who has real confidence, can remain in a small room totally relaxed and at ease, feeling assured that, "No matter what experience I will encounter, no matter what happens at the time of death and the bardo, I know how to be free. I know how to liberate all kinds of states of mind that may occur. I have no fear, I am not intimidated in any way whatsoever." From the outside, the person may look very relaxed and simple. Another meditator may dress up in all kinds of fancy attire, and prop himself up with conceptual thoughts like, "I am a Dzogchen meditator, I know the view. I have practiced a lot. I can do this and that." This artificial way of building up courage is totally unnecessary for a meditator with real confidence.

We need confidence, otherwise we cannot really be free. And this confidence only comes about through some experience of being free. We need to have some sense of freedom, otherwise that confidence doesn't come. Free of what? Free of thought. What is thought? Thought is habitual tendency. What is habitual tendency? Karma. Karma and habitual tendency together are called confused experience. That is what we need to be free of.

How to be free? Recognize self-existing awareness. After recognizing self-existing awareness, we need to settle that this is it. We need to feel sure about it. How does this certainty arise, and where do we get it from? Through training, through practice. Where does the practice come from? It comes through recognizing. Where does the recognizing come from? It comes from receiving pointing-out instructions from a master, and from one's own effort in practice. It's not something we are given by a master; rather, the master shows you what you already have by pointing it out.

What do you need to do? You need to acknowledge, you need to recognize what you have: "Oh yeah, I've got it." We need to know this. After knowing it, we need to take charge of it nicely. Not by wrapping it up in a lovely piece of cloth and locking it up in a treasure chest or a safe deposit box, or by putting it on the shelf next to the other books, but by growing used to it. How do we grow used to it? By being un-distracted while now meditating. Undistracted nonmeditation — that is crucial, because if we meditate, that is conceptual, and if we get dis-tracted, that is delusion. When we train in a way in which we don't meditate by holding a focus, and at the same time we don't allow our attention to wander off in distraction, that is what is called true pres-ence of mind, true mindfulness.

This true mindfulness is the single sufficient king. We can also call that equanimity, the meditation state. Equanimity literally means 'placing evenly.' What is placed evenly? It is rigpa, awareness. Placing rigpa in evenness means leaving it alone. It's not placing it as being aware of something other. Just leave your awareness as it is, alone. It's not a sense of nowness; nor is it a sense of the past or the future. Rather, it is something which embraces past, present and future, which embraces the nowness but is not the nowness itself.

In terms of seeing, it is not the seeing of a thing with concrete at-tributes, because the ground does not possess any concrete attributes. That is why it is said that "seeing of no thing is the supreme sight." When seeing in this way, one needs to have trust that this is it. Other-wise, one will think, "There's something other to see, something I haven't seen yet." And that is a mistake.

When we train in this way, further and further, sustaining this continuity, whatever thoughts and habitual tendencies take place simply dissolve; they are liberated. That is how to gain confidence in liberation. In short, this is called recognizing the true view. Having recognized the true view, we train again and again, not by meditating with a focus, and not by being distracted, but by being more and more undistracted, yet less and less focused. The state of rigpa starts to last longer and longer. The moments of confusion become shorter and shorter.

We train in short moments, repeated many times. It's like collecting water drops in a bucket, one after the other ... drip ... drip ... drip. Leave a bucket under the tap the whole night, and in the morning the bucket is full. In the same way, we need to kind of "collect" authentic moments of rigpa, again and again. It's not so helpful to train in a way where one is not really sure or certain, but is always thinking, "Maybe this is it." That is called double delusion: first one is deluded in general, and on top of that one is training in extra delusion. Don't do that!

Developing the strength through training means we grow through the stage called 'innate nature in actuality,' or 'manifest dharmata.' Next comes 'increased experience.' After that is 'awareness reaching fullness,' or 'culmination of awareness.' Finally one reaches what is called the 'exhaustion of phenomena and concepts.' That you can call real stability. At that point, there is no longer any such thing as letting be into equanimity and rising from equanimity into post-meditation. Such divisions no longer exist.

The dividing point we experience between the meditation state and post-meditation is made by confused experience. When confused experience dissolves, that is called the meditation state. When confused experience reoccurs, that is called post-meditation. When confusion is purified, dissolved, there is no dividing point between meditation and post-meditation. Even when looking for a confused state, you won't find one!

At the same time, whatever appears is perceived exactly as it is. While being undeluded oneself, one perceives the delusion of others. That is how the Buddha-mind is. Imagine there are two people in the same room: one is asleep and is dreaming, the other is awake and has clairvoyant powers that allow him to know the minds of others. The clairvoyant person knows what the sleeping person is dreaming, whether it be elephants, men, women, houses, or whatever. The clairvoyant person knows exactly what the first person is dreaming — but he doesn't have to be asleep and dreaming himself in order to know. In the same way, a buddha, without being deluded himself, can know the delusion of all other beings very exactly and precisely, through the wisdom that perceives whatever can possibly exist.

That is what is called Buddhist enlightenment. It is not necessarily other types of enlightenment. Buddhist enlightenment is when a meditator has gone through the four stages of innate nature in actuality, increased experience, awareness reaching fullness, and the exhaustion of concepts and phenomena. At that point, what was previously the ground has been realized as the dharmakaya of fruition, and the sambhogakaya and nirmanakaya are manifested in order to act for the welfare of other beings.

Because sentient beings are uncountable, numberless, the emanation bodies, the magical creations of nirmanakayas to benefit others, are also beyond count. The example often given is that in the one hundred billion universes there are one hundred billion different emanations of Padmasambhava. This is what is called 'the realization of dharmakaya for self, and the manifestation of rupakaya for the welfare of others.' That is the ultimate attainment, the complete purification of all delusion.

STUDENT: How is it possible to benefit other beings by training in emptiness?

RINPOCHE: Right now we are still on the path, and at present we need to train in rigpa as the single sufficient king. No matter what problem we encounter, no matter what situation we are in, the recognition of rigpa can solve everything. Everything is included within rigpa as a spontaneous presence. Honestly, everything is included within rigpa. Renunciation and compassion are included within rigpa. Because within this state of being wide awake and holding onto no thing, there is a natural reaching out towards all sentient beings. There is no turning away from other beings, no turning one's back on beings or forsaking anyone.

Also, there is a deep appreciation of the very source of this instruction on how to recognize. There is a deep appreciation of the transmission of the teaching through the lineage. That is devotion.

The letting be without reference point, the recognition of empty essence, itself perfects the accumulation of wisdom. At the same time, there is no blocking off. All experienced perception unfolds unobstructedly — that is the accumulation of merit with reference point. The simple training in rigpa itself without any effort whatsoever — that is the perfection of the completion stage. Everything is perceived vividly and clearly, without holding onto any substantiality, without fixating on anything. The perfection of the development stage is that there is no division made between the perceived and things being empty. In this way, all aspects of practice are effortlessly and spontaneously perfected within the training of rigpa, within the authentic state of rigpa.

So, how is it possible to benefit other beings by training in emptiness? It's because the nature of emptiness, this unformed nature of mind, is identical in buddhas and in all sentient beings, including ourselves. We are naturally connected with everyone, and by the training in the recognition of emptiness, we actualize this connection with all sentient beings. As a matter of fact, we are connected not only with other sentient beings, but with all enlightened ones — all buddhas, all lineage masters, and so forth. In the moment of simply letting be in the nature of emptiness, we are connected with them.

It's like all the enlightened masters, all buddhas, are connected to this electric wire of emptiness. All we need to do is to leave the switch on. The moment that we flip the switch on — the moment we disengage from being occupied with thoughts of past, present and future, with any conceptual frame of mind — we are naturally on, naturally electrified, and the current of blessings automatically flows through from all buddhas. At this point there's no barrier; nothing to block the flow. We're already connected through the nature of unformed emptiness.

This is also exactly how sentient beings are benefited through your realization of emptiness. If you want to truly benefit other beings, simply let be in the state of rigpa without any focus whatsoever. That is how to be *on*, how to be connected, so to speak. It's like when you switch a tape recorder on. All its activities and functions take place quite naturally. It will record, it will play, whatever — but only if the button is on. Our job, our task is to simply be on.

To continue the analogy, what is the electricity? It ignites when we remain in the nowness, free of the thoughts of the three times. We already have the wiring, but the ends of the wires need to connect. The way to reconnect the wires is by receiving the pointing-out instruction from a master, and recognizing. Some knowing of how it is occurs at that point, which is the current flowing through the connected wires. What we need to do is to stay on, shining brightly at all times.

STUDENT: If recognizing the essence is the single sufficient method for attaining enlightenment, what is the role of other methods, like the preliminary practices and yidam practices?

RINPOCHE: Their role depends entirely on the individual. If the training in simplicity is sufficient for you, that is fine, it is okay. But if it isn't, you may feel the urge for more elaboration and detail. Some people are not happy with straight simplicity; they don't feel that this is enough, and therefore they need to do other, more elaborate practices. For some people, it's only by going through more elaborations that they become more and more simple, until they finally reach full simplicity.

We can know this very easily by examining ourselves. Are we totally satisfied with the explanations I have given of what our experience is? Can we be with it? Are we totally convinced on how to continue the training, without a speck of doubt remaining? If we are completely at ease and comfortable with that, it's fine. But if we start to wonder about what actually is the basic ground, about the nature of confusion and how it happens and how to deal with it, then all these suspicions, doubts and uncertainties will come up and disturb our practice. We need to have our questions answered; we need to get more details. If we are like that, we should seek out more details in order to be satisfied.

The Nagi Gompa retreat is mainly taught for older students, by which I mean students who have already done the preliminary practices, and who have already done or are involved in yidam practice. Rigpa is pointed out in addition to this, not as a substitute or a replacement; but as a way of showing what is real. Don't be attached to these methods.

But there are also some new people here who I feel may benefit from hearing teachings that give an idea of rigpa, a taste of it. Later on, when these people begin the preliminaries or yidam practice, they will put these practices into the framework of rigpa. They will know how to fit them into the context of rigpa. We need to get to the point of integrating the two approaches, either by starting training from above, from the perspective of rigpa, or from below, with particular practices which we fit into the context of rigpa. It sounds like you have started from the top instead of from the bottom. Still there remains some bottom to be integrated. There is still some buttocks to be explained!

STUDENT: How does resting meditation combat disturbing emotions?

RINPOCHE: When we get totally caught up in a strong disturbing emotion, it doesn't help that much to have trained in some resting or stillness. However, the training in stillness does make it more difficult for disturbing emotions to arise quite so strongly.

STUDENT: My thinking is rigpa.

RINPOCHE: It isn't rigpa. Thinking rigpa is an idea, right? It does help a little. Because that idea occupies you from having another idea. Otherwise it doesn't help that much, it doesn't liberate. It doesn't allow for the primordially pure unimpededness of basic space. It helps a little bit. It is like when you are really hungry, imagine you are eating food and imagine that you already ate and it tasted good. Breath in and hold it a little bit and imagine that your stomach is full. It does help a little bit; it eases the hunger slightly. But you haven't really eaten, so your hunger has not gone. You are only imagining that your state is rigpa. You engender a feeling of confidence that this is rigpa while it actually isn't. You show off a little bit; you walk around as if you were embodying the state of rigpa. It occupies your mind, but because you are already occupied, it is more difficult to be occupied by another disturbing emotion, a small one. But if it comes really strongly, the whole thing collapses, because it was an imitation. It is not unimpeded. The main crucial point is the unimpededness.

A lot of people train in a way that they confine their awareness to either being vacant, or being conscious of something. Or they try being absentminded or oblivious, try to confine themselves to being the unknowing quality of the all-ground. That 'confinement training' doesn't allow them to be totally open, unimpeded. In the same way, dwelling on the nowness and convincing oneself this is the awakened state and being totally focused on the nowness, being in the present, that is a way of confining awareness. It automatically blocks off the intrinsic qualities of the enlightened state. You can't really be blamed for doing that; it does happen. We do it, others do it, it happens like that. But the important thing is how to deal with it. Because even if we sit and think, "This is rigpa," if you don't hold onto that thought either, it also clears; it vanishes, slowly, slowly, and the real rigpa is present. This is something that is eliminated through practice, not through learning and reflection.

Any other questions? The nuns? You must have listened really well.

STUDENT: In this song *Calling the Guru from Afar* which we recite by Jamgön Lodrö Thaye which says "Though thought is the dharmakaya, I didn't recognize it." How do I recognize it?

RINPOCHE: A thought becomes the dharmakaya only when recognizing the real nature of what the thought is. As a matter of fact, there is no real thought, ever, it only seems like there is a thought of something. It is this seeming presence that fools us into believing that actual thoughts are taking place. If one really looks into what a thought is there is no thing there whatsoever. It is more *as if* there is something. You can say that a thought is a mask, it is like a fake expression of rigpa, it is like an imitation of what rigpa actually is, like making a face. It is not the real thing. Because there is the real thing is it possible to be mistaken about the imitation. In this way, because there is rigpa, we can say that there are thoughts. It is because of rigpa that there is the thinking mind, because of dharmakaya there is all-ground, like that. If one is really clear about what thought is, then thought is dharmakaya. But because such a statement could create some confusion, it is often better to say that the identity or the essence of thought is dharmakaya.

I did actually hint at this before, the day before yesterday I was speaking of that, at some point the seeming movement of thought is no longer experienced as a real thought, that it is the play or the unfolding of original wakefulness. Otherwise it would be that the Buddha would have no awareness, that the Buddha would be totally oblivious of anything; not have any idea what is going on anywhere. That is not the state that we are training to be like. The omniscient wisdom of a buddha is aware of everything that takes place, and that awareness is not like a concrete thought, but yet everything is perceived. Every little detail. You could say that this awareness is a thought, but it is better to say that it is the play of basic wakefulness.

Other questions?

STUDENT: Can rigpa manifest without being recognized?

RINPOCHE: Yes that is possible. It does happen, because rigpa is our innate nature. Sometimes we are not occupied by thinking something in the past, sometimes there is no thought of the future, there is no thought of the present. We are in a moment without thought, but it is not recognized as being rigpa. It does happen again and again during one day. Unless there is some knowing of what it is, it doesn't help. It is as if my throne is made of pure gold and but I am unaware of it, it doesn't help much that it is gold. Say I'm really poor and have no money to buy food. I may be about to starve to death, but because I don't acknowledge that I'm sitting on a huge piece of gold; it doesn't help me much. In the same way, rigpa or dharmakaya is never separate from oneself, not even for one instant. It is always with ourselves, but it is not recognized.

Here's an example *(Rinpoche holds up a book with a piece of paper tucked inside)*. Imagine this piece of paper is like is a small piece of rigpa. Now it is completely hidden inside the book. This is just like not recognizing it. Rigpa is a piece of dharmakaya, however. The principle here is that a piece of dharmakaya can be revealed, but it is still covered by habit *(Rinpoche moves the paper so that more of it is revealed)*. The training here is not in turning the pages until full rigpa is revealed. It's more a sense of letting or allowing it to be increasingly revealed.

STUDENT: I'm confused about the subject-object relationship.

RINPOCHE: To state it in general terms, it comes about because of mistaking something for being what is not. Dharmakaya is not only dharmakaya when you acknowledge it to be so. It's like gold: whether you know it's gold or not, it's still gold. But if the dharmakaya is not recognized by rigpa, it doesn't help us. In the moment of recognizing, a small piece of gold is visible. All the rest of the gold is still covered by habit. Recognizing rigpa slowly removes the rest of the covering. Rigpa has the quality of being cognizant. Knowing all three of its qualities simultaneously is rigpa. That is one piece, one corner, of dharmakaya.

STUDENT: I seem to lose some physical feeling when I recognize rigpa. Am I really recognizing or not?

RINPOCHE: What you experience doesn't mean that it isn't genuine a state of rigpa. It's simply that the physical sensations are not so strong or immediately present. It's very difficult to be as if there is no body from the very beginning. The different aspects of sensation, perception, formations and cognitions need to slowly and gradually be purified.

How you're practicing is probably okay. The technique is to recognize, then totally let be. Drop everything. That is enough. You don't have to recheck afterwards to make sure it is rigpa. It could be rigpa, or maybe not — it doesn't matter so much in that moment. We don't need to be as precise as a computer programmer, who has no room for error. It's not like either it is or it isn't, and if it isn't, you have to do something else to make sure. You just recognize, and totally let be. Sooner or later it will be the real thing. It's okay if sometimes it is the real thing, and sometimes it isn't. You don't have to impale rigpa on a spear to make sure you've nailed it down.

Sometimes recognition happens beautifully and immediately. Sometimes you create a cloud of concepts, and at that moment you are enveloped in clouds, in thoughts. But it doesn't really matter whether you are successful or not successful on any one particular occasion. If you carry on your training, all the different stuff that can happen will slowly wear off or clear up, like rust being removed from copper.

Sometimes it might seem really difficult to be free. It might seem like you are immediately caught up in thoughts. At that time it can be very useful to exclaim PHAT very strongly, slap your hands hard down on your knees, and drop everything. Don't get caught up in slapping yourself and how that feels like, either — it's only a method to interrupt the formation of thought. Thoughts are always something formed. Because they are conditioned, they can easily be interrupted and broken apart. It's a way of creating a short interruption, of abruptly cutting the flow of conceptualizing. At that moment you need to let be and recognize, recognize rigpa. If that doesn't happen, we might just as well use electric shock therapy! The point is not the shock that interrupts the thoughts, but rather that you need to recognize your basic nature.

Scattering the cloud of thought is not the main point here. Recognizing and letting that state continue, that is the main thing. Although we use the word 'recognize,' you don't have to stick to that word either. It's not like something is being recognized by something else. What it means is to simply *let be* in that state. Sometimes the Buddha would cease speaking and remain silent. Why? Because anything said is still a superficial form of Dharma. Any spoken word belongs to relative truth. In order to illustrate that point, sometimes the Buddha would remain in silence. Silence is also a teaching. To quote from the *Praise to Prajnaparamita*:

> *Transcendent knowledge is beyond thought, word and description.*
> *It neither arises nor ceases, like the identity of space.*
> *It is the domain of individual, self-knowing wakefulness.*
> *To this mother of the buddhas of the three times, I pay homage.*

These lines refer to the domain of original wakefulness, not the domain of conceptual frame of mind. Why is this original wakefulness called "this mother of the buddhas of the three times"? It is because of realizing this that all the buddhas of the three times became awakened. It is because of this that all the buddhas of the future and present are awakening or will awaken. It's not like there's an actual mother who gives birth to a baby that becomes a buddha, or that there is one big mother who is the literal mother of all the buddhas. Rather, being a buddha means free of confusion, and your individual, self-knowing wakefulness, that is the way to be free, is like this mother.

Who hasn't asked anything at all yet?

STUDENT: Are the three kayas present in a moment of rigpa?

RINPOCHE: To say that the three kayas are included in rigpa means that their seed potential or a piece of the fully formed kayas is present. The empty essence is the seed of dharmakaya, the cognizant nature is the seed of sambhogakaya, and the unconfined capacity is the seed of nirmanakaya. It is not yet the full-fledged three kayas; I am not saying that. The moment of rigpa is a piece of the ground. It is also a piece of the fruition, the final result. It is like the link between the ground and fruition. To be a link to the fruition means that something of the fruition is already present.

How are the three kayas of the fruition present in a moment of rigpa? The emptiness of your essence is how the dharmakaya is already present, and therefore included. The cognizant quality of your nature is how sambhogakaya is included. And the final quality of nirmanakaya, which is unimpeded or unconfined, sending out and reabsorbing, and always acting for the welfare of beings without any obstruction, is already present right now as your unconfined capacity. Unconfined means that perceiving and being empty is not confined to one or the other. That is what we chant in the innermost refuge. (*Rinpoche sings the refuge lines from the Kunzang Tuktig terma teaching*):

In the empty essence, dharmakaya ॐ
In the cognizant nature, sambhogakaya ॐ

And in the manifold capacity, nirmanakaya ⁙
I take refuge until enlightenment. ⁙

What this really means is that at the time of the ground, right now, your empty essence is what will be the perfect dharmakaya. Your cognizant nature is what will be the perfected sambhogakaya, and your unconfined capacity is what will be the perfect nirmanakaya. Therefore, since this is so, we say we will place our trust in these three qualities. Do you understand? What about the rest of you, do you understand? What about it?

STUDENT: Does this mean that in the future the three kayas will manifest?

RINPOCHE: Where are you now, right now? When you recognize rigpa right now and your obscurations are purified, and later on as you go along, what will you be when your obscurations are purified? Right now you are doing business, you have a job. If your business goes really well and is very successful, with more and more money coming in, what will you be?

STUDENT: Wealthy.

RINPOCHE: Yes, wealthy. When will that happen?

STUDENT: As I gather more and more and work more.

RINPOCHE: In the same way, as we train further and further in this, the obscurations are increasingly purified, until there is total freedom from obscurations. That is in the future. But what the future will be is based on what is now. What's your name?

STUDENT: Joel.

RINPOCHE: So we are talking about the present Joel, who in the future will be a buddha. We are not talking about the dharmakaya or the Great Perfection right now. We need to know a little bit more about the relative and ultimate level. Right now you are mainly occupied by relative truth; you are still on this side. You are not on the ultimate side, yet. There is still time. There is still the notion of time, right?

STUDENT: Yes.

RINPOCHE: We are talking about the Great Perfection of the person. In the Great Perfection itself, there is no past, present and future; nothing to be purified. But that's not our business. It's very easy to test what stage of the path you are on right now. Put your finger in a flame. If it hurts, you are still on the path! Or, make a small slice on your hand with a knife. If you are at the stage of final fruition, there is actually nothing being cut in your experience, because all conditioned phenomena have been purified. If not, it will definitely hurt.

Quite a few people these days claim to be enlightened. It's easy to test this claim by throwing them off of a high-rise, or into the middle of a big lake. Plenty of people have wrong views! It's all right to say "I am someone who has gone through part of the path and have some realization." But if you say, "I am enlightened; I am a buddha," or "I am beyond practice, I don't have to go through further training, I am beyond confusion," you are implying there is not a speck of confusion left in your stream-of-being, that you are not harmed by anything; not by any form, sound, smell, taste or texture, nothing at all.

Some spiritual teachers these days actually think they are enlightened. Of course, there are some who may just pretend to be enlightened, who act as if they are enlightened in front of others, but inside they know that they aren't. But I'm referring to the people who have actually convinced themselves that they are a buddha, a fully awakened one. They actually believe it. Their understanding of enlightenment is of something very tiny. That is not the Buddhist enlightenment. Maybe it's some kind of enlightenment, but it's not the Buddhist version.

The word 'enlightenment' is of course not Buddhist, but is English and applied by Westerners. The Tibetan term for enlightenment is *sangye,* which is also the term for Buddha. It means totally purified from all obscurations. Please be clear on this point and don't confuse enlightenment for anything else.

(A dog barks from outside) — The dog said it was enlightened! *(laughter)*

(The dog barks again) — Who knows? Maybe the dog thinks it is enlightened. It could be a rebirth of someone who thought he was enlightened! *(laughter)*

DIGNITY

TULKU URGYEN RINPOCHE was my father, but he was also my teacher. He gave many people a lot of instructions, using many methods. At first glance he looked just like any other old man, but his mind was that of a great Dzogchen yogi. He would use all kinds of different methods to make us understand. In particular, he would teach mind-to-mind. There are three main ways of teaching, called the mind transmission of the victorious ones, the sign transmissions of knowledge-holders and the oral transmission of masters. The first involves mind-to-mind transmission; the second teachings using gestures or symbols, and the third using words.

I don't have to praise aloud the high realization of my father, because many other masters have done this already. I don't have to add to that. But looking at Tulku Urgyen Rinpoche's behavior could teach us something as well; there is something to learn from examining his life. Before Tulku Urgyen died in 1996, I had the fortune to spend a few months with him, and during this time I became very clearly aware of how he conducted himself. There is a certain kind of natural compassion in someone who truly realizes emptiness, and Tulku Urgyen had this kind of great compassion. Through witnessing it, I felt I could better understand how compassion unfolds out of the understanding of emptiness.

Tulku Urgyen was quite sick in the last months; so sick that actually he should have been lying down and receiving oxygen. He had severe heart problems, but he didn't exclude anyone from his heart. He didn't forsake anyone, even up to his last breath. That is a sign of a true bodhisattva. A bodhisattva is someone who never forsakes other beings, never leaves them behind, never excludes them from his experience. Tulku Urgyen would always be teaching and receiving people, even when he was really sick. Even though he was not quite up to doing so, he would come and sit by his window and wave to people and give them an audience, although it was very difficult for him to even sit up. That's a sign of a true bodhisattva. Someone who has realized emptiness is naturally compassionate, and doesn't close off and become concerned with only him or herself. Like "Now I don't feel so well. I don't want to face anything, I don't want to see anybody, I don't want to do anything." Rinpoche was never like that, not even on the very last day of his life.

Rinpoche had a several health attendants, including American and German doctors, a western medical assistant and a few nuns. They emphasized that he needed to rest and tried to restrict his visitors. When they were present, Rinpoche was not permitted to see anybody. My brother and I have small children, and they were also prohibited from visiting their grandfather. Still, as soon as these attendants were out of the way, Tulku Urgyen Rinpoche would send for someone. He would instruct a different attendant to fetch the children, and would give them a hug or some sweets. He would call for other people as well, to see them or give them a few words of advice.

In the end he was extremely sick and in a lot of pain, but I don't think he ever had the thought, "I don't want to relate to anyone, I don't want to share any teachings, I don't want to be disturbed." I feel that kind of thought never entered Rinpoche's mind. He was like that until the last breath. That is a sign of a bodhisattva. Through that, one can catch a glimpse of the kind of master such a person is.

When I compare myself with Tulku Urgyen I can see a huge difference, and through this I understand something more about realization. Even though Tulku Urgyen was really sick, he was more concerned with others than with himself. If someone came to visit, he wouldn't talk about how sick he felt or how bad his health was. He would always ask how the other person felt and try to help them or teach them. Such selfless behavior is possible through experience and realization.

Tulku Urgyen Rinpoche lived in a simple way. He was very simple inside, so he didn't have to make a lot of fuss about his life. Still, he was able to do a tremendous amount. He built a lot of monasteries and gave many teachings and empowerments, to other masters as well. Yet he himself lived very simply, and because of that he never got tired of carrying out Dharma activities. Many of us make our lives very complicated with all the thoughts and ideas we have. If our thinking is very complex, even a small task can become too much. Even if we manage to carry it out, we find it quite tiring, quite exhausting. The opposite of this is very simple thinking, a very open and simple mind, which allows great activity. I have read about that kind of personality often in the teachings, in books, but Tulku Urgyen Rinpoche exemplified it. His life shows the need to be simple from within. Then, even if you do complicated work, it's okay. To supplicate the root and lineage gurus means to actually aspire to be realized like them, to use them as examples for how to be.

I feel that it was a great help for me to actually witness personally how Tulku Urgyen was. I was there when he died. Both before and after he fell ill, I never heard him say, "I don't want to help someone." He never expressed that. That's what a bodhisattva is.

A real practitioner is at ease in any situation, no matter where. Along with being at ease, there is some sense of being happy, but sad at the same time, kind of tender, in the sense of being weary of or disenchanted with samsara. Even if samsara has been left behind, there is still weariness with the entirety of samsara. This tenderness embodies devotion and compassion. This tenderness is what causes one to not turn one's back to even a single sentient being. To think, "I can't stand these people, they are annoying. I want to go home to my own retreat hut and be comfortable," means that one is turning one's back on sentient beings.

Tulku Urgyen Rinpoche would always see people, especially people who had come from far away, even when he was in retreat. It never occurred to him to exclude beings who wanted to have contact with him. He never had the attitude to exclude others. Even when he was so sick he could hardly take one step on his own, he had his attendants prop him up in front of his window so he could wave goodbye to people who had come to see him.

That was very annoying for some of the people taking care of him. They would say, "Rinpoche, why are you like that? Why can't you behave and not see people, it is for your own good." But now we realize it only shows his bodhisattva activity. He never considered himself as more important, but always held others to be more important that himself. Even when he couldn't walk or sit up by himself and had to be helped and supported, he would still pay attention to others, asking who each person was and where they came from. Usually when we are sick we are not like that at all, are we? We lock the door from the inside and we don't let anyone in because we want to be comfortable. In fact, we get angry when people come. When Rinpoche heard someone was coming, on the other hand, he was happy.

A lot of you met Tulku Urgyen Rinpoche, and you could see what he did for himself — not much. He was happy with very little, a very simple way of living. He didn't take much care or do much for himself at all. But on the other hand, he did a lot in his life. He accomplished a lot of activity, he did a lot of things, but all of it was for others. He never gave up on anyone or turned his back on anyone. Up until the time he drew his last breath, he was acting for the welfare of others. It's not easy to be a genuine bodhisattva, only concerned with others.

Tulku Urgyen was really like that. When very ill, he both directly and indirectly made himself available for others, even though he knew he might die in one or two days. To be so totally unselfish is very difficult. I spent a lot of time with Rinpoche, and I never saw him even once show any irritation with the prospect of having to meet somebody. And he would often see people from six in the morning until nine at night.

Right now we are not talking about what Tulku Urgyen's realization was, his view, his way of meditating, and so forth. Let's totally set those aside. What I do know is what I saw — how he behaved, his behavior. We should take this example to heart. Make the wish, "May I be like such a bodhisattva." Sometimes, when we train in the view and when our meditation is good, we should recall the life example of masters like that. To sum up, the more loose and free you can be inside, the more deeply relaxed and open, the better. To the extent that this freedom arises from within, we can help others that much more.

AFTERWORD

WHEN YOU'VE READ THIS BOOK and you want to take something with you, take this view, meditation, conduct. You need to know what these mean. We may not know what the ground is, we may not know how it is at the time of fruition. However, we do know that right now during the path there is confusion. In order to deal with and be free of confusion, we need view, meditation and conduct. We need to know what these mean and how to practice. A famous summary of Buddhist teachings says,

Do not commit any evil,
Do what is perfectly virtuous,
Fully tame your own mind.
That is the teaching of the Buddha.

What I have taught in this book is chiefly about the third line — how to tame your own mind, fully tame your own mind. That doesn't exclude the first two. Of course, we should follow the general principle of avoiding what causes harm to others, what is negative, and what is unwholesome. Also, through our thoughts, words, and deeds, we should try our best to be of help to others, to carry out the first five of the six *paramitas*. When it comes to taming our own mind, when it comes to being free from within, these three points — view, meditation and conduct — are indispensable. You should really know how to train in these.

Honestly, if we truly tame our own mind, not only will we not cause harm to others, but we will automatically and spontaneously do what is necessary to help them. We may not have gotten to that point yet. We are still beginners at this; we just started. We're trying to tame our own mind. If we pretend to ourselves that we already have fully tamed our mind and that everything else is delusion, then when we hear about avoiding causing harm to others, we might think, "What harm? Harm is only a concept. There is no real harm. There is no real benefit. Who is there to benefit?" That kind of conceptual plastering-over is a great danger, so please do your best to avoid that. As I said before, the time to have this attitude is when you no longer burn your finger when you put it in a flame. If you find yourself coming up with this attitude, you should make it a point to check once in a while.